1101
BUSINESSES
YOU CAN START
FROM HOME

WILEY SMALL BUSINESS EDITIONS

Kim Baker and Sunny Baker, *How to Promote, Publicize, and Advertise Your Growing Business*

Robert A. Cooke, *Doing Business Tax-Free: Perfectly Legal Techniques to Reduce or Eliminate Your Federal Business Taxes*

Fred Hahn, *Do-It-Yourself Advertising: How to Produce Great Ads, Brochures, Catalogs, Direct Mail and Much More*

Daryl Allen Hall, *1001 Businesses You Can Start From Home*

Daryl Allen Hall, *1101 Businesses You Can Start From Home*

Herman Holtz, *How To Start and Run a Writing and Editing Business*

Gregory and Patricia Kishel, *How to Start, Run, and Stay in Business*, Second Edition

John Kremer, *The Complete Direct Marketing Sourcebook: A Step-by-Step Guide to Organizing and Managing a Successful Direct Marketing Program*

Harold J. McLaughlin, *The Entrepreneur's Guide to Building a Better Business Plan: A Step-By-Step Approach*

Richard L. Porterfield, *The Insider's Guide to Winning Government Contracts*

L. Perry Wilbur, *Money in Your Mailbox: How to Start and Operate a Mail-Order Business*, Second Edition

1101 BUSINESSES YOU CAN START FROM HOME

Revised and Expanded edition

Daryl Allen Hall

John Wiley & Sons, Inc.

New York • Chichester • Brisbane • Toronto • Singapore

Copyright ©1995 by Daryl Allen Hall

Published by John Wiley & Sons, Inc.
All rights reserved. Published simultaneously in Canada.

Library of Congress Cataloging-in-Publication Data
Hall, Daryl Allen, 1938–
    1101 businesses you can start from home / by Daryl Allen Hall.—
Rev. and expanded ed.
      p.   cm.—(Wiley small business editions)
    Rev. ed. of: 1001 businesses you can start from home. c1992.
    Includes bibliographical references.
      ISBN 0-471-10241-5 (cloth/acid-free paper). — ISBN 0-471-10237-7 (pbk.)
      1. Home-based businesses—Handbooks, manuals, etc. 2. New
business enterprises—Handbooks, manuals, etc. I. Hall, Daryl
Allen, 1938– 1001 businesses you can start from home. II. Title.
III. Title: One thousand one hundred and one businesses you can start
from home. IV. Series.
HD2333.H35   1995
658'.041—dc20   94-15734

Printed in the United States of America
10 9 8 7 6 5 4 3 2

▐▌▌▌▐▌▌ PREFACE

WHY START A HOME BUSINESS?

What goes around comes around. There is nothing new under the sun. History repeats itself. If you stand in a stream long enough, the water that flowed by you in the beginning will flow by you once again. So they say.

And so it is with home businesses. Certainly the first businesses ever in history were home businesses. Until the industrial revolution, nearly all businesses were home businesses. In fact, both the United States and Canada were founded by millions of people running home businesses. The industrial revolution, with its large factories and office complexes, briefly disrupted the prevalence of home business. But now the tide has turned. The industrial trend, toward "bigger is better," is now reversing—smaller has become better. Indeed, millions are convinced that home businesses are best of all. We have come nearly full circle.

Today we see hundreds of large companies, such as IBM and General Motors, in the throes of downsizing in a desperate effort to remain economically viable. Besides downsizing, they are moving factory after factory to countries such as Mexico, Korea, and Indonesia in order to take advantage of cheaper labor and tax breaks. They are resorting to mergers, leveraged acquisitions, and reorganizations, which also cut jobs. This desperate trend will probably continue until few if any factories remain.

Plant closures mean massive job loss. We are in the midst of an unemployment crisis. At present, 2300 jobs are lost each and every day in the United States and Canada. Many of these are factory jobs. This translates to nearly 850,000 jobs lost each year!

About 23 million people in Canada and the United States are currently unemployed. The true, average unemployment rate for both countries is close to 17 percent and growing. During the Great Depression, unemployment peaked at 25 percent. Our governments would have us believe that unemployment is only half that rate, but their figures fail to include over half of the unemployed, those who are on welfare and have given up actively looking for jobs. Nor do their figures reflect the large number of people in low-paying, part-time jobs or people who are underemployed, for example, PhDs who are driving taxis. Both governments are using smoke and mirrors in presenting their statistics.

Many people believe these jobs will return someday. (But then they are optimists. And an optimist is a person who believes that a housefly is just looking for a way to get out.) But this belief is unrealistic. The job picture is nothing short of dismal.

On the other hand, the climate for setting up a home business has never been brighter. During 1994, 1.3 million individuals in the United

States and Canada will set up a small business, and most of them will be home based. About 26 million home businesses are already in operation. By the year 2000, over 40 percent of the workforce in the two countries will operate from homes.

Setting up a home business makes splendid sense for many reasons. The first reason is the fear of dismissal. It is clear that we can no longer depend upon spending our entire working lives with any one business or company. Currently, college graduates can expect to change career fields an incredible 10.4 times during their lifetimes. And every day we hear horror stories about hard-working people who are cruelly laid off just short of earning a retirement pension. It makes no sense to strive for a carrot that will be snatched away just before you reach it. It does make sense to start a business of your own as insurance against an unexpected layoff. After all, you can never be fired if you have never been hired.

Freedom from oppressive authority is another strong reason to start your own business. To many, this is probably the most important reason for starting a business. The taste for independence is something most of us share. We want to take control of our own lives; we want independence of both thought and action. We want to be masters of our own space and time. And we want quality time, which we lack when our lives are controlled by high-pressure jobs or meaningless details.

An enhanced paycheck is another reason to go it alone. Entrepreneurs realize there are distinct economic advantages in running a business from home. They search for new and creative ways to make homemade profits. In theory, there is no limit to the amount you can earn when you work for yourself. Perhaps you are tired of living from hand to mouth. Perhaps you are tired of moonlighting just to make ends meet and are now craving some rest.

Making money, however, is only one way of showing a profit. Money is not always the important kind of wealth. Some wealthy people are enslaved by their riches. Many intangibles are just as important as money. Of these, enjoying your work is the bottom line. Money is cold comfort if you don't enjoy what you are doing. Your home business may never have you rolling in money, but it may give you an overall sense of well-being which money can never buy.

Less stress is another major reason for starting a home business. It is much easier to commute downstairs than to commute downtown. It is usually less stressful to work in the confines of your own home than to work in a noisy factory or the Grand Central Station of many large office complexes. The high stress in many workplaces may cause emotional distress. The futility of knocking your head against a wall can wear down anybody. However, if you run your own business at home, nothing prevents you from taking a walk or from doing something else for a break when you run into an obstacle. If things get very tight, you can even declare your own holiday, if necessary. Just try that at a regular 8-to-5 job!

Many people seek the challenge of a home business. They want to discover who they are. They want to bet on themselves and their capabilities. They can learn what it means to be self-reliant. People may need to escape from an uninspiring, boring job. To escape job burnout, they might launch out into the deep, where the fishing is best.

To realize their own dreams, many people need to free themselves from old-fashioned management practices and business methods. They want to break free from these encumbrances and put their own fresh ideas and innovations to work. They want to stop following the herd and be an individual. Seeing their own ideas and work succeeding makes their struggle worthwhile. Someone who played a small role in a large company can quickly become an important person by running a home business.

Receiving recognition for hard work is another good reason people set up their own home business. Many people work hard at their 8-to-5 jobs and get little in return. Too often, go-getters who love to work and achieve are often thwarted in their efforts to get ahead.

Then there is the matter of saving a buck. Why make the tax people richer than they already are? The chance to deduct some home and car expenses can be a plus. High gasoline bills or high wardrobe expenses aren't likely, either. And who wouldn't be sick of paying high union dues and getting nothing in return?

Running a home business will definitely save you time. The time you formerly spent commuting back and forth to work can now be spent more productively. You can invest this precious time in the business, use the free time for yourself, or spend it with your family. You can be there to see your child take his first step or play in her piano recital. You can set your own schedule and keep it flexible. This is real freedom. Many people in 8-to-5 jobs feel as if they are serving out life sentences. They compare it to suffocating on a treadmill.

A choice bonus in running your own business is that you can create your own work space and use it how and when you will. This work space can be as informal as you like. If you want to work with your feet propped up on your desk, which could be just a packing crate, there is no one to stop you. Your most productive time may be at odd hours of the day; you can work in the wee hours of the night if you like. A home business can be an ideal opportunity for a single parent to work gainfully while the children are at school. Remember, it is you who will be running the show.

Another sound reason to start a home business is to do work that is important to you. Many jobs border on being meaningless. For most people, slinging hash at minimum wage does nothing positive for the mind (or the pocketbook). We all want to do something that makes us feel significant.

Technology makes many home businesses efficient to operate. Computers, Fax machines, answering machines, copiers, cellular phones, and the like are conducive to small workplaces. This user-friendly equipment makes working at home much more convenient and efficient than working in an office tower. This technology makes dropping out of the rat race not only possible, but very enticing.

These are just a few of the many good reasons that could motivate you to start your own home business. Now we turn to you. Ask yourself why you want to start a home business, and be completely honest with yourself. Think long and deeply. You should have a good understanding of yourself before you take that big step. Dispense with any and all cloudy thinking. Get rid of any pie-in-the-sky fantasies about a super-glorious future. Use good judgment and lots of common sense. Be hard on yourself. Be realistic. Finally, remember that nearly all successful home businesses are the result of hard work—lots of it.

Once you have decided to take that giant step, the critical thing for you to do is to get off your duff and jump. And keep jumping. It is simple as that.

Many people have ideas and dreams about starting their own business, but most people just keep sitting and dreaming. Few leap to their feet and take off. Most people's lives are consumed by procrastination, which is the art of keeping up with yesterday.

But for you it will be different. It will not be tomorrow, not next week, not next year—today. A true entrepreneur, having first dreamed, becomes a genuine doer. The entrepreneur knows that only dead fish swim with the stream—and that every stream is on its way downhill.

May you spend the rest of your life doing work that you love. Good luck!

▌▌▌▌▌▊ CONTENTS

used auto consultant ■ used car lot ■ van interior customizing ■ windshield repairs ■ computerized used vehicle listing and locating ■ antifreeze recycling service ■ mobile auto inspection ■ dent removal ■ quick paint repair

Children   30

children's letter service ■ children's library ■ children's party service ■ children's puzzles ■ children's used clothing ■ bedtime stories on tape ■ child care center ■ coloring books ■ doll houses ■ doll repair ■ fish pond for children ■ merry-go-round wagon ■ mini-lumber for mini-carpenters ■ piñatas ■ pony rides ■ rocking horses ■ time toys for tots ■ toddler staircase ■ wooden toys ■ children's resale store ■ child security systems ■ baby store ■ personalized children's videos ■ mail-order educational toys ■ cardboard playhouses

Cleaning   37

garbage can cleaning ■ janitor service ■ restrooms only service ■ steam cleaning ■ surface cleaning, mobile ■ vehicle cleaning ■ venetian blind cleaning ■ construction site cleanup ■ wall cleaning ■ ultrasonic cleaning ■ mini-blind cleaning ■ ceiling tile cleaning ■ house cleaning

Crafts   41

apple dolls ■ aprons ■ baby shoes in bronze ■ bird cages, ornamental ■ bird feeders ■ blacksmithing ■ bookshelves ■ boomerangs ■ braided rugs ■ bumper stickers ■ buttons for clothes ■ candleholders ■ caning ■ carving kits ■ clothes posts ■ coat hangers for fine clothes ■ coat hangers of aromatic cedar ■ concrete ornaments ■ cork crafts ■ corsages ■ cypress knees ■ decorative screens ■ decoys of papier mâché ■ doll miniatures ■ dolls of history ■ driftwood ■ eggshell knickknacks ■ flower stationery ■ fly tying ■ folklore figurines ■ fun novelties ■ handicraft manufacturing ■ handweaving ■ hooked rugs ■ lampshades ■ leathercraft ■ millinery ■ names of animals ■ nature crafts ■ personalized mugs ■ plaster casting ■ quilts, custom-made ■ resin casting supplies ■ rug maker, custom ■ seashell crafts ■ shade pulls ■ shoe planters ■ shoe recovering ■ silk-velvet pictures ■ trays, decorative ■ whittling ■ wishing well planters ■ youth crafts instructor

Entertainment   56

barbershop quartet for hire ■ booking agent ■ humor ■ one-person entertainer ■ song writing ■ wholesale party goods ■ antennas ■ baseball batting range ■ recording studio service

Food   59

baked beans, home style ■ barbecue specialty ■ bottled water ■ butcher at the client's ■ candy apples ■ candy store ■ caramel corn shop ■ cider ■ cookies-only shop ■ croissant shop ■ dining and party

catering ■ donut shop ■ egg culls ■ egg production ■ ethnic food
shop ■ fast health-food takeout ■ food by mail order ■ food-
preserving service ■ food specialty ■ fortune cookies ■ fruit roadside
vendor ■ gingerbread products ■ gourmet natural coffee and tea
shop ■ holiday goodies ■ home bakery ■ homemade cakes and
pies ■ homemade candy ■ juice ■ low-calorie bakery ■ lunchbox
home-cooked service ■ lunch-in service ■ maple syrup ■ natural foods
bakery ■ no-alcohol bar ■ old-fashioned ice cream parlor ■ omelette
restaurant ■ pasta place ■ peanuts ■ pickles ■ pizza ■ portable
restaurant ■ rural rustic dining ■ salads and exercise ■ salads-only
lunch restaurant ■ sandwich route ■ sandwich wagon ■ sassafras tea ■
snack bar ■ snacks by paddle ■ soup restaurant ■ soybean sprouts ■
spaghetti takeout ■ specialty bread shop ■ stuffed potato restaurant ■
submarine sandwich shop ■ vegee pies ■ wild berries ■ computerized
nutrition ■ food delivery service ■ peanut butter and jelly sandwiches
■ global candies

Health

cough remedies ■ first-aid kits ■ foot massage ■ hairpieces ■ health
resort ■ health tips ■ hearing aids ■ home convalescent care ■ lanolin
■ massage salon ■ medicinal herbs ■ no-sun tanning center ■ nursing
equipment rentals ■ nutrition counselor ■ optical discount shop ■
physical fitness center ■ reading glasses ■ reducing salon ■ rent-a-hot-
tub business ■ stairway lifts/elevators ■ stop smoking clinic ■ stress
clinic ■ vitamin store ■ waterbeds ■ weight control clinic ■ wild herbs
■ personal image consultant ■ sun protection ■ ambulance contractor
■ funeral advisory service ■ pain relief consultant ■ stress relief
consultant ■ hair care products ■ disability consultant ■ home health
care agency ■ medical claims consultant ■ craving control consultant

Horticulture

bedding plants ■ beneficial bugs ■ bonsai (ming) tree collecting ■
cactus ■ compost ■ drip irrigation systems ■ earthworms ■ exotic
plants ■ floral arranging ■ florist shop at home ■ flower trees ■
fuchsias ■ garden sales ■ giant seeds ■ glads ■ gourds ■ green
plant service ■ herb boxes ■ herb gardening ■ holly ■ horseradish ■
house plants ■ landscaping plants ■ lawn grass ■ manure ■ mums ■
mushrooms ■ mutations for profit ■ nursery (plants) ■ nuts ■ orchard
management ■ orchids ■ palm trees ■ plant collecting ■ plant shop ■
pollination service ■ potting soil ■ pruning service ■ roadside produce
■ rototilling ■ sawdust ■ seed potatoes ■ soilless gardening ■ soil
testing ■ strawberries ■ survival seeds ■ topsoil ■ totem pole planters
■ tower gardens ■ tree planting ■ tree pruning service ■ tree removal
■ violets ■ watercress ■ watermelons ■ weekly flowers ■ winterizing
plant service ■ woodlot manager ■ weed control

Household

carpet laying ■ carpet recoloring ■ carpet/upholstery cleaning ■
chimney sweep ■ china repairs ■ concrete repair ■ consignment used

furniture ■ countertop repairs ■ economy interior decorating ■ energy loss prevention service ■ floor refinishing rentals ■ furniture stripping service ■ glass etching ■ household machine rentals ■ house number curb painting ■ housewares service ■ interior decorating ■ kindling ■ landscaping ■ lawn and grounds service ■ maid service ■ menu service ■ microwave cooking instruction ■ moving service ■ new neighbors ■ pine cones ■ preserves, homemade ■ root cellars ■ roto-rooter service ■ rubbish removal ■ sauna ■ solar sales and installations ■ stenciling ■ storage expert ■ used carpet sales ■ vacuum cleaner shop ■ wall fabrics ■ wall murals ■ wallprinting ■ water treatment systems ■ well drilling ■ window shades ■ wood splitting ■ creative window treatments ■ voice-activated home automation ■ custom closets ■ home computers and software ■ new home interiors ■ kitchen tune-ups ■ wireless speakers

Housing 117

barn lumber ■ beams and posts ■ home installations service ■ building houses ■ cabinets of arborite and formica ■ decks and coverings ■ drywall ■ fences ■ home improvement contracts ■ home office management ■ house painting ■ house restorations ■ kitchen cabinets ■ kitchen cabinet refacing ■ log houses ■ rooming house ■ sawmilling ■ stone sales ■ suspended ceilings ■ home ownership facilitator ■ staircases ■ building demolition ■ construction estimation service ■ skylights ■ garage interiors ■ mortgage payment consultant

Instruction 125

accent in speech service ■ aerobic instruction ■ astronomy ■ ballet school ■ camp counselor ■ computer camp ■ crafts school ■ dog obedience school ■ driving school ■ essay coaching ■ first aid instruction ■ foreign language school ■ freelance substitute teacher ■ gardening by video ■ gourmet cooking instruction ■ ham radio instruction ■ home business counseling ■ homemaking instruction ■ home safety counseling ■ home schooling counselor ■ homesteading school ■ horsemanship ■ horse training ■ house building instruction ■ hobby school ■ industrial arts tutoring ■ knitting instruction and supplies ■ manners instruction ■ music school ■ parenting instruction ■ penmanship instruction ■ reading clinic ■ real estate school ■ remedial instruction ■ ropes and knots ■ sailing instructor ■ secretarial school ■ sewing school ■ speech improvement ■ stocks and bonds ■ teacher's agency ■ test coaching ■ tour guide instruction ■ trade school ■ tutoring ■ used correspondence courses ■ pilot training ■ aptitude testing

Mail Order 138

classical music mail order ■ coins ■ formulas by mail order ■ how-to books by mail order ■ licorice ■ mail order ■ mail order gourmet foods ■ stain removal service ■ plastic bags by mail order ■ postage stamps ■ translator by mail ■ wall coverings by mail order ■ wind chimes

Manufacturing   **142**

archery supplies manufacturing ■ baby packs ■ brooms and
brushes manufacturing ■ burlwood tables manufacturing ■ canoe
manufacturing ■ custom case making ■ cutting boards ■ doghouses
■ electronic assembling ■ fish lure manufacturing ■ flower pots ■
food dryers ■ formica signs ■ formula products ■ furniture prefabs
■ garden hand tools ■ grain-raising tools ■ greenhouse kits ■ hot tub
sales and manufacturing ■ lap desks ■ lawn ornaments ■ lice-killing
scratch posts ■ license plate frames ■ litter bags ■ martin houses
■ metal creations ■ moccasins ■ musical instruments handmade ■
neckties for sportsmen ■ patchwork pillowcases ■ photo lampshades
■ pictures on plates ■ pillow making ■ pillows, throw ■ pine pillows
■ plastic stained glass ■ polyester cast crafts ■ portable furniture
■ pottery ■ pun plaques ■ puzzles, wooden jigsaw ■ pyrex glass
art ■ rolltop desks ■ rustic furniture ■ scenic products ■ sewing
beachwear ■ shampoo and soap manufacturing ■ sign letters ■ spoons
■ stenciling ■ store directory systems ■ street signs ■ stuffed animal
kits ■ suggestion boxes ■ sundials ■ swimming pools ■ teddy bears ■
t-shirt shop ■ utility trailers manufacturing ■ wall plaques, blanks ■
wood products ■ gold electroplating ■ vending vehicles

Novelties   **159**

artifact sales ■ baby handprints ■ balloon vendor ■ button badges
■ candid keychain photos ■ canned surprises ■ coats of arms ■
concession rack manufacturing ■ custom puzzles ■ doll clones ■
historic replicas ■ national emblems

Pets   **163**

bird boarding ■ bird talk ■ boarding kennel ■ bugs ■ canaries ■
cat-nippers ■ cat scratching posts ■ chipmunks ■ dogs by air ■ exotic
pets ■ parakeets ■ pet cemetery ■ pet food service ■ pet hotel and
grooming service ■ pet photos ■ pet sitters ■ pet taxi ■ poodle
grooming ■ poodles ■ puppy consignments ■ dog pooper scooper
service ■ private pet control contractor ■ zoo

Photography   **170**

accident photos ■ antique photo studio ■ baby pictures ■ birthday
photo albums ■ business photos ■ business picture calendars ■
calendar booklets ■ color slide sets ■ construction photos ■ feature
photos ■ flower photos ■ microfilming service ■ minilab photo
finishing ■ mobile photo studio ■ paper doll photos ■ photo agent
■ photo booth ■ photo copy shop ■ photos of new homes ■ pony
polaroid photos ■ portrait studio ■ postcard photos ■ promotional
photos ■ publicity photos ■ real estate photos ■ slide sets (35mm)
■ snapshooting baby ■ spot news photos ■ tintype biz ■ trick photo
cards ■ wedding videos ■ winner photos (animals) ■ aerial photos ■

Travel 290

backpacking vacations ■ boat tours ■ cabin rentals ■ campground ■ canoe trips ■ convention tours ■ escorted camping trips ■ farm vacations ■ freighter hand ■ gold prospecting trip guide ■ home travel agency ■ interview sales ■ jobs by long distance ■ job creation ■ job fair ■ jobs for youth ■ luggage rental service ■ translator rental agency ■ travel agency ■ travel by TV ■ cruise-only travel agency

Typing 296

legal home typing ■ secretarial service ■ steno service ■ typing instruction ■ typing school papers

Vending & Jobbers 298

duplicate key stand ■ fishing tackle vending ■ advertising specialties ■ office supplies ■ packaged popcorn ■ plastic laminating ■ popcorn vending ■ produce vendor ■ rack merchandising ■ rawleigh, fuller brush ■ rose vendor ■ seafood vendor ■ shoes ■ sunglasses ■ toy stuffed animal vendor ■ vending machines ■ wagon vending ■ personal care vending machines

Writing 303

ad newspaper columns ■ biography writing ■ business rating guide ■ club news service ■ collection letter writing ■ complaint service ■ condo newsletter ■ freelance news reporter ■ ghost writing ■ guidebook publishing ■ hand lettering ■ handwritten works ■ hiking guidebook ■ home histories ■ household hints service ■ instant language booklet ■ instruction manual ■ letter writing service ■ literary agent ■ logos ■ magazine article writing ■ mail addressing ■ mailing lists composing ■ manuscript prepping ■ name lists sales ■ newsletter writer-publisher ■ newspaper column ■ parents' guide ■ pen pal matching ■ personal histories ■ poetry ■ PR brochures ■ research specialty ■ résumé service ■ rural news reporter ■ specialty manuals ■ survival book ■ tour guide ■ who's who local directory ■ writing social letters ■ writing space fillers ■ writing speeches ■ writing story plots ■ personalized books ■ home nursing directory ■ writing business plans

▌▊▐▊▌▌▊ INTRODUCTION

HOW TO START A HOME BUSINESS

Welcome to the Age of the Entrepreneur! In this book, *1101 Businesses You Can Start from Home,* you will find how to achieve a simple, contented life, on your own terms, on your own time, and, in most cases, in your own home. You will find 1101 selected business summaries or job descriptions. The entire selection of listings has already proven satisfying and profitable to hundreds of people who have put them into practice.

There are dozens of potential jobs here for both the active and the handicapped, male or female, younger or older. Most of these jobs are suited for communities of any size. Most have low start-up costs.

This is a new book intended to revitalize and refresh our work force with 1101 special ways to use your home and your present skills to make a living. With proper input from you, the job ideas can provide a new way of living for you.

Well over a million new small businesses and industries will be started this year in North America. And, by far, the vast majority of them will be started by individuals, perhaps like yourself, who will operate out of their own homes.

If you dream of becoming your own boss or simply of boosting your present income, you may be pleasantly surprised to learn that it is a lot easier to change your dream into reality than you may have thought. It doesn't matter if you don't know the first thing about business. With the proper attitude you, too, can learn. Although it takes far less work to get rich by marrying a millionaire or buying a winning lottery ticket than it does to run your own business, for most people the rewards would not be nearly as satisfying.

Starting and running your own business will, of course, require some honest work on your part, especially at first. If you like honest work, it will be easy for you. On the other hand, if you have never learned to work and you are just looking for pie in the sky, this book is not for you.

This book will help you choose a home business. It is very possible, though, that the business will choose you because of something you are already doing that wins a great response from other people, such as making brownies, for example.

All of these 1101 special businesses or jobs can be put into one of two categories: selling *products* or selling *services.* These, in turn, can be further subdivided into two other categories: working for yourself, or working for some other company.

Selling products or services *for another company* has many advantages. These products or services are the easiest to sell, especially if they are well-advertised and reputable. You don't have to uphold any warranties.

The company usually provides good support with items, such as catalogs. You can usually set your own hours. There are usually good bonuses in return for good sales figures. Little training is usually required. It is a good option for unskilled people and those working only part-time.

Possible disadvantages to selling products or services for other companies include poor product return policies, supply problems, difficulty for you in believing in the product or service, initial cash investment requirements, and the need to work evenings and on weekends.

There are countless ads in most of the media claiming big bucks for simple menial tasks, such as stuffing envelopes. Most of these businesses are legitimate, but you should realize that the profit returns are usually small. It is true that these jobs usually require a minimum of thought, talent, or creativity. This mindless work gets old pretty fast for most people. But you don't have to go out looking for customers, and usually all your products and/or materials are supplied. And it is ready cash if you are desperate.

Nearly every business, whether it offers a service or a product, can be found as a franchise offering. The advantage of the franchise is obvious—it is a concept that has been tried and proven. Obviously, McDonald's, with its 5000-plus hamburger stands, knows what works. It knows where to locate and how to advertise. The franchisee has the advantage of buying into something that is going to succeed more than 80 percent of the time. For that success guarantee, franchisees pay. They pay in the form of a franchising fee and an ongoing royalty. They also must follow standards and rules set down by the franchisor. Although they may be operating their own business, they are still subject to the franchise agreement, and in many cases it can be more restrictive than an employer-employee relationship.

Not every franchise is a sure success. Even McDonald's closes an occasional restaurant. To determine which franchises are the best, contact the International Franchise Association (IFA) in Washington, D.C. The IFA maintains statistics and records on the industry and facts on many of the franchisors.

Selling a home-based product usually involves a product that has been a crowd pleaser for you, perhaps for years. It will possibly be a product that you have been giving away free until now, and which you enjoy making. Perhaps it is an unusual recipe for jam, or an outstanding pattern for a lap desk.

Selling your own wares has its drawbacks, however. You and your product will be little known outside your local area, which means you will have to do your own advertising. Also, your old friends and family may resent now having to pay for what used to be free.

Homemade products sell especially well through mail order if you have something unusual to sell that is not readily available elsewhere.

Many people like to receive things through the mail, judging by the fact that mail order is a $70-billion-a-year industry.

Here are some tips on mail order. The most successful mail-order businesses cater to repeat business. Know what your competition offers and at what prices by obtaining their catalog. Make friends with your customers through the mail; this will bring repeat sales. Make friends with the postal people, who can advise you on the least costly shipping methods. Advertise, advertise, and then advertise some more while staying within your budget.

The biggest single area of home-based businesses or jobs is in the area of *selling your own services*. This book is especially strong in that area. These businesses usually require little or no cash outlay apart from advertising and transportation. It is usually easy to set your own hours in this type of selling. These jobs often require repeat servicing on a weekly basis. These businesses usually involve some skill or trade that you have already more or less mastered. However, just because you don't have a certain package of skills before you start doesn't mean that you can't pick them up as you go along on the job. Mastery always requires some on-the-job training.

If you wish to sell a service, you should ask yourself these questions: Is the service I am offering something I just "fell into"? Am I selling my service just because I am expected by someone else to do it? Can I put my heart into performing this service? Am I doing this service only because I don't have any choice? Is my personality right for the service I plan to sell? Will my health stand up to all the stress this particular service will require? Is there a solid market for my service? Will I be able to get along with the kind of customers I will have to deal with? You will be able to think up other similar questions.

Whichever business you decide to enter, you would be well advised to talk to people in the business, especially to the pessimistic ones. Find out what can go wrong so there will be a minimum of unpleasant surprises.

The biggest problem facing you will probably be getting started: getting in gear, beginning to act on your ideas, and breaking free of procrastination. It should comfort you to realize that each and every job or business described in this book has both its own particular advantages and its drawbacks. No matter which work you enter, you will be faced with obstacles and problems and hassles. That's life. But look upon these setbacks as tests of your character that will force you to grow stronger in coping with life. Look upon them as opportunities and you will always come out the winner.

It is highly recommended that you *select more than one* job or business to operate. You know the adage about not putting all your eggs in one basket. I have a number of entrepreneurial enterprises going simultaneously, including three major ones. Using this approach, you will have more variety of activity, which will keep a sparkle in your attitude toward work. This will have a very telling effect on your sales and public relations, as well as the quality of your work. You won't have to worry about job burnout. Nor will you have to worry about a downturn in a specialized market when you have other sources of income for backup. So strive for several compatible jobs or businesses that you can dovetail together.

No matter which enterprise(s) you decide to enter into, you will obviously have to invest some time and money. Without *working capital*, it is almost impossible to proceed with most businesses. You may be able to start up with just your savings. On the other hand, you may have to borrow some money for start-up. In this case you will have to convince someone else that your idea is sound.

Before approaching someone else for money, you should have solid answers to these questions: Why are you starting up this particular business? Are you going to be in it for just a short spell, or are you going to try to stick with it over the long haul? Does your background of skills and experience lend itself to your proposal? What competition will you be up against? What evidence is there that there is room for your business? How much will you need to get under way? What will be your monthly expenses? What are your plans for the first year? For the next three years? What is your market? How will you obtain and maintain your piece of the market? Is this a seasonal business? If so, what will you do the rest of the year? How will a downturn in the general economy affect your job or business? Be prepared for other, similar questions.

Many people think you should only think big. I think differently; I believe it is wise in our day to think small. Try to find a market or markets that have been overlooked by the bigger businesses. Don't make the often-made mistake of trying to compete with long-established companies with huge budgets. Find markets that are not being serviced, or are not being serviced properly, by the competition.

You may have determined that you are right for a given business. But you should also ask yourself if the business is right for you. Are you the only person who can do the job, or can someone pitch in if necessary and sub for you? Would the business fall apart without you? Can you obtain a steady supply of whatever materials and logistical support you will need for the project? Will you always be able to afford them? Is your product or service ever likely to cause a client any harm? Will you be able to control the costs and the quality? And so on.

You will have to give special thought as to *how much your product or your service is worth*. Don't let your ego or inadequate research get in the way. If you think too highly of your product or your service, you will price yourself out of the market. The opposite is equally true. Although we all like bargains, we do become suspicious when companies drastically undervalue their products or services. So do your homework—check your competition's catalogs and flyers, price-check stores, and take careful notes.

Naming your business can present special perils. Your business name will often be the very first impression you make on your customers, so make it good. The name must have clout. It must be catchy, individual, easy to remember, and reasonably short and easy to say. Don't pick a name that will go out of date. Try out the name on your friends for their response. Live with it for a while before you go public with it. Don't use the phrase "and company" unless you are properly registered. And don't use "Inc." or "Ltd." unless you are actually incorporated.

Starting up a business is much like starting up a household. There are fairly big *costs* right up front. But after the bigger, one-time costs, the regular operating costs should become manageable.

The type of business you undertake will determine the actual start-up costs, but these are some of the costs you may likely consider:

- Renovations and decorating
- Furniture, shelves, counters, and so on
- Signs
- Equipment and installation
- Legal fees
- Accounting fees
- Inventory (or materials for product manufacturing)
- Licenses, dues, permits
- Advertising and promotion
- Rents
- Insurance
- Office supplies
- Taxes
- Loan payments
- Utility bills
- Wages
- Cash reserve

Don't dash your dream to pieces just because you don't have the funds to get started. It is ideal to get started without going into debt whenever possible. But if necessary, it is easier than you might think for someone opening up a business to obtain a loan.

If you carefully learn the art and science of *borrowing money*, you can actually have lenders competing with each other to give you your needed funds. Making the right approach is what matters.

Having earlier established a good credit rating is the key to success. It is obvious to you and me that it is better to never have needed to borrow before, but bankers simply don't think like you and me. They want solid proof that you know how to fulfill your obligations concerning loans by making payments promptly. Therefore, if you don't yet have a credit rating established, you can apply for a department store or a bank charge card or a small car loan. Make sure you pay back these small loans promptly, or you will have defeated your original purpose. Banks will also be more friendly if you establish savings and checking accounts with them.

Besides your friendly banker, you might consider others who might lend you your start-up funds: your friends, friends of your friends, your life insurance policy, grants, the small business governmental agencies, credit unions, or your own credit cards.

No matter whom you approach for the needed funds, here are some basic pointers:

- Avoid the services of loan brokers, as you will likely do just as well as they can do. This will save you time and money.
- Seriously consider consulting an accountant to help you select the best cash sources. They can also help you with your financial statements, your cash flow projections, and any audits.
- Demonstrate that you are thinking ahead by exhibiting a list of major orders or prospects.
- Make a good first impression by looking your best in conservative attire and show that you are well organized and have a responsible attitude.
- Stay cool. Discuss your qualifications and your needs carefully. Then don't ask for any money, but do leave your business card and invite the person to contact you if he or she is interested. Whatever you do, never give the impression that you are desperate for money.

The *goodwill* of your clientele will be your most important asset in business. Do all you can to generate word-of-mouth recommendations. You can do this by always meeting any deadlines and keeping all promises no matter what. Be careful to never overcommit yourself. Know your own limitations. Never hesitate to ask experts for advice when you know you are in over your head. Avoid doing shoddy work—always. Never give an estimate until you have thoroughly researched a prospective job. Make your customers feel special by giving something extra, some kind of a freebie; nearly everyone likes to have frosting on his or her cake.

If you decide to run your business out of your home, you will be faced with a set of *problems all work-at-home entrepreneurs must solve* in order to succeed. Being your own boss means you will have to ignore your nearby refrigerator. It means you will have to put the alarm clock out in the hallway so you will not be tempted to catch just a few more winks. Put a timer on your TV, if necessary, so it won't come on until you've put in your eight hours or whatever. Don't let yourself do any housework or any yardwork. Your paying work must always come first. Remember that it is your bread and butter.

Set up some area in your home for a workplace or office for your new business. You can deduct any associated expenses for it at tax time. You might select part of the den, or a spare room, or part of the garage or even inside your motor home. This special workstation will allow you to drop your work and not have someone interfere with it until you return.

Home businesses can create a lot of tension in the home between the family members. Your family members may be frustrated to see you around the house all day, every day, and yet be forbidden to have access to you personally most of the time because you are working. It will be wise to sit down together from time to time, especially at the start of your business, and talk over any problems that have arisen and that you anticipate will happen. Try to involve your family in some way in the responsibility of making a success of your new business so things can flow more smoothly.

An excellent source when checking on the pitfalls of a business is *Entrepreneur* magazine, located in Irvine, California. *Entrepreneur* has several hundred start-up manuals on various businesses, and although they do not cover every one of the ins and outs, they provide enough inside information to help the budding entrepreneur evaluate a business opportunity.

Good *communications* are a must for any business. Don't depend on your family for taking messages, if possible. Rather, get a good answering machine and perhaps even a fax machine. A second telephone line and phone number should also be considered.

The idea of *selling* makes most people break out in a cold sweat. But when you think it through, you quickly come to realize that everyone is in the business of selling something. If you have ever interviewed for a job, you were selling yourself. If you have ever had a date with someone, you were into a form of sales. If you ever had a debate with someone, you were trying to sell others your idea. And so it goes; we are all salespeople.

Good salespeople are always trying to sell better. They are always learning how to use better body language, sharper intuition, more sensitive listening skills, and, that rarest gift of all, plain common sense in order to get other people to see things their way. Good sales records are not just a matter of luck; they are the result of careful learning and practice of the best sales techniques.

Along with good technique, you will need to demonstrate a high level of energy, enthusiasm, polish, credibility, confidence, and momentum. You will strive to avoid being fearful, or showing procrastination, forgetfulness, dishonesty, carelessness, talkativeness, overfamiliarity, and lack of sparkle.

As your own boss, you will likely have to be your own coach as well. As coach, you will have to give yourself pep talks, as required. You may already realize that success usually comes to those who first believe they will succeed. So start out believing in yourself and your success. In other words, sell yourself on success.

The idea of building an entire house from start to finish might overwhelm the average person. However, a carpenter realizes that the house goes together just one nail and just one board at a time. Your business will come together in the same manner—just one item sold to just one customer at a time. So set very limited and specific goals for yourself that you can easily achieve each day. Take the best care you can of just one day at a time. Tomorrow will generally take very good care of itself.

Here are some very good *pointers on successful selling* that you would do well to memorize:

- Always look for the most likely prospects. You can do this by phone, by mail, or in person. Combining all three approaches might be ideal for your particular business.

   If you contact prospects in person, the first impression you make on them is of supreme importance. So dress very neatly and conservatively and be well groomed. Be careful with your posture and the manner in which you "talk" with your body. Don't slump while sitting or standing. Folded arms and legs suggest you are anxious or negative.

   If you contact prospects by phone, which can be the most efficient means to sales, always be polite and professional. It is wise to keep careful notes of the basics of most business phone conversations for future references. Check your own voice by listening to it on a tape recorder so you can improve areas where you are weak.

   If you contact prospects through the mail, you will be off to an excellent start by introducing yourself and your product or service. This approach shows both a personal and a professional touch that most buyers will appreciate.
- Be sensitive to the timing of your prospective customer. If the customer is not ready to complete a deal just now, be prepared to back off until he or she is ready. No one likes to be annoyed when not ready to purchase. Just leave your card and try again later.
- Keep it simple—probably the best advice ever given. Don't overload your prospect with nonessential details. This is the surest way to lose a sale. Simplicity is the hallmark of genius.
- Rehearse your presentation until you feel at ease with it. Practice with a tape recorder or a friend or in front of a mirror. Try to package

your entire presentation in color—colorful language, colorful dress, colorful brochures—because color sells.

- Strive to get the upper hand over your prospect in one of several possible ways. You might bring the prospect to the point of feeling obligated to you by doing some favor for him or her. Then again, you might call upon authority to sway your prospect by citing testimonials and good words from people who are in authority, such as teachers or doctors, or you may hold up a series of statistics and numbers to impress your prospect, citing how well others have accepted your product or service. If you are selling security items or health care products or services, you may bring up facts that may justifiably alarm your prospect, such as how a certain water filter can solve polluted-water problems. Finally, you can make your prospect feel that he or she will somehow be special by purchasing your product or service.

- Learn how to field any objections. This will often require fast thinking on your part. Some objections can only be countered by showing other virtues of your product or service that will more than compensate for any of its shortcomings. With more and more experience you will soon find ways around any objection.

- Try to tune in to where your prospect is. You can do this by asking a few simple questions that will enable you to size up your prospect.

- Learn positive closing techniques that will hit your target in the bull's-eye. Whatever you do, never ask your prospect a question they can answer with the word "no." Rather, ask questions such as, Will you want the blue ones or the red ones? or Will you be paying by cash or by credit card? Assume, in your talking, that a purchase will be made as you close. The momentum of asking this type of question can carry an interested prospect right into a sale.

- There are many different kinds of closings to sales. Here are just a few. First, you can just act as if the sale is an accomplished fact by starting to fill out the sales forms while you ask if it will be cash or charge. Or you could try to persuade the prospect that now is the time to buy because tomorrow may be too late because of your low stock or your unavailability for some reason. Then again, you might consider throwing in something free to sweeten the deal: "If you buy today, then I'll throw in a free widget."

- Everyone is interested in most or all of these seven things: family, money, job, fun, health, security, and social status. No matter what you are selling, it will appeal to virtually everyone in at least one of these areas. Find out which areas your prospect is especially interested in, and your sale is already half made.

And now a word about *keeping the books* for your business. Unless you have the bucks to hire a secretary or a bookkeeper to do it for you, you will have to do your own books. Running your own business is work, and for most people keeping the books is the hardest part because it borders on drudgery. Lists and lists of numbers are not exactly exciting to most of us.

It would be too bad if you were to lose your exciting go at business just because you were too uncaring to hit the books for a few minutes each and every day. Your profits could take a real clobbering just because you couldn't be bothered. So if you have to, grab yourself by the scruff of the neck and have at it. In a week or so it will become a habit you will be forever happy with. As a successful businessperson, you must know your profit situation and which products or services should be eliminated. Your carefully kept books will point out any problems before they turn into disasters.

Any good bookkeeper will help you set up your bookkeeping. A bookkeeping course at night school will show you the ropes. It is imperative for every business to keep basic written records of every business transaction for future reference. In fact, the government insists on your doing this.

Insurance for your new business requires the help of insurance experts. Whatever you do, be careful that you are not jeopardizing your homeowner insurance by starting up a business in your home. Check this out carefully. Be especially careful about the third-party liability clause in your present homeowner policy. Check out malpractice insurance especially well.

It would be well to consult with a licensed CPA about all your business money matters, including your need for insurance. These people are well-trained experts, usually well worth their cost.

Starting up your own business involves more than just hanging up your freshly painted shingle. You will need to know a few things about *business law.*

Most self-employed people run what is called an *individual proprietorship,* which is the form of business in which an individual puts up the capital, starts and operates the business, keeps all the profits, pays all the taxes, and assumes all the liabilities of the business.

In this form of business, your main obligations are to obtain the necessary license, permits, and appropriate tax numbers allowing you to operate. Any of your profits will be taxed as personal income. If you are not using your personal name, you may have to register the business name with the appropriate authorities.

In a *partnership,* two or more people come up with the required funding, operations, and responsibilities of the business. In this case, each partner is responsible to each of the other partners. Any partnership should have a carefully worded agreement between all the partners involved covering all aspects of the business. Partnerships should be finalized with the help of a lawyer who is conversant with business law.

Partnerships end the minute one of the partners dies. Therefore, you should carefully agree with each other what will take place with the business in the event this should happen.

Incorporating your business is the third and most complicated form of a business. It will also provide the most protection for the owner(s). An incorporated business is really a phantom legal person who is totally separate from the people who own and control it. This allows the corporation to do whatever a real person might do, such as operate a business, own property, file a lawsuit, or obtain a loan. The big advantage of this sort of arrangement is that, in the event the business collapses, only the money invested in the business is lost—any personal property cannot be attached and lost. This means your house and your jewelry are safe.

You will have to check locally for the fees required to help you incorporate your business. If you are in a big tax bracket, it may be worth your while to suffer the extra paperwork. Legal help is advised.

Zoning may affect you in setting up your new business, especially if you live in an urban setting. The various governments set up special zones that affect different regions and neighborhoods for the purposes of traffic flow, noise pollution, street safety, privacy, and property values. Often these same well-intentioned zoning laws can adversely affect a careful individual running a home business in a quiet, responsible manner.

Zoning committees can often rule in favor of your new business if you present your position carefully and with due respect to all concerned. If you are uncertain of your position, then check with a zoning lawyer for advice.

There are always *special laws* dealing with any business that involves *food* because of the need for careful sanitization and product freshness.

Certain types of businesses require licenses to protect the safety of the public. These include hairdressers, plumbers, commercial contractors, pilots, and chauffeurs. These licenses are granted upon satisfactory passing of special tests. *Check with your local authorities to see if you need licensing.*

Self-employed people must also pay into social insurance programs in both the United States and Canada.

One last warning to you as you start up your new business. The law is constantly being updated, revised, changed, and even reversed. Never assume that what was legal for your grandparents 40 years ago is still valid and permissible for you today. You must check out the law thoroughly for yourself.

A true entrepreneur, it has been said, is a person who would rather work 80 hours a week for himself or herself than work 40 hours a week for someone else. This person, in striving for independence, often has only a smattering of entrepreneurial sense, but has loads of raw intestinal fortitude and determination; is willing to take the plunge with all its risks; is usually willing to be very poor for at least a while; realizes that even if you aren't into selling, even if you can't sell gold bricks for 10 cents a piece, that you can still start up a business in which the product sells itself, like popcorn does; knows there is a price for going against the tide; realizes it is never too late to make a fresh start; knows that the freedom of not being tied down is worth taking the big step; and it is possible to combine one's business with one's play so closely that one will be hard pressed to tell which is which. And most importantly, this person knows that if you screw your courage to the sticking place, you can't ever fail!

Both the author and the publisher of this book assume no responsibility whatsoever for the results of any business you may decide to start. You, the reader, assume all responsibility for any information you decide to take and use from this book.

Careful planning is a must for any business to be successful.

Your happiness and independence are well worth the bargain price of this invaluable handbook.

The very best to you in your enterprise!

▌▌▌▌▌▌LEGEND

At the end of each job/business listing you will find certain symbols that will allow you to quickly size up each listing according to your individual needs.

First of all, there will be one or more dollar signs:

ESTIMATED START-UP COSTS CODE
$—Shoestring Operations
$$—$1000 to $5000
$$$—$5000 to $10,000
$$$$—$10,000 to $20,000
$$$$$—$20,000 and up

Other symbols are defined as follows:

  ♿   = appropriate for handicapped people

  ⚒   = requires permission of local authorities/laws

  🏙   = good for urban locations

  ⛰   = good for rural locations

  🏞   = good for all locations

IIIIIIIIIADS

1 AD CLIPPINGS

This is a very simple business to run in your home. Merely clip all the best advertising pertaining to specific products (such as TV sets) from leading newspapers and magazines each month. Collect them by category and then sell each package of clippings to advertising agencies. These agencies specialize in promotional campaigns and advertising, and they will pay you well for your work. Get these agencies to subscribe to your service on a monthly basis. Charge by month, or accept prepaid annual subscriptions.

$ 🔥 ▩▩

2 AD FOLIOS

Collect newspaper advertising on big-ticket items such as appliances, cars, furniture, and clothing. Print ten-page folios showing the ads you have collected. Then sell these sample ads by category at nominal cost to dozens of advertising agencies. If the response to your sample folios is satisfying, proceed to solicit subscriptions from these advertising agencies for your advertising ideas service, in which you send out new folios each month to the subscribers. This can be a most satisfying home business.

$ 🔥 ▩▩

3 BENCH ADVERTISING

Build benches and then rent advertising space on the back of each bench. Install the benches at busy corners such as bus stops. Each bench is, in effect, a miniature billboard. Anyone waiting there or going by can see the ads. Cities, like individuals, like to get something for nothing, so try contracting with your city government for citywide exclusive rights for your benches. Free benches that you maintain would be hard for any city to pass up!

$$ ◤ ▩

4 ENVELOPE STUFFING

Most readers will have, at some time, received bulk mailings of envelopes stuffed full of various flyers advertising a variety of things. You can contract to work at home stuffing the same kind of materials into the same kind of envelopes for bulk mailing. This would be a good job for a handicapped person. Look for ads in national magazines for openings in this well-paying field.

$ ♿ 🏙

5 HANDBILL DISTRIBUTION

Contract with supermarkets, dry cleaning firms, independent grocery stores, and so forth, advertising in flyers as follows: "Supervised handbill distribution. Try our new service. It works. Call Tad at 426-6305." Mail your flyers to prospective customers. Hire young people to distribute the contract flyers. Pay something like one cent per flyer, but charge two cents to your customer. A profit of 50 percent will be yours. Constantly spot-check to see if your hired distributors are actually doing their jobs and not dumping the flyers. Eventually, you will acquire an honest crew. A good living can be had.

$ ⚒ 🏙

6 LITTER CAN ADS

Supply your city or town with free trash receptacles in this business. In exchange for this service, you are granted the right to paint advertising by the silkscreen process on all four sides of the square shell that surrounds the garbage can. Sell these advertising spaces to local businesses and keep the ad signs in good repair. The advertising is done on a yearly basis by contract. The litterbugs will have no more excuses. And everyone will benefit—the city, the local merchants, and especially you.

$$$ ⚒ 🏙

7 TOURIST VIDEO DIRECTORY

Tourists arriving in a city want to get a quick, overall idea of where to go and what to do during their stay. You can run a business that both answers their need and gives you a fine income. Videotape all the amusements, eating places, recreation areas, sightseeing tours, concerts, and other attractions in your area. Have various businesses sponsor each short film clip. Then transmit this information to cooperating motel and hotel rooms on an in-house TV channel, free. Your income comes from your paid advertisers.

$$$ ♿ ⚒ 🏙

8 TRAFFIC STOPPERS

People will stop at roadside stands and elsewhere if they can see something that is unusual and eye catching. You can start a specialty business in which you build or arrange for these spectacular traffic stoppers for your clients. Imagination suggests no end of them—huge balloons tethered at the place of business, zoo animals, huge replica dinosaurs, a discarded plane, an old passenger railcar, or a full-size spacecraft. Work on a cost-plus contract with the required working capital up front.

$$ ◣ ▙▌▐

9 WINDOW DISPLAYING

Attracting customers is the biggest job any retailer has. A good window display out front is a must. Many businesspeople are too busy or too unskilled to set up good window displays month after month, year after year. If you are artistic and creative, you can set up your own well-paying business of making customized window displays for business clients. Strive for fresh, eye-appealing displays appropriate for each business. Avoid controversial displays for best results.

$ ▛▜

10 BANNERS

Flying banners on which you have painted paid advertising is making a comeback. You can fly these giant ads from tethered balloons; this creates lots of public curiosity. Or you can trail these banners from low-flying aircraft along waterfronts and beaches. However you decide to proceed, there is big money to be made in this spectacular form of advertising. Find out local regulations before setting out.

$$ ◣ ▙▌▐

11 FAST SIGNS

Fast signs can make fast money for both you and your clients. The standard way signs have been made in the past can take days and even weeks. But techniques and durable materials available today can allow you to make an average sign in as little as one hour. Some of these techniques involve using a computer. In this business, your main selling point will be speed. Your client will normally want to hang the sign up just as soon as possible and start making a profit just as soon as possible. If you can beat the competition at a reasonable price, you will soon have the lion's share of the sign business in your area. Little training is required.

$$ ♿ 🏙️

12 BULLETIN AND DIRECTORY BOARDS

Many business establishments offer some form of a public bulletin board, even if it is only the privilege of putting a poster in a display window. It is a good public relations device for a business. Sometimes there is even wall space dedicated to a bulletin board. But you have probably noticed that there is often only lip service given to the idea. You can set up a business in which you make decently sized bulletin and directory boards and sell them to various businesses. You could offer follow-up service in which you will keep postings current and neat.

$ 🏙️

13 PLACING ADS ON RENTAL VIDEOCASSETTE CASES

This business is just what its title suggests. You simply arrange with managers of video rental outlets to place ads of all types on the cases or jackets in which their videocassettes are protected. You are paid for each ad you place by the business whose ad you've placed. Then you pass on to the manager of the video store a cut of the money you have received for placing the ad. Everyone gains in the exchange, even the consumer. If possible, try to work with several video outlets for best results.

$ ♿ 🏙️

14 CLASSIFIED ADS FREE PAPER

Most newspapers have a classified advertising section. But few papers are just all classified advertising and nothing else. This business is simply a paper of classified ads—nothing else. You sell the ads by undercutting all your competition. Then you select how you will circulate the paper. Perhaps you will decide to set out stacks of the papers in corner groceries, convenience stores, and gas stations free for the taking. In this business you will need a small office location in which you will sell the ads and in which you will make up the master layout of the paper for each edition. You can contract out the actual printing of the paper.

 **$** ♿ 🔨 🏙️

▐▌▌▐▐▐▌ ANIMALS

15 ARTIFICIAL INSEMINATION SERVICE

This service (A.I.S.) will save larger animal producers thousands of dollars every year. They will purchase registered semen from you, which will save them enormous stud fees or the considerable costs of keeping bulls and stallions. Flexibility in changing blood lines or in creating new breeds of animals is also enhanced. You must find a reliable source or sources for low-priced semen before you start up. Add on vet supplies for double profits.

$$$ ◤ ▐▛

16 BUTTERFLIES

A good butterfly collection can be worth $100,000 or more. There is a great demand for butterflies from scientists, museums, laboratories, and private collectors worldwide. Of the 20,000 species in the world, 700 are found in North America. Collectors pay handsomely for species that will complete their collections. You can import breeder butterflies from any part of the world, raise them from eggs, and then sell the adults by mail. This is an ideal business for someone who loves nature and enjoys country living. Your main expense will be a good set of books about butterflies.

$$

17 SPECIALTY DOGS

Dogs can be put to many uses. If you are fond of dogs and have a background in working with them, this business may be for you. Raise special breeds of dogs, such as German Shepherds, and train them for specific functions, such as guard dogs, tracking dogs, or seeing-eye dogs. These dogs are far more valuable when they are properly trained to do special jobs, than they would be as just ordinary dogs. This can be a most satisfying business and service.

$$

18 CRICKETS

Live gray crickets are the ideal bait for bass, trout, and other game fish. You can raise and sell them very inexpensively. In just two years, starting with 200 breeder crickets, you can have 100,000 crickets for sale at $30 or more per thousand. The critters are fed in little plywood boxes on dried chicken mash and leafy greens. Supply all the local fisherfolk through the resorts and sporting goods shops, but sell most of your crickets through ads in national sports magazines to dealers all over the continent.

$$

19 EXOTIC BIRDS

Fanciers and breeders of strange, exotic birds are scattered all over North America. Some of these people make a full-time living at their pleasant pastime. There are hundreds of different birds they collect, breed, and sell—many radiantly colored, all from romantic places, all gorgeous and excitingly different. You can set up and sell eggs, chicks, or breeding stock to other breeders who are just getting started or who wish to increase their variety. Special newspapers deal strictly in these birds. You build up a reputation for shipping only the finest, healthiest birds and bring in $500 and more per breeding pair.

$$$

20 FISH FARMING

Gourmet restaurants almost always have fresh trout on their menus. The demand for gourmet trout dishes usually outstrips the supply of the fish. Excellent money can be made by raising these fish and then selling them live or freshly dressed on ice. Air freight shipping is commonly used for this delicacy. You will need a small, steady supply of spring or creek water, two big ponds, and lots of inexpensive commercial feed. A full-time, steady income can be yours with only an hour or two of work each day.

$$$

21 FISH RESTOCKING

In many areas of North America, various government fish and game departments take care of restocking lakes and streams with new fish. In many other areas private fishing resorts require their ponds, lakes, and streams restocked from private enterprise. You can contract with these businesses to raise the fish they desire for their restocking needs. Contact these businesses and see if they can make it worth your while to raise the fish they need for their fishing clientele. They may even fund the necessary start-up costs to get you going.

$$$$

22 FROGS

If you have a bit of swampy land going to waste, you could turn it into a virtual goldmine by raising bullfrogs for sale. Frog legs will delight any gourmet cook as he prepares to sauté them. You can also sell them for breeding purposes. For very little input from you, this can be a highly remunerative business. The croaking of your frogs will be sweet music indeed to both your ears and your patrons' once you are well under way.

$$

23 GOATS

Goats are lovable pets that will more than pay their way, and your family's way as well, if they are carefully managed. Goat's milk is always in short supply in nearly every area. It is frequently prescribed by doctors, because of its superior digestibility and nutritional values to invalids, babies, and elderly persons. Its market price is double that of cow's milk because of its scarcity. It is often pasteurized and then sold to hospitals, health food stores, and individual homes. There is a great deal of literature, including several magazines, that will provide all you need to know about starting a goat dairy.

$$

24 GUINEA PIGS

Guinea pigs are used as "guinea pigs" by colleges, hospitals, and scientific laboratories for studies connected with making serums, blood studies, and various other experiments. If you plan to mass-produce guinea pigs for the above institutions, first study what the institutions' specific requirements are and then obtain contracts with them before proceeding. Guinea pigs are also fine pets for children, as they are very clean. They are easy to keep, but they cannot tolerate temperature extremes. Guinea pigs breed prolifically.

$$$

25 HAMSTERS

Hamsters multiply faster than any other mammal. A single pair can produce more than 60 offspring per year. They live for about three years and are vegetarians, eating inexpensive grains and lettuce, carrots, cabbage, and so on. They sell well as pets because they are small, alert, clean, and gentle, as well as inexpensive. You can sell them to colleges and research and hospital laboratories, where they are used in medical research. You can start with only $10 and eventually build it into a steady living, if you work the market carefully.

$

26 HOMING PIGEONS

Many people have reached the point where they depend on their homing pigeons for their entire livelihood. Some homing pigeons, when trained as qualified racers, sell for $2000 and more. These beautiful birds have a peculiar homing instinct that allows them to fly directly back home when released up to 700 or more miles from home. They are commonly used in racing. Raise and train the pigeons and then sell those that aren't brood stock. It will cost about 20 cents per bird per month to feed them. A loft is necessary to house them.

$$

27 HONEY

Bees will literally work themselves to death for you. During peak nectar flows, worker bees last for only six weeks before their little wings become tattered beyond use. Learn how to channel all their energies into supporting you and your chosen lifestyle. Fickle weather will give you boom and bust years alike. Be prepared. You will come to love the little hustlers in their own right just watching them.

$$$

28 MINNOWS

Minnows, or shiners as they are sometimes called, are dandy live bait that can sell well, especially if you have easy access to a fishing resort area. You can raise them in small ponds and sell them wholesale to resort owners for about $10 per hundred, or you can retail them directly to fishermen for $2.50 per dozen (most fishermen will be only too happy to get them at these prices). A single female minnow will lay eggs for 300 hatchlings a year. You can sell any leftover fish to other fish farmers to be used for forage for game fish.

$$

29 PHEASANTS

For health reasons more and more people are switching away from red meats to poultry. Dining on roast pheasant is no longer fare just for aristocrats—gourmet pheasant dishes are now widely popular. With six hens and one cock you can sell 200 or more birds in the first year alone. After three years of building up your flock, you can have a thriving and profitable pheasant farm on less than one acre of land, which will provide you with a most comfortable living. You will be selling to fine hotels and restaurants, in addition to providing quick-frozen birds to individuals.

$ ◣ ☐

30 PONIES

Ponies are down-sized horses for the younger set. There are dozens of different kinds, each with special, attractive traits—Shetlands, Welsh, miniature Sicilian burros, donkeys, fjord horses, and so on. You might do well to consider raising one or more types of ponies as a home business if you have access to a bit of acreage. Well-trained ponies for pulling wagons or carts and well-broken riding ponies fetch better prices than most larger horses do.

$$ ☐

31 QUAIL

The current wholesale price for quail is about $30 a dozen. You can raise them quite inexpensively from eggs you produce, incubating the chicks until they are mature birds. When they are mature, dress the birds, quick-freeze, and ship them, frequently by air express, to hotels and restaurants serving exotic gourmet dishes. For health reasons, people are switching away from red meats to poultry, and quail (bobwhite) are considered to be among the better-tasting birds. This project can pay off handsomely. Some careful know-how is necessary.

$ ◣ ☐

32 ANGORA RABBITS

Many people raise rabbits for various reasons. But raising angora rabbits is in a class by itself. The very fine, silky hair from these rabbits can be made up into the very softest of garments, which are quite valuable. The wife of the author raises these rabbits and she does very well with them. She carefully keeps the best stock, culling each litter carefully. Colors range from pure white to black. She combs each rabbit each month, collecting the long hairs. She then spins the hair into yarn. The yarn is then knitted into various clothing items. Sweaters bring in $300 and more. Caps can bring in $40. And of course, the choice manure enriches our garden each year. Just one good angora rabbit can bring in as much as $1000 a year with the proper care.

$ ◤ ▌

33 SALMON FARMING

Salmon are among the choicest of eating fish. Fish is replacing red meats for health reasons. If you live beside a body of salt water and have access to a freshwater stream as well, you can farm salmon. Salmon begin life in freshwater and then normally migrate into salt water, where they grow to maturity. You can set up wire pens to confine the fish in bays and inlets of salt water. Simply feed the fish and harvest and market them when they are mature. It is becoming one of the fastest growing businesses in western Canada today.

$$$$$ ◤ ▌

34 SIAMESE CATS

Siamese cats are unique in the cat world because they remain playful throughout their adult life, unlike other domestic cats. With proper care and training, a Siamese cat will be just as affectionate, just as companionable, and just as watchful as any dog. You can raise them for profit. More than 30 kittens a year can be bred from one female Siamese. Young cats sell for $100 and more, depending on pedigree and markings. You will experience many rewards besides financial ones if you elect to breed these cats as a business.

$ ♿ ▜▌

35 SQUABS

Squabs (young pigeons) are considered to be a delicacy, and they are served in gourmet dishes by most of the finest hotels and restaurants throughout the world. A well-managed squabbery can be highly profitable. You will need a pigeon house and an exercise yard or pen, which allows for exercise without escape. You can produce about 6000 squabs per year from a brood flock of about 500 pairs. Price a squab dish at a nearby restaurant, and you will quickly see how a full-time living can be made in this business.

$ ◤ ▌

36 TROPICAL FISH SALES AND SERVICING

Tropical fish is a hobby second only to photography for consumer sales. Capitalize on this steadily booming business by opening a tropical fish store. An aquarium setup can cost between $25 and $1500, depending on tank size, fish species, and decorating accessories. Markups average 90 to 200 percent! You can begin by servicing home and office aquariums for those who want the beauty of fish without the work. You can do this right out of your own home.

$$$$ ♿ ⛰

37 TURTLES

Gourmet dishes using genuine turtle meat and turtle eggs are now found on the menus of finer hotels and restaurants. Culinary delicacies such as real turtle soup have spawned turtle farming. To date there is almost no competition in this field. All you need is a boggy area of ground good for nothing else. The turtles and eggs will sell for fantastic prices—the demand is far in excess of the supply. Write the Department of Agriculture in Washington, D.C. for further information on turtle farming.

$ ◣ ⛰

38 WORM FARMING

Nearly everyone laughs at worm farmers except their bankers and their families. Here is a farmer who can live and work in the city. A backyard will make a fine place for raising the creatures. A hundred dollars of boards and nails, some rich black soil, some starter parent worms for "brood cows," and some garbage (such as old oatmeal and coffee grounds) to feed the crew, puts you in business. Work the places that sell fishing equipment and licenses. Gardeners, too, will pay for worms, as they willingly work 24 hours a day tilling the garden soil.

$

||||||||APPLIANCES

39 AIR CONDITIONING AND REFRIGERATION

How air conditioners, refrigerators and heat pumps work is a mystery to at least 95 percent of our society. You can easily enter into this field with a home correspondence course, and then open up a well-paying business in your own home. You can sell new units, install them, and make repairs to existing units for low overhead and high profits. Much of your business will be service calls to commercial businesses.

$$ 🛠 🏭

40 CEILING FANS

The energy crisis is here to stay, and any product that can save on heating and cooling costs is a winner. Ceiling fans fill this bill perfectly and use no more electricity than a light bulb consumes to do the job. You can run a fine, upbeat business specializing in ceiling fans. You can even make your own ceiling fans to sell by simply buying only the motors and then adding your own blade sets with fancy woods in fancy designs. The market will not peak in most of North America for several more years, so you can ride the crest of the wave to real success.

$$$$ 🛠 🏭

41 PAGER RENTALS

Renting electronic paging devices (commonly called "beepers") is a brand new business possibility with almost unlimited potential for making money. You can purchase a number of these clever devices and then rent them out to people needing daily paging service. All sorts of people need them—service personnel, executives, doctors, nurses, motel and hotel guests, guided hunters, people at trade shows and conventions, staffs in large-spread outbuildings, staff members and pet owners at animal shows, and so on. You can work through special switchboards and phone answering services and share the action.

$$ 🛠 🏭

42 RENT-AN-APPLIANCE SERVICE

Many people today prefer to rent their major appliances rather than buy them. Students in dormitories, military personnel in barracks, new couples in unfurnished apartments, and others are looking for someone to rent major appliances from. You can snap up an inventory of used major appliances, make any needed repairs, and then rent your units out as real money-makers. Provide pickup and delivery service. Advertise your appliances in regular and college newspapers.

$$$

43 SMALL APPLIANCES

New and different small household appliances arrive in the marketplace every week. And there are the standard ones—juicers, grinders, toasters, mixers, irons, electric frying pans, can openers, blenders, and so forth. All of these will eventually need some servicing. You can make a fine business repairing and selling these products in your home. You can sell new units or good used ones that you have bought cheaply at yard sales, flea markets, or discount stores. You will be your own boss and your salary, once you are well established, will be among the best in town.

$$

44 MAYTAG HOME APPLIANCE CENTER

The name Maytag stands for quality and durability. Maytag home appliances have been a leader for many decades. You can attach yourself to their reputation by opening up a Maytag Home Appliance Center in which you retail nothing but their home appliances. It will take a minimum investment of about $20,000 from you, but the products will nearly sell themselves thereafter. It is possible to run this business from your home if you are adjacent to the downtown core and if local laws allow you to do so.

$$$$$

▌▌▌▌▌▌ARTIST

45 ANIMAL REPLICAS

A business that makes life-size elephants? Yes! And any other animal that will sell! Make full-size animals out of plaster. Over the plaster model, lay several layers of fiberglass. When it is hard, remove the fiberglass outer shell in two halves. Then cement the two halves back together at the seam, and you have a full-size animal replica. Paint it realistically. Imagine one of your replica deer standing in front of a taxidermy shop— or a Holstein on top of a dairy barn! Sell them for $500 or more each! You can build a fabulous business with no competition.

$$ ▐▜▐▛

46 CANDLE SCULPTURE

If you have just average creative ability, you can shine with this new, exciting gift item. Original-design sculpted candles are easy to make, and each one offers uniqueness, unlike molded candles. Profits can be quite sizable. A candle costing you about $1 may retail from $12 to $15. Anyone can start for less than $200. There is a huge market already and you can work right out of your own home.

$ ♿ ▐▜▐▛

47 CARTOONING

Cartooning ranges from brutally hard work to deliriously wonderful play. It could be the drop-out-do-your-own-thing for you. Freelance cartooning can be a mainly mail-order business, a work-at-home dodge, that you just may happen to get paid for. Avoid trade schools. The best cartoon instruction in the world is only as far away as the nearest printed cartoon. A fun way to take the plunge of kicking the 9-to-5 habit.

$ ♿ ▐▜▐▛

48 CHAINSAW SCULPTURES

Michelangelo would laugh himself back into the grave if he saw you sculpturing with your lightweight chainsaw in large red cedar logs. But if he caught a glimpse of a check from one of your sales, he would choke to a stop. You can learn to carve whatever will sell, in the form of big 6- to 10-foot sculptures—the head of Lincoln, Easter Island Tiki heads, animals, or free forms. Torch the wood lightly after sculpting, wire brush

14

it, and then wax it. Expect fantastic prices to be willingly paid, as each creation will be unique.

$

49 CHARCOAL PORTRAITS

People especially prize portraits of themselves. Charcoal portraits are usually flattering because they project warmth and softness. You can master the drawing of charcoal portraits if you are average or better. Then you can set up wherever people pass by—on sidewalks, in parks, or wherever—and offer to draw charcoal portraits of passersby in about five minutes for a fee of about $10. You can make 40 to 50 drawings per day. This can bring in exceedingly good income. You can sell other charcoal drawings at the same time on the side.

$ ♿ ♮

50 FEATHER FLOWERS & PICTURES

Feathers offer a fantastic range of exotic colors, textures, and patterns with which you can let your imagination run riot. You can set up easily at home and make gorgeous flowers, mosaic pictures, or whatever your imagination allows. You can then sell those creations—the ones that you will let yourself part with—to interior decorating firms and gift stores. The secrets of using feathers creatively can be found in instruction books from public libraries and craft supply stores.

$ ♿ ♮

51 FELT ART

Unusually beautiful wall hangings and collages can be made by cutting different colors of felt into special designs and pictures and gluing the pieces onto velvet-textured backgrounds. You can frame the creations or leave them simple and unframed. You can create animal studies for children's bedrooms, or scenic portrayals for other rooms in the house. Strive for an artistic style of your very own in this medium and one day you may have your own art show, which will double your income almost overnight.

$ ♿ ♮

52 FLORAL PICTURES

Original work really goes over well. Here you can use your eyes and imagination to create and enjoy. Flowers are usually fleeting delights, but you capture them in their prime and turn them into long-lasting, attractive floral pictures. Pick the flowers, press them out carefully between paper towels, mount them in creative arrangements on black velvet glued to cardboard, and mount in inexpensive frames that you have spray-painted behind glass. Keep them small, 5 × 7 inches or so. They will sell themselves; take them anywhere.

53 HAND-PAINTED HOSIERY

People will buy whatever appears to be *not* mass produced. One-of-a-kind products have special appeal. You can purchase all kinds of hosiery—nylons, pantyhose, stockings, and so on—at wholesale prices, and then hand-paint interesting and attractive designs on them using acrylic paints. These washable items can then be resold for three to ten times what you originally paid for them to boutiques, lingerie shops, and department stores. Add on customized painted designs, as well, for increased sales.

$ 🦽 📊

54 HAND PAINTING

Clever is the only word for it. Find just any old pot or pan or kitchenware or whatever in secondhand stores or elsewhere. Then rehabilitate the items by first cleaning them, then painting them, and then painting fancy decorations over the base coat of paint. What was once just junk becomes a saleable object of beauty, which you will sell easily. Just about any old item will become "buried treasure" after you have given it your artistic best!

$ 🦽 📊

55 INSTANT PORTRAIT DRAWINGS

Even if you can't draw, you can! You can purchase a special machine from Norton Products, 271 N. Ave., New Rochelle, N.Y. 10801. The machine will enable you to draw a portrait of a person in one minute flat or less with a bit of practice. Imagine setting up in a mall with a booth selling one-minute drawings for $2 a piece! That is about $100 per hour after overhead. Only lawyers and doctors make that kind of money. Check it out for yourself.

56 KEEPSAKES

Everyone has a collection of keepsakes that needs to be organized and perhaps even set up for display. You can set up a business in which you take your client's memorabilia and organize it in some meaningful way for display. You can create collages, scrap books, wall hangings, displays under glass, and so on, so that your client's treasures can be properly displayed in his or her home or office. Stress the nostalgic in your keepsake creations. Strive for good balance and color combinations also. Humor may help.

$$ ♿ ▀▙▐

57 PAINTINGS, BROKEN ROCK

Pictures are usually made from paints of different kinds. But you can "paint" pictures by using natural rocks of many different colors that have been broken up into a variety of small sizes—from mere powdered dust up to pea-sized bits. Using a real picture or perhaps a lovely photo for inspiration, glue (with clear spar varnish) your rock "paints" into place on a stiff art backboard. Take your time, and you, too, will be amazed at the incredible beauty possible. Sell them for $100 or more without the slightest sales resistance!

$ ♿ ▀▙▐

58 PAINTINGS, RENTAL

Simply purchase (or rent inexpensively) good copies of famous paintings and then rent them out to art lovers who are reliable. The art lovers benefit because they can have new works or collections from time to time. You can build up your inventory as you proceed. You will need storage space in your own home for all the works not in circulation. A brochure showing the works available will solve your selling problem. You might add on being a broker for others owning works of art and for others who would like to rent the same works temporarily to hang in their own homes.

$$ ▀▙

59 PAPIER-MÂCHÉ

Papier-mâché has definite commercial possibilities in the right hands. For example, well-shaped and artistically painted nativity scenes for window and fireplace mantel displays will certainly sell well. Mannequins, toy helmets, trays, boxes, dolls, even flower pots with tar coating inside, doll houses, toy furniture such as stoves, fridges, and so on, are both practical and decorative items that can be made from papier-mâché and then sold for profit. Follow your imagination; experiment!

$ ♿ ▐▜▐▜

60 PEN AND INK DRAWINGS

Most everyone would like to have their own personalized greeting cards and stationery to send out to friends. You can combine average artistic talent with ingenuity to make an extremely successful business. Make pen and ink drawings of people's own homes. You can work from ordinary snapshots that you have taken yourself or that have been sent to you by your client. If you advertise nationally, you will eventually find it impossible to fill all your orders unless you hire extra help. This job will really move out.

$ ♿ ▐▜▐▜

61 SEED PAINTINGS

Even the most physically restricted can keep happy and useful making seed paintings. You can supplement your income by making and selling them. First, put the bold outlines (by tracing or another method) of a picture on a stiff backboard. Then fill in the enclosed spaces with seeds of various types (corn, millet, peas, and so on) that you have dyed in various colors, gluing them in place. With patience and a good eye for color and texture, you can turn out lovely art works, which, by being unusual and pleasant to look at, will sell well.

$ ♿ ▐▜▐▜

62 SOFT SCULPTURES

Everyone knows what a teddy bear is. Just apply the idea of a stuffed object to all sorts of other everyday items such as beds, chairs, large house plants, large 8- and 10-foot animals, lamps, screens, tables, and the possibilities are endless. If you are even mildly artistic you can create these soft sculptures and sell them to higher-income people who are collectors of art or the unusual. Stores will buy them as eye-catchers for display windows. Interior designers will flock to your creations. This is a brand new market.

$ ♿ ▐▜▐▜

63 TEXTILE PAINTING

The chances of selling handpainted textile products are truly excellent. You will need to practice painting fabrics if you haven't already, as practice makes perfect. Experience will be your best teacher. As you become more and more professional, your creations will begin to merit quite high prices. Dresses, handkerchiefs, ties, blouses, and skirts are just a few things that can be handpainted. Equipment costs are fairly negligible. Fabrics will be your main expense. Try painting fabrics with stencils as well.

$ ♿

64 UNIQUE GREETING CARDS

High prices are inevitable for anything that is not mass produced, but is one-of-a-kind. You can go into business making one-of-a-kind greeting cards with just about anything in the way of small objects as takeoff points, such as paper clips, rubber bands, buttons, and so on. You can work out simple catchy designs of faces, figures, or designs in conjunction with these small objects, which are glued onto the parchment paper card. Make up a batch of unique cards and you will be able to sell the entire lot as is at any greeting card shop or finer gift store at good prices.

$ ♿

65 WALL PLAQUES, FINISHED

This can be a full-time job, which will bring you a full living. Slice up smaller trees or large limbs on an angle so you can see both the inner wood grains and the outer bark around the perimeter. Sand smooth. Print messages, quips, animals, and the like on the best side by silkscreen process. Finally, coat it with clear spar varnish to protect it. Install a rustic piece of leather to hang it from. Make different sizes. Gift shops and other tourist shops will gladly retail them for you.

$ ♿

|||||||AUTOMOTIVE

66 AIRBRUSH

Painting with an airbrush is a whole new experience based upon a new technology. With an airbrush paint setup you can quickly make lifelike pictures and designs that formerly were almost impossible to do. It is this procedure that has made it possible, for example, to give unique and attractive paint schemes to automobiles. If you have the quickly-learned skills required, you may consider doing custom airbrush painting with dozens of applications. A good living is certain in a well-run business of this kind.

$$ 👨‍🦽 🎨

67 AUTO DETAILING

This endeavor is little known, but it is a real sleeper that can be incredibly profitable. Clean and polish cars inside and out. You can "prep" new cars, or recondition used cars, on a volume basis, or perform high-quality cosmetic maintenance upon a fine auto owned by a proud private party. Build a regular clientele, giving complete, thorough jobs for about $150. Work almost anywhere—parking lots, garages, alleys, and so on. Two to three hundred dollars will start you shining!

$$ 🔨 🎨

68 AUTO-PAINTING SHOP

New car prices are climbing sky-high with no end in sight, which makes this business boom as well! Start a high-quality, low-priced paint center for automobiles. Offer pickup and delivery, use of a substitute car, and quick, local service, and you won't have to worry about any competition. New paints, such as acrylics, make painting a car a snap. Custom add-ons such as pinstriping and airbrush effects will double your profits.

$$ 🔨 🎨

69 AUTO SECURITY

An automobile is one of the most expensive purchases most people ever make, second only to their homes. With the rising cost of fine cars, more and more people are concerned for automobile security. The underworld thrives on stolen vehicles in particular. In this business, stock all the latest and the best security devices for automobiles.

$$$ 👨‍🦽 🔨 🎨

70 USED CAR SALES PAPER

Look in the classified section of almost any paper and you will normally find that the largest category of listings is that of used autos. All car owners know that they will get more by selling their car privately than they will ever get on a trade-in. In this business, you provide a pulp brochure monthly or biweekly with used auto listings for your area, in which you provide better pricing and ad space than any of your competition.

$$

71 AUTO PARKING SERVICE

Hire students to provide this service for the better restaurants in your area. Restaurants will gladly sign up for your service—it helps attract patrons. Also the restaurants are usually happy to let you hire and supervise your own attendants to provide the service. You will soon be having your own car parked by your own attendants as you and yours begin dining in style at these fine restaurants!

$$

72 AUTO REPAIRS

The cost of auto repairs is becoming prohibitive to most customers. More and more smart auto mechanics are setting up an auto repair shop in their backyard or are setting up a mobile service in which they fix cars at the home of their clients. You will need a good set of tools and some initial ads run in your local paper. Flyers in laundromats, and the like, will bring you steady work. Your much lower prices will attract dozens of people in distress who will see to it that you make a much better living than you would working in someone else's garage.

$$$$

73 AUTO SOUND SYSTEMS

Installing and troubleshooting sound systems in cars and other vehicles can provide a good living. You will need to understand basic electronics. With this basic knowledge you can set up a simple business in your home shop or garage working with these special sound systems. A few newspaper ads will get you under way and later on word of mouth will probably bring you over half your business. Flyers in laundromats and elsewhere will also bring customers to you.

$$$

74 AUTO SWAP MEET

Simply turn a vacant lot next to your house into a swap meet for automobiles only. You charge people who wish to display their auto in your lot a flat fee for a specified day or week. The public is admitted to the display at scheduled times only. You have nothing to do with the selling and buying or trading. Your only cost will be your ad to attract car sellers and possible buyers. You could add on a food concession for increased profits.

$ 👤   ⚒   🏙

75 AUTO TRANSPORT SERVICE

People often want their car or cars delivered from one part of the country to another. Used car dealers often have this problem. Retired people going south for the winter and north for the summer who want to fly back and forth and still have their car waiting for them at their destination have this problem. Contact reliable drivers with good driving records in need of free one-way transportation and hire them by subcontract to deliver the auto cross-country.

$ 🏙

76 AUTO TUNE-UP INSTRUCTION

The cost of auto tune-ups and minor repairs is becoming exorbitant. Many books have appeared recently with information to help car owners do their own tune-ups and repairs. But these books tend to belabor very simple jobs. People can learn much more easily and more quickly if they can be shown person-to-person how to do something. If you know auto tune-up and repair, you can sell this ability and know-how to private auto owners so they can learn how to ultimately save hundreds of dollars by adjusting and repairing their own automobiles.

$$ 👤   🏙

77 AUTO TUNE-UP IN THIRTY MINUTES

More and more gas stations have quit offering repair service. This has forced the growth of specialty repair shops. You can set up a precision operation, offering 30-minute tune-ups only, for around $5000. Call yourself Autotune, or whatever, and be prepared to tune-up your lifestyle in short order. Every major neighborhood has a need for this time-saving service.

$$ ⚒   🏙

78 BATTERY RECONDITIONING

You can buy discarded batteries for about two dollars or less, restore them for another two dollars or so, and then market the same battery for $25 to $40. That is a humongous profit to be sure! You can run this goldmine in your backyard workshop with just a few hand tools. You can restore about 20 batteries a day. You can rework batteries for service stations, used car lots, farmers, homeowners, contractors, and truckers. With new batteries costing up to $100 and more, you can see that the market is ready for you to set up this business in your area.

$

79 CAR CLEANING

People will pay you well, not to have their car washed, but rather to have it thoroughly cleaned, inside and out. You can set up in conjunction with a local service station or garage. You can shampoo the engine compartment, sponge clean and vacuum the interior, and wash and wax the exterior. Repeat business will be a certainty. People buying used cars will seek you out without delay. You may get contracts with used car dealers for this special service. You can always go door to door offering this service. You will keep busy!

$

80 CAR WASH

An ideal absentee-owned business. No inventory to be pilfered and no heavy labor costs. This is a service 63 percent of car owners use regularly, and researchers say that usage rates are steadily increasing. With $1.80-a-gallon gas prices, the gross profit on a combination fill-up and single car wash can reach $7.40. There are many car washes that clean up on more than 20,000 cars a month! Add-on sales such as headlights, wiper blades, and so on, can boost you even further.

$

81 CONSIGNMENT USED CAR SALES

Last year about 8 million cars were sold in North America, yet over 34 million used cars changed hands. This is a ratio of about 4 old cars to every new car. It may start out as a "poor man's car business," but it won't stay that way long if it is run well. Consignment means you sell it first and pay for it after. People consign their autos to you with the agreement that they will receive a certain amount of money when the vehicle is sold. A huge profit can be made when you sell the auto at the best price you can get. Net profits of $3000 a month are not unusual!

$ 🔧   🏙

82 CROSS-COUNTRY TRUCKER

This is a huge, growing market that offers tremendous opportunities for the sharp, aggressive person who likes the freedom of being his or her own boss out on the road. Profits average around $30,000 on start-up costs ranging from $0 upwards. You can be an independent owner-operator, or you can contract out with large freight companies. If independence and accumulating solid capital is for you, then this may be what you have been looking for.

$$ 🔧   🏙

83 DO-IT-YOURSELF AUTO REPAIR SHOP

The high cost of new cars plus the high cost of even questionable labor will make this new business boom for you! Your unique business will rent out bays, a complete line of automotive tools and service manuals for all cars, giving step-by-step instructions for the repair or replacement of every part. Add on basic parts sales. Some even have a professional mechanic as manager who can give additional help as needed.

$$$$ ♿   🔧   🏙

84 GLASS TINTING

Most homes have windows and glass doors that cause excessive heat or glare or interior color fading problems. Many auto windshields are also in need of tinting. You can set up a business to provide a window tinting service. You can first practice and experiment on scrap glass until you feel confident. You can check the yellow pages for your tinting materials, or you can learn to make your own inexpensively. Keep your prices within reach of average homeowners. Many businesses also need their windows tinted, so check around.

$$ 🏙

85 MUFFLER SHOP

Work out of your own home garage, making your tailpipes from scratch without stocking a large complicated inventory, and you can rest assured that you will beat your competition with their own deadly overhead.

Unlike costly franchises, you can get started with less than $10,000. You will have even the major franchisors running scared!

$$$

86 OIL RECLAMATION

Getting into the oil business is usually very expensive. Not so with this oil business. All gas stations dispose of used motor oil. You can provide free tanks for them to dump this used oil into. You can then haul the oil away, set up a machine to filter it in your backyard, and then resell the oil by the gallon to large construction companies with heavy equipment such as earthmovers, bulldozers, and so on, or to companies with fleets of trucks. You will be making nearly clear profit. Check your library to find where to purchase the necessary oil-purifying equipment.

$$

87 PROPANE CONVERSION CENTER

Each gasoline crunch makes conversion to propane more and more sensible. Propane burns cleaner, is 30 percent to 50 percent cheaper than gasoline, requires up to 50 percent less engine maintenance, and best of all, the reserves of propane in the ground will far outlast the petroleum reserves. Install propane-only kits or dual-fuel (propane and gasoline) systems in all types of motor vehicles. You will become the "energy czar" in your community in the business everyone expects to take off during this next decade!

$$$

88 RENT-A-JUNK-CAR BUSINESS

Call your business Lease-A-Lemon, or Rent-A-Heap, or Rent-A-Wreck, or whatever. Get a fleet of inexpensive heaps (and even antiques) and rent them out at dramatic savings to patrons. Hertz charges $24.95 per day plus 22 cents per mile just for a compact. You can beat that by charging about $9 per day, $52 a week, or $224 a month for one of your choice ugly ducklings. In weeks you will probably be expanding. Works well out of a home!

$$

89 SELF-SERVICE GAS STATION

This new concept was brought about by the high cost of gasoline. Hire minimum staff and promote volume sales by discounting in various ways, which can include giving away free premiums. Start up with less than $6000. Annual net profits frequently approach $40,000. Add-ons of take-out food and drinks or a car wash make your piece of pie even bigger.

$$$$ ◣ ᳀

90 SHUTTLE SERVICE

With an air-conditioned van or a minibus you can quickly get into this business. You will cater to people who want the service of a limousine but who are willing to share their uncrowded comfort and convenience with other people. These clients want to avoid public buses and taxis and finding parking and buying expensive gas and rush-hour traffic and so on. Add on prepared lunches if you like. Cater to groups of shoppers, or office people, or airport passengers, or restaurant row clients, or whatever you can find. Have regular routes with flexible schedules.

$$ ◣ ᳀

91 TEN-MINUTE OIL CHANGE

This business is here to stay. Go into a gas station that has gone self-serve and rent the service portion of the station for as little as $300 per month. Your customer simply drives through. You and your employee work as a team. One works underneath, draining oil and lubing, while the other is under the hood changing the filter, lubing, cleaning battery terminals, and checking wiper blades and other fluid levels. Pump all your fluids in to save time. Stand up for less than $5000 and call yourself the Lube Pit Stop or whatever.

$ ◣ ᳀

92 TRAILER RENTALS

You really build up this business yourself by making utility trailers out of used parts (or have a backyard mechanic do it for you). Paint them bright and keep them attractive. For $1000, using used parts, you should end up with six to eight trailers. Rent them out at a busy service station, paying the station owner 25 percent of gross receipts. Few people own their own trailers and nearly everyone needs one from time to time to haul things they can't get into their car.

$$ ◣ ᳀

93 TRUCK DRIVING INSTRUCTION

Truck drivers are generally the finest drivers you will find in North America. Most of them are professionals in every sense. If you have survived in this profession for a number of years, you could put your expertise to work for yourself so you can work out of your home without having to go back out on the road. You can teach others how to become professional truck drivers. Special instruction in defensive driving, air brakes, and so on will be what you will sell from now on, so you can stay near home.

$

94 UPHOLSTERY

This is an ideal "back room business." Stay at home with this one for meaningful profits. (Secret: You can sew heavy fabrics on any machine if you first spray the seam line with silicone friction reducer.) Start small and simple. Later, you may want to expand into fancy seat covers for autos and boats, boat canopies, snap-on protectors for pickup truck beds, gun cases, and so on. Keep your quality up and folks won't mind waiting while you catch up to their job.

$

95 USED AUTO CONSULTANT

All you will need to start this business is expertise in auto repairs. Advertise that you will help prospective used car buyers find a sound used auto. You will offer to go with them on a tour of used car lots and help them select a dependable car. Or else they can bring a car to your home, where you will carefully inspect it for them. Either way, charge them by the hour. There are many cautious buyers who will be glad to find your expert service available.

$

96 USED CAR LOT

Buy low—sell high. It is simple. A good knowledge of mechanics is a must, especially body work. Most people are more interested in how a car looks than how it runs. You will need a place to repair cars and the necessary tools. Buy from individuals for cash for much less than the asking price. Know the market value of cars well. Close bargaining is the real key to success in this business, just like it used to be in horse trading!

$$

97 VAN INTERIOR CUSTOMIZING

A van can become a comfortable, relatively inexpensive home-away-from-home if it is thoughtfully furbished inside. You may be interested in forming a business to customize the interior of vans for well-paying customers. You will need to have the skills of an interior decorator and a mechanic and a finish carpenter combined. An artistic flair will be a big bonus. Circulate flyers at all new and used car dealers, at car shows, and so on. Study other customized vans for ideas you can sell for a satisfying income.

$$ 🔨 🏙

98 WINDSHIELD REPAIRS

Windshields are always vulnerable to flying rocks. Replacing windshields that have pockmarks in them can be very expensive. If a windshield has only chips and pockmarks in it, and it doesn't have any cracks developing yet, it can be repaired inexpensively in just a few minutes with special new materials and techniques. You can get into the good-paying business of repairing chipped and pocked windshields quite easily. For about $50 you can start right away. A small continuous newspaper ad will keep you busy in larger centers.

$ 🏙

99 COMPUTERIZED USED VEHICLE LISTING AND LOCATING

Many people searching for a used automobile have their minds set on a certain make and model. In some of the big city newspapers, you may find that the classified ads for automobiles are listed by year, make, and model. In medium-size and smaller newspapers you will not find this convenience provided. Using a computer, you can create your own listing that provides this special service for prospective buyers of used automobiles in your own locality. You can market your listings through 24-hour convenience stores and most magazine stands.

$$ ♿ 🏙

100 ANTIFREEZE RECYCLING SERVICE

Antifreeze does not wear out, despite what you may have been told. It is now possible to buy a machine that recycles this product. This will be a real plus for the environment because every year thousands of gallons of this toxic material are dumped out somewhere. This will also be a plus to the consumer because the cost of the product is not exactly cheap. You can set up a business in which you simply go from client to client selling them on recycling their antifreeze and flushing out their car's radiator at the same time. This is a relatively inexpensive home business to start up.

$$ **▀▜▐▛**

101 MOBILE AUTO INSPECTION

There is a concerted effort all over North America to remove older, marginal, or nonroadworthy automobiles from operating on the roads. This removal is especially being pressed in larger cities, where air pollution is a real problem. It is imperative in many of these metropolitan areas to have your automobile tested on a regular basis for safety and for emission control. Much of this testing is performed at large centers where the drivers must sometimes wait many hours to have their cars tested. If you can be licensed to perform the testing yourself, you can set up a mobile car-testing business. The convenience you offer car owners would be most welcome.

$ **◣** **▀▜▐▛**

102 DENT REMOVAL

It takes just a tiny dent to undermine a new car owner's pride. The same thing is true of a dent in the main entry metal door to a fine home. There are special tools and techniques now available to remove nearly all dents wherever they may be found. With minimal study you can become an expert on dent removal. You can then set up in business to rid your community of them. You can simply cruise around looking for them. You can then approach a given dent's owner and offer to remove it for your fair fee. Most people will not be hard to sell.

$$ **▀▜▐▛**

103 QUICK PAINT REPAIR

Most people needing small paint repairs made to their automobiles will put off having the job done because it often ties up their vehicle in some distant shop for an entire day or longer. You can become educated on how to make these special repairs. You can then organize a business in which you provide mobile, quick paint repair service. This will mean that you will have to protect any new paint job from environmental dust by using a plastic frame. It also means you must have a good eye for color. And you must also use fast-drying paints such as acrylics.

$$

▮▮▮▮▮▮CHILDREN

104 CHILDREN'S LETTER SERVICE

As soon as you run your ad for this business in a national parent's magazine, parents will purchase one-year subscriptions to your "Uncle Ben" or "Aunt Mae" letter-writing service. You, who love to communicate with the younger set, will faithfully write a personal letter to the client's child each month especially intended to please just him or her. A special birthday letter will be included in the subscription. You will be keeping many, many youngsters all over North America happy with your monthly letters. Some of them will one day want to come visit you!

$ ♿ ▮▮▮

105 CHILDREN'S LIBRARY

If you love both children and books, this business can be a happy combination for you. You convert a room of your home into a library for children. You will need lots of low shelves, cushions to sit on, lots of wholesome books, new and used, and a bit of local advertising. Provide a story hour several mornings each week and perhaps some good quiet games for children. Charge each family a flat fee per month for your range of services. Stick to a reasonable schedule. You will likely be able to handle 50 or more family subscribers.

$$ ♿ ▮▮▮

106 CHILDREN'S PARTY SERVICE

If you are a self-starter with good energy, imagination, and ability to plan and conduct festivities for children, this business can be what you have been waiting for. Many working mothers or mothers of means will gladly hire you to move right in and conduct a given party for their child and friends. You will handle the invitations, the refreshments, favors, decorations, games and prizes, supervision, and the clean-up. You can look forward to a good demand for your services and very little competition, if any, in this exciting business.

$$ ◀ ▮▮▮

107 CHILDREN'S PUZZLES

It is difficult to find puzzles for children that are (1) durable, (2) interesting, (3) graded by ability, (4) at reasonable prices, and (5) that have wholesome pictures. If you can combine these five features into puzzles you make, you have unlimited possibilities throughout North America to do a genuine booming business. If you can mass-produce the above type of puzzles, then you will soon be set for early retirement!

$ 

108 CHILDREN'S USED CLOTHING

Used clothing for children makes good sense, because children will usually grow out of a garment long before it is worn out. You can set aside a special room in your home in which you can display your collection of good used clothing for children. Purchase your selection from thrift stores, garage sales, and so on. Plan to resell at 300 percent markup or better. Repair, clean, and press each garment. Buy out of season for bargains. Sell by appointment only, serving only one customer at a time. In this way you can schedule the use of your free time wisely.

$

109 BEDTIME STORIES ON TAPE

A well-selected bedtime story will help an active child to wind down so he or she can go to sleep. You can find tasteful, wholesome stories and read them in a relaxing, quiet manner onto cassette tapes. These tapes can then be mass-produced easily and marketed as wholesome bedtime stories. They could also be customized by using the child's real first name within an introduction to the type. There are many children with the same first name. You could sell these by mail order from home if you prefer. They would retail most anywhere.

$

110 CHILD CARE CENTER

In North America there are about 9 million working mothers with about 11 million children under the age of six. Nearly 70 percent of these children, who need full-time day care, spend the day with neighbors or babysitters. Most parents want their children immersed in a more stimulating environment than is usual with the average babysitter. You can begin small at home, offering a more stimulating and educational setting for client children.

$$$$

111 COLORING BOOKS

If you look carefully at the content of existing coloring books on the market you will notice quite inferior products—they are too often filled with pictures from the occult—witches, ghosts, fairies, and the like. Or they are given over to violence like *Star Wars,* and so on. You will be able to have the market for truly wholesome coloring books almost all to yourself if you go into this business. It would be so simple to come up with an entirely wholesome collection of pictures for children and publish them as a coloring book worthy of the name. The market is waiting for simple, wholesome products!

$$ ♿ ♲

112 DOLL HOUSES

Doll houses are perennial favorites with children. Many plans for doll houses and furniture are available in library books and magazines and even in hobby stores. You can work up several styles and sizes and show them around as samples. If you can work to custom-order you will be assured of a sale before you even begin the project. Try to match house styles with furniture styles. You can make up an inventory and market it in the fall before the holiday season rush. The furniture will sell itself in toy and department stores.

$$ ♿ ♲

113 DOLL REPAIR

A child becomes quite attached to his or her doll. Parents are usually willing to replace the doll but the child won't even think of giving it up. So parents will pay well to have a child's favorite doll repaired. You can take up the specialty of doll repair as a home business. Practice on restoring several dolls needing new clothes or their faces repainted until you are ready to go public. Average talents will get you into this business. You may want to specialize in restoring antique dolls or dolls from foreign cultures or even museum dolls.

$ ♿ ♲

114 FISH POND FOR CHILDREN

The chance to catch real live trout will excite any boy or girl. You can open up a very profitable fish pond just for young people to come catch live trout if you can provide the country or rural site, plus water for the pond. You will need two ponds—one for fingerlings to grow up in, the other for fishing in for the mature trout. You advertise your business and parents will bring their children to fish your pond, paying for each fish caught, renting the equipment from you, and buying the bait from you. Keep well stocked and you will not lack for repeat customers.

$$$

115 MERRY-GO-ROUND WAGON

Build a merry-go-round on a low trailer or truck, which you pull from residential block to block giving "pony" rides to little tykes. Give a five-minute ride and then move on. Perhaps you can specialize in birthday parties, where you charge by the hour. The neighbors will all be gaping. The kids will be squealing with delight. The doting parents will gain prestige by providing the merry-go-round for the occasion. Or perhaps you can work through supermarkets, giving free rides to customers of the supermarket. Work group picnics, too.

$$

116 MINI-LUMBER FOR MINI-CARPENTERS

Young boys often receive sets of carpenter tools for gifts, but they quickly become frustrated when they have no boards to saw and nail. Simply collect scrap lumber, cut it into proper lengths, package it in bundles, and sell it as lumber kits to toy stores and other retail outlets for the holiday season. Check sawmills or new home sites for mill ends. Those carpenter tool kits will be far more meaningful to the young carpenters with your kits as gifts.

$

117 PIÑATAS

The focal point of a party for children can be a Mexican-style piñata. It will add a welcome, festive touch. You can make piñatas easily from papier mâché, which are then festively decorated. Customers purchase them for birthday parties and hang them from the ceiling. Children take turns being blindfolded and trying to whack the hanging piñata down with a stick. The first one to succeed gets first choice of the goodies hidden inside the piñata. You can make them to order, as well as sell them to various retailers. Think of novel twists in making and using them to enhance sales.

$

118 PONY RIDES

If you like ponies and children you can do well in this business. Buy 8 or 10 ponies for about $50 each. They will live for 20 years or more. Location is very important—large mall parking lots, fairs, public parks, amusement parks, the beach—wherever there are lots of children. You will need the ponies, saddles, a ticket booth, and a corral (fence) that encircles the ride area. A boy or girl who knows horses could be your ride-hand sidekick.

$$　🏹　📊

119 ROCKING HORSES

A rocking horse heads the list of most desired toys for many children. Hundreds and hundreds of different designs are in existence. You can make and sell rocking horses as a fine home business. Creating one outstanding design and putting it into mass production is one approach. Another approach is to make a variety of models and sell them, perhaps through national advertising of a free catalog in which your selection is displayed. Another approach is to work with collectors of rocking horses who pay big prices for rare or unusual rocking horse designs.

$　♿　📊

120 TIME TOYS FOR TOTS

Children are often placed in positions where they have to wait for long periods during which they are expected to be quiet. They have to wait for the doctor or the dentist to see them, or they have to wait until the long trip is over. You can make and sell toy kits that will help occupy children quietly during these waiting periods—coloring book kits, knitting kits, play clay kits, book kits, and so forth. Package your kits in clear plastic bags with snap-lock tops. Sell them at bus, train, or plane depots. Parents and children alike will appreciate their existence. This could be a business that explodes!

$　♿　📊

121 TODDLER STAIRCASE

The world is designed for adults. Children can do a lot more on their own if they have a few helping tools specially designed for them. Design and make from plywood a little three-step staircase stool for young ones. With it they can climb up and wash their own hands and face at the sink. They can also climb up and see what their parents are doing in the kitchen or at a work table. You may soon have a small factory for building these staircases for little tykes who are eager to get up in the world!

$ ♿

122 WOODEN TOYS

Patterns for all sorts of wooden toys can be found in books in craft shops and public libraries. There are the standard toys that always sell well—jigsaw puzzles, doll beds, animals, and pull toys. However, if your imagination is up to it, an original idea could be even better. Get to brainstorming and see if you can come up with a new toy that can be thrown, or a new type of pull toy, or a new type of a doll, or something novel with wheels on it. Don't be timid. You may be the creator and maker of a brand new fad toy!

$ ♿

123 CHILDREN'S RESALE STORE

Children grow so fast that they seldom wear out anything. This is true of their toys, most of their clothes, and most of the equipment, such as cribs, they use. Most of these products can be used again and again by other children. A fine business can be made buying and reselling all of these items in almost any community. It will benefit not only you as the businessperson, but also the former owners and the new owners. Best of all, landfills will fill up less quickly.

$$$ ♿

124 CHILD SECURITY SYSTEMS

Children are naturally inquisitive, and this curiosity gets many of them into trouble. With a little foresight and with proper attention, most parents and guardians can help prevent most child distress. It is possible to operate a business in which you sell various technologies and information that would prevent most child distress. For example, there are methods for tattooing identification on a child in case the child should get lost or kidnapped. It is possible to run a business that specializes in giving both parents and children more peace of mind by enhancing the child's security.

$$ ♿

125 BABY STORE

A baby store could retail all items that a baby would normally consume. This specialty business can make one-stop shopping for baby products possible. Even basic food items could be carried in stock. In a town where there is a sizable young adult population, this business could be run profitably. It may be necessary to rent a retail space in which to set it up properly. Competitive pricing of your inventory would be a must in order to build up your clientele.

$$$$ ▥

126 PERSONALIZED CHILDREN'S VIDEOS

We all like to shine or be in the spotlight sometime in our lives. Most people do have their minute in the sun. But you can extend this minute into hours by making personalized videos. A child will really eat up a video in which he or she appears in a major way and is the hero or heroine. It is possible to make a video in such a way that you simply tack on the ending scene or scenes to portray a child client as the hero or heroine. A comedy plot will go over especially well.

$$ ♿   ▥

127 MAIL-ORDER EDUCATIONAL TOYS

Most toys being sold today are of poor quality—poor quality in terms of how they are made and poor quality in terms of what they teach children to think about when they play. Many of these toys teach violence and killing and immorality, which no one needs. If you share this same concern about toys, you may consider starting a business in your home in which you retail good-quality educational toys. Not everyone will appreciate what you are doing, but stick with it and your clientele will gradually grow. Just stick with quality at all times.

$$$$ ♿   ▥

128 CARDBOARD PLAYHOUSES

This is a very clever business to be in. You make cardboard playhouses that are large enough for smaller children to play in. You build them in such a way that they can be shipped flat by freight. You can then sell them mail order from your home. Your clients assemble these cardboard playhouses, and the children themselves paint the playhouse. You can draw outlines of animals and flowers and other items on the outside of the cardboard and the children simply color in your outlines.

$$

▮▮▮▮▮▮CLEANING

129 GARBAGE CAN CLEANING
Contract with restaurants, cafes, grocery stores, and other firms to steam-clean their garbage cans on a monthly basis. You can do the job either on location with a portable steam cleaner, or you can take them to your home to steam-clean them. Owners will appreciate the reduction in stench and flies from your service. Larger garbage bin containers can also be steam-cleaned. Contact the firms who rent them out to see whether you can clean all their units each month as well.

$$

130 JANITOR SERVICE
Before you start this business, get a job working for an established jani-torial business so you can learn the tricks of the trade! You will contract with commercial establishments—stores, theaters, offices, and restaurants—to work a certain schedule. You can start from your home with a few cleaning tools. Later, you can hire cleaning crews to subcon-tract under your business. Some janitor services keep a dozen crews busy constantly and are on their way to being rich!

$$

131 RESTROOMS ONLY SERVICE
Clean public restrooms are difficult to find in any community, whether it is large or small. Businesspeople should realize that one of the best attractions for repeat customers is to maintain neat, clean restrooms. You can purchase a few basic supplies and tools and then open a restrooms only service. You would sell businesses, especially gas stations and eating establishments, on your ability to provide the best complete restroom service in your area. Give a demonstration of what you can do for free and your client will find it hard not to hire you.

$$ ◣ ▦▮▌

132 STEAM CLEANING
A portable or mobile steam-cleaning business would be hard to beat as a home business where you are your own boss. You could go door-to-door cleaning auto engines—there is excellent money in this approach. Or you could work at truck stops cleaning truck engines and undercar-riages. Or you could work late nights steam-cleaning restaurant kitchens, which become encrusted with grease and grime. Many opportunities will

present themselves as you keep your eyes open for them in this business. A portable steam-cleaning unit will cost $300 to $600. You can pay for it easily with about one week's work.

133   SURFACE CLEANING, MOBILE

You clean up big in this business. Office buildings, houses, bridges, billboards, restaurant kitchens, and so forth are always becoming discolored by aging layers of dirt and grease. You can operate from a self-contained van unit. Jobs are easily found. Work from an office at home!

134   VEHICLE CLEANING

If you already have a van or a pickup truck, all you will need are some cleaning tools and supplies—soaps, cleaners, brushes, rags, and, perhaps, a propane-fired hot water supply. You can then specialize in cleaning all types of vehicles on the spot—airplanes, cars, trucks, and boats. You could get contracts to clean fleets of vehicles from government agencies. A portable steam cleaner would double your reach, as you could then clean engine compartments more readily. You could add on the cleaning of public washrooms, if you like.

135   VENETIAN BLIND CLEANING

Fashions often go in full circles. This is true of Venetian blinds, which are once again big sellers for home and office interior decorating. You can start a business very inexpensively in which you specialize in servicing these products. You will make minor repairs and adjustments, and you will wash and clean them. You can purchase special, inexpensive equipment that will quickly and efficiently clean these blinds, thus saving considerable drudgery. Advertise your services in the yellow pages and under "Services Offered" in the classified ads.

136   CONSTRUCTION SITE CLEANUP

Construction sites require good cleanup. They always need after-the-job cleanup, but they sometimes need cleanup even before the construction job begins, or even while the job is in progress. You can run a business in which you subcontract to take care of this portion of the construction job. You will need a few basic hand tools and probably a reliable pickup truck. You will often be allowed to salvage many of the building materials, which can increase your profits. Attention to detail will assure you of further business down the road.

$$

137 WALL CLEANING

No sooner is a wall painted than dirt and grime start to show up on it, especially if it is a light color. One way to get rid of the dirt is to simply paint over it. But a cheaper way is to simply clean the wall using an inexpensive cleaning compound mixed in water, such as TSP. You will need buckets, sponges, dry mops, and not much else to go into this business. The start-up costs don't get much smaller. Expect to have to move furniture to the center of most rooms you will be working in. You could join this business with a wall-painting business in which you paint the walls that have passed the point of no return and need more than a mere cleaning.

$

138 ULTRASONIC CLEANING

We all know how difficult it is to clean an oven when it is coated with baked-on crud. Self-cleaning ovens have mostly solved this problem. But there are many other items that get cruddy and are not so easy to clean. Using a new process, called ultrasonic cleaning, most of these cruddy items can now be easily cleaned. You can purchase the equipment to do it. It is normally a steel tank about the size of a medium-size fish aquarium. You put the dirty item in the tank and turn the apparatus on. In only a few seconds, you turn the machine off and remove the item, which is now spotlessly clean. No more need for elbow grease and ferocious scrubbing and harsh solvents. This process can form the nucleus of a fine home business.

$ ♿   ▀▜▛

139 MINI-BLIND CLEANING

Mini-blinds are very practical items to have installed on windows in both the home and the office. They are very reasonably priced. They do a good job of providing privacy and blocking out excessive light. But they do collect their share of dirt and grime. Cleaning them can be a very distasteful chore under normal circumstances because of all the nooks and crannies which need to be wiped clean. There is technology now available which makes cleaning them a relative breeze. You can purchase this equipment and use it daily in your mini-blind cleaning business.

$$

140 CEILING TILE CLEANING

Ceiling tiles are almost always flat white, so they show dirt almost from the moment they are suspended in place. Some of them are called acoustical tiles because they have a highly textured surface to reduce noise levels. These tiles are particularly difficult to clean because of their rough surfaces. There are special cleaning methods and technologies which clean tiles quickly and thoroughly. The cleaning devices can be the backbone of a sound home business.

$$

141 HOUSE CLEANING

Life is filled with irony. For example, in order to clean something it means that you have to make something else dirty. But have you noticed that anything can get dirty without anything else getting clean? If so, then you know that there is one other thing certain in life besides taxes and death, and that is house cleaning. When people can escape from it, they often will. Many working people are too busy to look after their house cleaning and are willing to hire the job done. You can run a decent business cleaning houses for these people. You might even hire others whom you supervise.

$

▌▌▌▌▌▌▌CRAFTS

142 APPLE DOLLS
Unlike mass-produced dolls you will never see two dried apple dolls that look exactly alike. Each one has unique features that depend completely on the imagination of its creator. Peel the apple under cold water to keep it from turning brown. Carve the facial features with spoons and knives. Soak in salt water for two days. Remove and hang to dry for three weeks. Now decorate the face. Add a sawdust-filled body and clothes, and coat the apple face with floor wax to preserve its appearance. You will end up with nifty, unusual, wizened creatures that are highly saleable.

$ ♿ ▐▜▐▛

143 APRONS
Aprons are selling better now than they did in grandmother's day. You can start up a nifty home business of making and selling aprons for all occasions—the fancy pinafore type for general use, to the tiny little decorative type for special dinners, to the denim models for backyard cookouts, etc. You can operate well from your own home or you may want to open up a tiny storefront retail outlet. Add on apron patterns and fabrics for more profits.

$ ♿ ▐▜▐▛

144 BABY SHOES IN BRONZE
Preserving baby's first shoes in bronze (or gold, or silver) has become a permanent tradition in North America. All parents have a sentimental attachment to these dear shoes with all their scuffs and wrinkles. They are a memorial of memories parents wish to capture and cherish forever. You can start up this business for about $40. You can bronze coat a pair of shoes in less than an hour for less than one dollar. Mount the shoes on an interesting plaque or set of bookends and sell them for $30 or so. You can run this home business through direct mail advertising if you choose to do so.

$ ♿ ▐▜▐▛

145 BIRD CAGES, ORNAMENTAL
You have maybe seen one of these before, hanging in a florist shop, a gift shop, or some private home. They are artificial birdcages housing artificial birds—parakeets, parrots, etc. They are incredibly beautiful arrangements of pastel color—made of ribbons, nylon netting, pipe

cleaners, feathers, etc. No two are necessarily alike. The variety possible is surely endless. The birds don't sing, but then you don't have to feed them or clean their cages either. People will love them in their breathtaking loveliness. They will sell themselves.

$ ♿   ▙▌▐

146   BIRD FEEDERS

People will want to laugh at you if you tell them you make a good living by making and selling bird feeders! But your bird friends and your friendly banker won't be laughing! Collect a variety of plans. Select a few of the best and start producing and selling by mail order. Knockdown kits go well and ship easily. Supply tallow-seed mixtures as well by mail order. Obtain a list of pet stores and wholesale through them. Add on birdhouses, bird feed, and so on.

$ ♿   ▙▌▐

147   BLACKSMITHING

Wrought iron and decorative ironwork are finding their way into most modern homes for things like banisters, railings, plant hangers, and so on. You can pick up this reviving trade and become a modern day black-smith making a respectable income. Several correspondence courses are available.

$$ ▙▌▐

148   BOOKSHELVES

There are hundreds of different ways to build bookshelves. But a few simple styles will put you in business making them and selling them. A small ad will bring customers your way. Build them to order for quickest return on your investment. This is a specialty product that can keep you profitably employed full-time in a center of any size.

$ ♿   ▙▌▐

149   BOOMERANGS

You can make good boomerangs for about 15 cents apiece and then proceed to sell them for about $3 apiece—a gross 2000 percent profit! Study the different kinds of boomerangs and experiment yourself with making them and throwing them. Find the best type for general use. Specialize in it and go with it. Spray paint them in bright yellows and oranges. Fluorescent paints are eye-catching. Peddle them wherever kids of all ages congregate, such as at fairs, flea markets, air shows, etc. Boomerangs always return—excellent profits!

$ ♿   ▲▮▮

150 BRAIDED RUGS

Machines make all kinds of braided rugs today, but their results simply cannot match the beauty of old-fashioned, hand-braided, woolen rugs, which you can learn to make for profit. Machines cannot match the wide range of color and design that you can. For these and other reasons, many people will prefer to have you braid rugs to their order. Use only good wool. Presell your rugs by getting enough deposit up front to cover materials before you begin. Get a braiding tool, which will speed up the work considerably. Strive for uniqueness in your designs.

$ ♿   ▲▮▮

151 BUMPER STICKERS

Bumper stickers are here to stay. They are a very effective way to get messages of all sorts across to the public. You can set up a small home business in which you print and sell them to various clients. Presell your orders in most cases to special tourist spots and businesses, to politicians, to church groups, and the like. Certain general interest stickers will sell well through gift and novelty shops. Your overhead costs will be negligible compared to your potential profits.

$ ♿   ▲▮▮

152 BUTTONS FOR CLOTHES

Every eye is attracted to the beauty found in wood grains and rock patterns. You can set up inexpensively to make buttons of beautiful, polished gemstones and agates, petrified wood, and regular wood. You can then sell these in matched sets attached to display cards to exclusive shops dealing in unusual findings of all kinds for the tailor and the seamstress. You could finance a trip around the world, selling these as you go. Work them up in the winter and they will provide the means for an extended summer vacation!

$ ♿   ▲▮▮

153 CANDLEHOLDERS

Candleholders can be made from an enormous variety of materials. Among the nicer-looking holders are those made from fine wood and brass. Others are made from beautiful grained woods turned on a lathe. Develop an entire line of fine decorative candleholders that you can duplicate over and over again, and set yourself up in a home factory business in which a good living is possible if you learn how to work the market you wish to corner.

$

154 CANING

Wicker furniture has recently made a solid comeback. Today there are specialty stores that deal strictly in wicker. The trade of recaning the seats of cane, or rush, or splint seats is practically unknown. You can quickly master this trade and then go on to recane chairs and other items for individuals, antique shops, and secondhand stores. The only tools you need are an awl, a sharp knife, and a few wooden pegs. You will make a handsome return from your work because your cost of materials will be exceptionally low.

$

155 CARVING KITS

Lots of people have plans to take up wood carving "someday." But "someday" often never comes, because people don't know how to begin wood carving. You can get them started with one of the more rewarding hobbies you will find. Sell would-be-whittlers whittling kits that contain plans, pictures, proper tools, and even a piece of wood that you have already begun to carve for the customer. If a customer still procrastinates after all you have done to get him started, then maybe he can make a healthy batch of toothpicks.

$$

156 CLOTHES POSTS

This business is not one to get rich in, but it can be reasonably profitable. Most women have clothes dryers, but most of them prefer to hang their clothes outside to dry whenever the weather permits. Fabricate backyard clothes posts from steel that rotate in a two-foot-deep-in-the-ground socket hole secured with concrete. Make up a sample, keeping track of your time spent and your materials costs to determine selling costs. A good part-time job to begin with.

$

157 COAT HANGERS FOR FINE CLOTHES

Fine clothes need fine closets with fine accessories. You can do well selling exquisite garment hangers made in various tasteful ways. One way is to wrap an ordinary wooden hanger in foam rubber sheeting, over which you sew a sheath of fine pastel satin. Paint the hook to match the satin. For a final touch, hang a small sachet made from the same satin together with a small ribbon bow and a flower to the hook. Sell them at local women's apparel shops and gift shops. Try other materials besides satin. Make others for men's fine clothes, too.

$

158 COAT HANGERS OF AROMATIC CEDAR

Aromatic cedar often ends up in hope chests, jewelry boxes, and hand-kerchief boxes. These items keep right on selling well year after year. In addition to these, aromatic cedar works nicely made into coat hangers, as the scent of the wood repels moths from the closet, and the pleasant smell refreshes a normally stuffy closet. These cedar coat hangers are not only practical but they are also good looking if made well. They will sell well in men's clothing stores and nicer department stores.

$ ▓▐▌

159 CONCRETE ORNAMENTS

This business is similar to molding ceramics, but on a much larger scale. Purchase ready-made molds of various objects, fill them with concrete, let the concrete set up, dismantle the mold, clean and oil mold, let the concrete item cure, and then paint the item or just leave it natural, depending on customer tastes. Mold bird baths, urns, animals, chairs and tables, statues, flower pots and planters, stepping stones, and so on. Sales of some items will bring in $300 or more. Sell to mortuaries, gift stores, florists, garden supply firms, and so on. See public libraries for more information about molds and related subjects.

$$ ▓▐▌

160 CORK CRAFTS

You can turn this business into a corker! Pressed cork is one of the easiest and least expensive materials to work with. You can purchase it in flat sheets of different thicknesses, or various shapes, such as balls, cubes, or ovals. It can easily be cut to any shape. You can make all sorts of saleable items from it—coasters, toys, novelties, place mats, desk sets, hot-dish pads, and so on. Colorfully decorate them with local motifs, landmarks, and the like with lacquer or woodburning tools. Sell wherever tourists look for such items.

$

161 CORSAGES

Corsages are portable little bouquets, which, being pinned to you, are like your shadow, accompanying you everywhere you go with their lovely fragrance and beauty. Make them very inexpensively at home and sell them with permission in restaurants to dining patrons. Make them in batches and sell them all. Then make another batch, and so on. Rose corsages and gardenia corsages are the standards, but many other ones are possible. Experiment. (Gardenia corsages must be kept in water until just before they are sold.) Sell 50 or more an evening if you can produce that many. Undersell floral shops and you will have a sweet-smelling business!

$

162 CYPRESS KNEES

Many people turn to nature to provide them with a job for making money at home. Cypress trees grow in swamps in the southern parts of North America. They send up special roots above the surface of the water called cypress knees. These knees grow into all sorts of grotesque and surrealistic shapes, which are easily carved or arranged into pieces of art or made up into craft items such as lamps. No two knees are ever alike, so each product you make to sell will be one-of-a-kind. These products can be sold locally or even by mail order.

$

163 DECORATIVE SCREENS

You can create and sell decorative screens if you have average artistic talent and the ability for minor carpentry. A standard screen is simply three decorated panels connected by metal hinges. You can hand-paint them, wallpaper them, install glass or louvers in them, or whatever will sell. Wholesale them to department, furniture, and gift stores. Make up a prospectus using color pictures of your designs to save packing actual samples about. You can conceivably grow into a small, busy factory and you can make a very nice living at it while enjoying it at the same time.

$

164 DECOYS OF PAPIER MÂCHÉ

This winner is not for the birds. Bird hunters will love them because they are unusually lightweight for carrying. Make duck or goose decoys from simple papier mâché and paint them using realistic colors. Then waterproof them with lacquer or shellac. An honest living can be made making and selling them. Women will also buy them if you cut a hole in the back of each decoy and coat the inside with silicone so they can be used as planters. These two ideas will go together for an ideal home business.

$ 👤 ⛰

165 DOLL MINIATURES

Miniature doll replicas of famous people—Beethoven, Queen Elizabeth, Napoleon, and so on—can keep you very profitably employed. You may have to practice this art form to get your replicas just right, but persistence will definitely pay off handsomely. Patience with the facial details, and authentic clothing and accessories for each tiny doll—eyeglasses, canes, umbrellas, hats, and the like, will bring your characters to life. You may find your art works showing up in art galleries and even museums!

$$ 👤 ⛰

166 DOLLS OF HISTORY

Many adults, both men and women, are avid collectors of dolls. They often buy dolls representing certain periods in history called period dolls. Some collectors purchase dolls representative of the variety of present-day cultures. Learn to fashion these dolls so they will be truly historically authentic or culturally accurate. Work up only one doll a day and it may well sell to an avid collector for $100 or more. There are many books available on this fascinating topic. There is currently a revival in period dolls.

$$ 👤 ⛰

167 DRIFTWOOD

Half of the fun of this business is searching for the driftwood. Look for pieces of unusual shape and design; the more twisted and gnarled, the better. Turn them into lamps or other useful items. Or trim them for wall hangings or bookends, artful decorations, and so on. Driftwood often resembles animals or humans, and you can bring out these resemblances with due artistic care. If you become good at this, full-time work is a real prospect for you.

$ 👤   🏙️

168 EGGSHELL KNICKKNACKS

There has been a revival of the popularity of eggshell art in the past few years. It is really fun expressing an artistic bent in this delicate medium. You can use real eggshells or substitutes made of clay, styrofoam, plastic, or even papier mâché. Save useful bits of ribbon, lace, cellophane, beads, rickrack, dried flowers, or old greeting cards. Use your imagination to create new combinations that are unusual and saleable. Each eggshell creation will be unique and handmade, so if you work well at it you should be able to profit accordingly.

$ 👤   🏙️

169 FLOWER STATIONERY

In this home business you simply join two good things together and sell them. Collect flowers in their prime, such as pansies or violets, and press-dry them. Then purchase pastel-colored bond paper, already boxed if possible, and with nonyellowing glue, mount the dry flowers in the corner of each page of bond paper. Then market the special exquisite stationery, to which you have added considerable value, for a dramatic profit. Sell by mail order and through gift shops and variety stores.

$ 👤   🏙️

170 FLY TYING

Fooling fish is an ancient art. Artificial flies are one of the more interesting and colorful ways of tricking them. You can make hand-tied flies and sell them on a full-time basis. Many people do. The market is impossible to saturate, because you can create new patterns of flies that can make current patterns obsolete. You can make up a select inventory of them during the winter and display them on large cards and then market them in fishing tackle outlets just prior to the opening of fishing season.

$ 👤   🏙️

171 FOLKLORE FIGURINES

With time and patience you can easily learn to carve tiny folklore characters from soft wood. Peter Piper, Snow White, Humpty-Dumpty, Little Miss Muffet, and hundreds more. You can bring them closer to life by painting their faces and tiny articles of clothing. You can specialize in just a few, or strive for a well-rounded variety. Sell them in sets in gift stores and toy stores. Appeal to customers to try collecting your entire line. And then get busy sharpening your knife!

172 FUN NOVELTIES

Buy up all the waste scraps of material from tailoring shops and turn on your imagination as to how you can make good money with these scraps. One thing you can do is take scraps and sew them up into doll's clothing—coats, matching muff and hat sets, capes, dresses, and so on. For the "big set," make special items, such as cloth covers to protect sweaters, from your scraps. This business can expand until you have to hire help!

173 HANDICRAFT MANUFACTURING

If you have been looking for a fun hobby/career that can bring you an excellent steady income, then open your mind to this one. Imagine making $2000 or more a weekend just selling artistic items made from tree bark and broken mirrors, or whatever can be scrounged even from a garbage dump! Picasso did it with all sorts of discards and became wealthy! Sell at fairs and swap meets or contract with exclusive gift shops or art galleries.

$ 👤 ▉▐

174 HANDWEAVING

Handweaving is an ancient art that is experiencing a modern revival. Modern looms and methods and materials make it possible for nearly anyone to create truly beautiful hand-loomed treasures. You can learn this art-craft through books or adult classes or correspondence school. Once you begin to master the techniques, you will be able to make saleable items—place mats, draperies, garments, upholstery, rugs, and the like—for which you will find a ready and lucrative market in gift stores and shops with discriminating customers.

$$ 👤 ▉▐

175 HOOKED RUGS

Hooking rugs can be an enjoyable and creative way to make a good living. Tools now available make the task both easy to learn and quite productive. New abstract and modernistic designs will suit modern tastes. You will use new colorful woolen yarns. Have some of your creations made up as samples. Show these around and you will get custom orders from which you can earn generous commissions. Try to sell direct to customers for best profits. Furniture stores may buy some of your cleverly designed rugs.

176 LAMPSHADES

Lampshades are vulnerable at the best of times. They are one of the most frequently damaged articles in a household. What do people do when they are damaged? You can make lampshades to order right in your own home. Sometimes old wire frames just need recovering. Experiment until you have reasonable proficiency. Wire forms can be purchased ready-made. Use various coverings—silk, linen, parchment, plastic, fireproof papers, even denim! Advertise under the "Services Offered" newspaper column. This service is needed nearly everywhere.

177 LEATHERCRAFT

Leather lovers always prefer hand-tooled, genuine leather articles instead of mass-produced, machine-stamped leather items. They are always in demand by people seeking quality and the personal touch. Modern methods and tools vastly simplify working with leather, too. Billfolds, purses, belts, pet collars, gloves, bookcovers, bookmarks, coin holders, slippers, and a host of other usable items will always sell well in gift and novelty shops. Look through a catalog of leather supplies and you will be impressed by how limitless the opportunities are!

178 MILLINERY

Milliners create headwear for ladies. If you are a virtuoso artist you may find yourself right at home in this business. Take bits and pieces of all sorts of interesting small objects—feathers, lace, flowers, or fur—and create a smart chapeau that will lighten any head it adorns. Original creations will earn top dollars. You can specialize in wedding millinery if you like. Recommendations will keep you steadily and profitably busy at home at work you thoroughly enjoy.

$ & ▀▐▌

179 NAMES OF ANIMALS

If your last name is Wolf, it is likely that you have a special liking for wolves. And perhaps you even have possessions with pictures of wolves on them. This is only natural. You can build a business around this special affinity of people for animals they have received their last names from. If it is Wolf, search through phonebooks for all the people on the continent having the last name of Wolf, and then proceed to sell them products bearing pictures or other representations of wolves. The same principle can be used for dozens of other last names. This can be a real money-maker.

$ ♿ ▓█▐

180 NATURE CRAFTS

A walk through the fields and woods will supply you with all sorts of goodies from nature—pine cones, tree roots, seeds, nuts, acorns, needles, leaves, grasses, flowers, ferns, and so on—on which you can turn your imagination loose and create all sorts of crafts that will sell if done well. One example: Make wreaths out of what-have-you and spray-paint with gold or silver to make them more appealing and durable enough to last several holiday seasons. Try to schedule marketing about two months before the main holiday season.

$ ♿ ▓█▐

181 PERSONALIZED MUGS

We have all seen inventories of ceramic drinking mugs in drug stores with a variety of names on them. Unfortunately, about 60 percent of people can never find their name in the inventory, which usually has only the more common names like Sam or Sue. You can solve this problem by taking custom orders for personalizing drinking mugs with unusual names. With the right stencils and paint you can take a glazed plain cup and inscribe any name requested on it easily. Pay shop owners commissions on sales and ready yourself for a steady income.

$ ♿ ▓█▐

182 PLASTER CASTING

With plaster casting you can reproduce and even create literally thousands of durable art objects. This rapidly expanding industry may be for you. Profits in plaster casting are very good because your materials cost only a small fraction of your finished products. It is an ideal home business! You could quickly find yourself inundated with orders from wholesale distributors and interior decorators from many miles around.

$ ♿ ⬛⬛

183 QUILTS, CUSTOM-MADE

If you are an avid needleworker you can find a lucrative market in making quilts to order for people wanting the best. Advertise widely and send out a catalog so customers can choose their pattern and color combinations. Take a healthy deposit before you begin in order to cover at least your materials. Many people will use your creations as decorative coverlets only and not for warmth. Charge for individuality, superior quality, and many, many hours of meticulous labor, especially for quilts with finer patterns.

$ ♿ ⬛⬛

184 RESIN CASTING SUPPLIES

Hobbyists and craftspeople are turning out all sorts of products that require polyester resin casting supplies. These products include everything from key chains with small animals encased in polyester to beautiful, exotic wood table tops. You can retail from your home all the supplies and equipment necessary for this fascinating hobby. The resin can be purchased by the 45-gallon drum and resold in smaller containers at 300 percent profit. You will stock all sorts of molds, colored crushed glass, polished stone slices, and so on. You may want to produce some polyester cast products yourself to sell for even more profit.

$ ♿ ⬛⬛

185 RUG MAKER, CUSTOM

A rare, low-investment business that can easily be successfully operated from a person's home, even on a part-time basis. The market is open ended. Companies and individuals alike will pay high prices for individualized rugs on which you have emblazoned their own trademark, logo, or name. Can be used as attractive wall hangings at eye level.

$ ♿ ⬛⬛

186 SEASHELL CRAFTS

The world's beaches abound in beautiful shells that are there for the taking. Clean and polish them and turn them into various products that will sell—lamps, bookends, paperweights, tabletops, and so on. You can buy shells cheaply in bulk if you are not near a seashore. Artistic ability and a reasonable ability to work with tools will be a plus. Sell in tourist outlets.

187 SHADE PULLS

Window shades are making a big comeback. They not only provide privacy and block out strong sunlight, but they save a lot of energy in terms of heating a house, especially at night. A variety of decorative shade pulls can be made at home in a variety of media. Use 2-inch clear glass circles, or octagons, and glue on colored tiny chips of glass in mosaic effects to form pictures. Drill a hole and attach to shade. The colors will catch the eye as they reflect sunshine into the room. Each of your creations will be one-of-a-kind. They will sell well most anywhere.

188 SHOE PLANTERS

You can take any old shoes you can find or purchase and change them into nifty planters by encasing them in fiberglass polyester resin. Look for old work shoes, cowboy boots, running shoes, baby shoes, slippers, and so on, that you can get free or cheaply at thrift stores. Simply dip the shoes into a pail of resin and then allow them to dry. Sell them with plants in the planters for best profits. Accept custom orders for special shoes having special meaning to clients. This is a sure money-maker.

189 SHOE RECOVERING

People will think you are a magician or an alchemist of old shoes in this business. Take a pair of old shoes and cover them with fabric chosen by your client. First practice on some old shoes until you get good at it. Learn to tuck the fabric tightly in between the sole and upper and then glue the fabric into place until at last you bend the upper edge of the fabric down in between the upper and the lining. You will need scissors, glue, a utility knife, strong thread, and a screwdriver. Shoe repair shops will send lots of customers your way as they won't want to do it. Advertise with samples on display.

190 SILK-VELVET PICTURES

One of the richest looking types of picture you are likely to see is silk appliqué on black velvet. You can purchase kits to make these pictures. They go together much like paint-by-number pictures do. They usually include a fancy frame as well. If you get good at it, you will want to start from scratch creating your own pictures. These originals will put you in the professional category eventually, where you can make an actual living selling what you create. This would be a satisfying occupation for a handicapped person.

$

191 TRAYS, DECORATIVE

Unusual ideas are the best ideas to build new businesses around. Purchase any size and any shape of baking pans as cheaply as possible. Apply enamels of interesting colors to entire back and outer edges or sides. Then buy inexpensive prints of famous paintings, or cut pictures out of wallpaper or greeting cards, and cement these pictures inside each pan. Add several coats of shellac to waterproof. Can be used as unusual serving trays or wall hangings. You should make 300 percent profit easily.

$

192 WHITTLING

Whittling out a living! You can do it. A sharp pocket knife and a supply of good soft wood is all you really need, although a rocking chair to sit in while you work will enhance things very much! Specialize in things like animal heads or walking canes or letter openers. Polish them well and move them through gift stores or tourist novelty stores. Learn to whistle while you whittle for added earnings!

$

193 WISHING WELL PLANTERS

Start with just a one-pound coffee can. Add upright posts and a roof of local pine or cedar. Attach a plywood base sticking out about one inch farther all around the can. On this base, heap up a cement mortar mix surrounding the can; embed small colorful stones in the cement. Paint to taste. These unique stone wishing well planters are ready for market in florist shops, gift shops, tourist shops, and the like. Put plants in for sample looks. They will be snapped up without delay.

$

194 YOUTH CRAFTS INSTRUCTOR

You will love the living you will make in this business. The response will overwhelm you. You must love children and enjoy working and playing with them. Simply teach crafts to children, individually or in groups. To any children, or to disabled, confined, and cognitively impaired children. Ages six to twelve years, or thereabouts. Children who have some handicap will especially benefit from the manual work involved in your crafts projects. You will not only do well financially, but you will collect some wonderful memories.

$ ◤ ♿ ▞▀▌

▐▌▐▌▌▌▌▌ENTERTAINMENT

195 BARBERSHOP QUARTET FOR HIRE
The beautiful, intricate harmonies in barbershop quartet music have no equal. Everyone sits spellbound while listening to this form of music. If you can organize one of these quartets you can run it as a business. You may be one of the quartet, or you may be the business agent for the quartet. As soon as the group has half a dozen old-time favorite songs in its mastered repertoire, you can hire the group out to practically every group, organization, club, and convention in your area. You can even go on overnight tours into neighboring centers if desired. You should be able to pay your way easily.

$ ♿ ▐▀▌▐

196 BOOKING AGENT
Get local engagements for all sorts of entertainers. Your normal fee is 10 percent of the client's fee. Usually all you need is an office with a telephone! There always seems to be room for one more agency. Many booking agencies have gotten fabulously rich, especially in larger cities. How far you go depends on your salesmanship, your energy, and your personality. Start with just $300 or so.

$ ◤ ▐▀▌

197 HUMOR
From time to time we all need the comic relief that comes from good, clean, wholesome humor. Most people have a good sense of humor. If you have an above-average ability to concoct new, original humor, you may want to try marketing it. Many trade journals, magazines, newspapers, comedians, cartoonists, and radio and TV entertainers solicit new and good humor. They will usually pay well for material that appeals to them and is well suited to their purposes. Librarians can direct you to prospective clients.

$ ♿ ▐▀▌▐

198 ONE-PERSON ENTERTAINER
Churches, schools, clubs, and many organizations require special entertainment from time to time. If you have the open personality for it, you can set up your own business offering a variety of wholesome family-style entertainment. Offer decent music and wholesome humorous readings,

for example. You will need good portable sound equipment. Advertise with form letters to all the organizations in your area of intended operations. You may find yourself suddenly booked well into the future.

$

199 SONG WRITING

Really good songwriters are few and far between. However, even average songwriters can make good with the right connections. You will need to have something a bit unusual before the market will recognize you. Good wholesome music that the entire family can safely listen to is sadly lacking. You would be doing everyone a favor by producing this type of music. By writing both the lyrics and the music you can double your possible income in this field.

$

200 WHOLESALE PARTY GOODS

When people decide to have a party they are frequently frustrated because they have to go shopping to a variety of stores for all their list of party goods. A good home business can be built around becoming a wholesaler of party goods. You could offer the convenience of all the party goods in one handy location. You might dedicate a large room or perhaps your basement for storing and displaying the goods. Stock all the standard goods used in parties, but try to include unique items that will add something special to a party. And don't overlook children's parties, which could become your main bread and butter.

$$$

201 ANTENNAS

Antennas pose lots of problems for most people needing them. They are almost always difficult to install. They need to be secured against high winds and lightning strikes. They are often installed on rooftops where the footing is dangerous. There are many kinds of antennas: satellite signal reception, TV, FM radio, shortwave listening (SWL), HAM radio, microwave, cellular and radio phone, and others. You may already have a background working with them. Get a well-rounded knowledge of the different types and how to install them most effectively. There are few people working generally in this field. Most service technicians work only with one type of antenna.

$

202 BASEBALL BATTING RANGE

Every baseball fan would like to see how close he or she measures up to Babe Ruth, Mickey Mantle, or Hank Aaron. The most enjoyable way to find out is to try out your swing in a baseball batting range. You simply stand at the plate while a machine pitches baseball after baseball over the plate. You will find out how often you can make contact with the ball as well as how far you can send the smacked ball. These batting ranges are now available in franchise form. But you may be able, after purchasing just the pitching machine, to set up the rest of the batting range yourself at much less cost. Batter up!

$$$ ♿ 🏙

203 RECORDING STUDIO SERVICE

There are many different kinds of recordings. Most of the time we think of audio recordings, such as tapes, CDs and the like. But you could also include video recordings as well. Recordings could include new technologies, such as CD-ROM. In this ideal home business, you would probably set up the electronic equipment required to make original sound and/or video recordings. You would probably also have equipment that could edit these recordings and mass-produce them as well. A soundproof recording studio would be a must for professional results. A home basement could be used for this business.

$$$$ ♿ 🏙

▌▌▌▌▌▌FOOD

204 BAKED BEANS, HOME STYLE
With so many TV dinners and similar food on the market today, real home-baked foods deliciously prepared are hard to find. You can start a home-cooked food take-out service right in your home with almost no start-up expenses. Offer the basic foods that are always scrumptious— real baked beans, homemade breads, homemade apple pies, and so on. If you like, have a certain food scheduled for each night of the week (Example: spaghetti every Monday evening, and so on). People won't eat on your premises, which simplifies your business immensely.

$ ♿ ◣ ▀▜▛

205 BARBECUE SPECIALTY
If you enjoy outdoor cookery and have a place out in the country with a picnic-like setting of shade trees, you may be able to offer a packaged barbecue program to interested organizations such as clubs, churches, fraternal groups, family reunions, conventions, staff gatherings, and the like. Cater to the group with foods you have barbecued in your large, open masonry barbecue pit, together with appropriate desserts and juices. Rent out your facilities and your expertise. The group will be happy to pay well for their good time.

$$ ▐▛

206 BOTTLED WATER
Bottled water is the newest "in" beverage and it is likely to stay in for years to come. More and more people are avoiding alcoholic drinks because they are so high in unwanted calories. You can take your local water from a spring or elsewhere, and if it is good-tasting water, you can simply bottle the water under proper sanitary conditions, attach a striking art deco label to the bottle and market it wherever finer bottled waters, such as Perrier, are selling.

$$ ♿ ◣ ▐▛

207 BUTCHER AT THE CLIENT'S
By having a mobile butcher shop you can custom-butcher meat for farmers right on their own premises so they won't have to haul the animal into town and then later on haul the meat back home again. Compose a letter, which you send to all farmers within 20 miles of your home,

in which you fully describe the butchering services you wish to provide, along with costs for each service. The response will be quick, and after a year you may be turning down work. Advertise by letter with hunters as well.

$$

208 CANDY APPLES

A good solid business. As simple a business as any—stick skewer sticks into good clean apples, dunk the apple into molten caramel or taffy, set out to air harden on wax paper. Take apples door-to-door at corner groceries, and the like. Or work fairs, air shows, and beaches. Many candy apple firms sell to several hundred stores regularly.

$

209 CANDY STORE

Several candy businesses that began in a home kitchen have grown into multi-million dollar operations. Each year North Americans, with their notorious sugar craving, turn more than four billion pounds of candy into an $11 billion market. The big trend is no-sugar and no-chocolate candy. Carob is a perfect substitute for chocolate and several sweeteners are replacing sugar. Use top-quality gourmet ingredients, have an informal retail atmosphere, and have on-site visible manufacturing. Every kid, from 2 to 102, likes to watch candy being made!

$$$

210 CARAMEL CORN SHOP

Rent a very small shop in a high-traffic area. Paint the inside of the shop gleaming white. Install very bright lighting. The attendant dons a snowy-white uniform. Install an exhaust fan which blows the delicious smell of the caramel corn (caramel-coated popcorn) out over the sidewalk! Fresh caramel corn is an impulse item. Passersby smell the delicious aroma and can't resist buying some!

$$$

211 CIDER

Apple cider is about the most popular of all fruit drinks. Everyone likes its tangy, sweet flavor. You can go into the apple cider business in a number of ways. You can set up a custom mobile operation in which you press out this succulent juice for people right on their own premises.

Or you can set up in your home or garage. You will need to crush the apples first, then press out the juice, then filter, and then package the juice. Use waxed cartons, like milk cartons, and the juice can then be frozen and later thawed as fresh juice, thus avoiding any preservatives. Solid income is all but certain.

$$

212 COOKIES-ONLY SHOP

Few people can pass up a cookie shop! Keep everything super simple. Offer only four or five kinds so no experienced baker is needed. Use only natural ingredients, which offer both better health and better flavor! One key ingredient is *pure* vanilla rather than the synthetic kind, because of its highly aromatic quality. The smelling ability of your patrons will be your best salesman! Many mall cookie shops average about one pound of cookies per minute!

$$

213 CROISSANT SHOP

A croissant is a type of delicious French pastry. It was comparable to a plain piece of toast until recently. It has now become a new craze in the food world because someone realized that you can stuff it with all sorts of other delicious foods, such as fruit, tomatoes, asparagus, mushrooms, and so on. You can appeal to the quest for good nutrition by using only fresh, natural ingredients. There is a virtual explosion in this market right now and the ground floor is still unoccupied!

$$$

214 DINING AND PARTY CATERING

You will learn to enjoy working hard in the kitchen while everyone else is eating, drinking, and socializing in the living room when you think upon the fact that, when you leave you will be anywhere from $800 to $10,000 (or more) richer than when you came, because you catered to the special needs of those at the party or special dining event. Build your confidence by beginning with small birthday parties for children.

$

215 DONUT SHOP

An independent donut shop can easily thrive with its 80 percent or so profit margin! Each year, about 744 million pounds of donuts are sold in North America—at a staggering value of about $1.8 billion. Many tiny storefront stores gross over $150,000 each year. Fifty-cent donuts cost only a few pennies to produce. It takes only a few days of practice to learn to produce tasty donuts efficiently. Hire part-time student help during peak periods to tend to the selling. Don't go with chains if you have a choice.

$$$

216 EGG CULLS

Egg farmers have a goodly percentage of their eggs that are culls. Sometimes the eggs are simply cracked. Other times they have odd shapes or sizes. They are just as good as regular eggs for eating, but regular retail outlets refuse to handle them. You can go into business buying these cull eggs and selling them. You can buy them for about 25 percent of the regular wholesale price and sell them for about 75 percent of the regular retail price to bakeries and restaurants and even budget-minded housewives who can save considerably by getting them from you.

$$

217 EGG PRODUCTION

Consumers like their eggs fresh. Most eggs are kept somewhere in cold storage for a period of time before reaching the table. If the marketing allows for it in your area, you can produce and sell eggs directly to consumers with a guarantee of freshness that will make your selling easy. By selling direct you will eliminate all middlemen, which will bring you significantly higher profits. You will need about half an acre, two chicken houses, and about 1000 layers to go at it full time. Establish an egg route door-to-door and sell fresh eggs exclusively.

$$

218 ETHNIC FOOD SHOP

If an ethnic group of any size, even 100 families or so, exists in your town or city, find out if there is a store that caters specifically to that group. Perhaps you can set up a store especially for them. A hundred families—whether Polish, Greek, Turkish, Puerto Rican, Japanese, or whatever—can consume a lot of groceries! Consider converting a room in your house into the store. Get to know the people well— work to gain their confidence. Your little venture might well prove quite successful!

$$$

219 FAST HEALTH-FOOD TAKEOUT

In this business you will combine a number of popular trends into one booming enterprise. The trends are gourmet food, natural food, fast service, and takeout service. You may set up with a few stools but you will stress high-volume takeout orders. You will prepare all foods on your menu very quickly from fresh inexpensive ingredients: soups, whole-grain breads, shakes, and so on. Set up in heavy foot-traffic areas for highest profits.

$$$$

220 FOOD BY MAIL ORDER

More and more people are finding out that organically grown food is far superior to the normal nonorganic food. For example, a tomato grown organically has nearly 2000 times more iron in it than a tomato grown by the usual nonorganic method. You can grow these highest-quality foods organically and then sell them, and the poison-free nature of your products will build you a clientele that will return to you again and again as they happily consume truly health-giving food!

$$$

221 FOOD-PRESERVING SERVICE

This business consists of contracting by the unit to process and preserve fruits and vegetables for paying customers. You will need the know-how and proper equipment to run what, in effect, is a home cannery. It is a service much in demand as more and more mothers become full-time employees. You can use and offer several methods of preserving: jars, tin cans, freezing, and drying. Charge per jar or tin can or package. It will be seasonal work at harvest time. Extend your production by making jams and jellies from frozen fruits.

$$

222 FOOD SPECIALTY

Here you will specialize in just one well-tried and tested food product. On the other hand, it may be a new innovative product you have created yourself and which has never been marketed before. You may be able to make a new breed of super-scrumptious coconut macaroons, for example, that beat anything on the market. Having perfected the recipe you then turn to packaging and marketing. Free, fresh samples will be your best sales staff. Work your samples hard, and return home and get your factory fired up for heavy production.

$$

223 FORTUNE COOKIES

You don't have to be Chinese to bake delicious fortune cookies. You can bake them yourself at home using a very simple recipe and sell them to restaurants of any type (not just Chinese), who can use them as a "special-touch" novelty treat for their dining customers. You can even sell them by mail order, as they keep well. Your main task will be to print catchy little sayings of fortune or misfortune on paper, which you will stuff into the cookies through a crack after baking. Businesses could cleverly use them for offering catchy discounts.

$ & ◣ ▮▮▮

224 FRUIT ROADSIDE VENDOR

Fruit simply sells itself to just about everyone. You can make a very good living buying fresh fruit from farmers in season and then trucking it into an area that can't supply its own fruit, where you proceed to sell it, either door-to-door or at a busy roadside rest area. A couple of signs placed along the highway in both directions will alert customers to stop in time. Have a good variety of tree-ripened fruit at reasonable rates on display; the rest is simple.

$$ ◣ ▮▮▮

225 GINGERBREAD PRODUCTS

Old-fashioned gingerbread products are as popular as ever. You can learn how to make all sorts of things with gingerbread—from gingerbread man cookies to gingerbread houses. Then you can sell these products far and wide, as there is a steady market for them. The houses sell year round but especially at certain holidays, (as birthday cake substitutes for children, for instance). You can work entirely from your home. Custom orders by phone will handle most of your local trade. Cook up some samples and display them in key locations.

$ & ◣ ▮▮▮

226 GOURMET NATURAL COFFEE AND TEA SHOP

A very high-ticket specialty business, gourmet natural coffee and tea stores are brewing up big profits wherever they appear. You can cash in on the growing rebellion against the ho-hum, stale supermarket coffees and tea blends, which are heavily laden with the slow poison of caffeine. With a complete line of safe herbal teas and coffee substitutes you can be a real winner. This market is wide open for small business operators because specialty-food retailing has little or no appeal to big chains. Profit margins are high and repeat customers are all but virtually guaranteed from the day you open shop!

$$$$ ◣ ▨

227 HOLIDAY GOODIES

Holidays are special times for special treats. All sorts of delicacies are welcomed—shaped cookies, fruit cakes, popcorn balls, candied apples, tree lollipops, wreath donuts, and so on; the list is limited only by your imagination. Make everything that preserves well as far ahead as possible. Most items can be stored in the freezer without damage to either flavor or texture. Wrap goodies in special colorful cellophane. Make arrangements for sales well ahead of actual deliveries for more perishable items.

$ ♿ ◣ ▨

228 HOME BAKERY

Pies. Cakes. Breads. Pastries. All tasting twice as good as commercial varieties. All easily commanding twice the price of commercial varieties. All coming from your very own home kitchen. People will cheerfully go out of their way (and budget) in order to patronize your famous products. Never lower the superior, top quality of your goodies; use the most healthful ingredients (whole grains, and so on) and you will be inundated with real flavor seekers!

$ ♿ ◣ ▨

229 HOMEMADE CAKES AND PIES

All you need is an oven, some tasty recipes, and a mailing list for your brochure. People are sick of mass-produced tasteless bakery products. They miss those home-baked goodies "like mother used to make" with the personal touch. Today, with working women and men being just too busy, there is a huge market just waiting to be satisfied. With cakes costing about 60 cents to make and selling for about $9, at the rate of 12 cakes per day, you will net about $100 per day or about $2,000 per month!

$ ♿ ◣ ▨

230 HOMEMADE CANDY

This can be a great part-time or weekend business. Simply sell candy made in your own kitchen. Requires just a few hours per week to prepare.

Start with about $100 or so of materials. Products will sell for ten times cost of materials! Net up to $500 each weekend! Very simple formula! Search out large public gatherings for sales.

$ ♿ ⚒ 🏙

231 JUICE

Fruit and vegetable juices are among the most nutritious of foods. The fresher the juice is, the better it is for you. The juice should be sipped slowly in order to do a person the most good. You can obtain a commercial juice extractor machine and go into the juice business. Purchase good, fresh fruits and vegetables locally and extract their juices. Sell the fresh juices in appropriate containers daily to a route of customers including health food stores and restaurants, sandwich shops, and the like. Keep your premises sterile. Experiment with fruit blends or vegetable blends to see what will sell best.

$$$ ♿ ⚒ 🏙

232 LOW-CALORIE BAKERY

This is a fine pie from which you can carve a dandy piece for yourself! Start a sugar-free local bakery catering to people such as diabetics and the overweight. These will form the nucleus of your customers. This business concept is long overdue. You will likely do better than your competition because they can't cope with the common problems of calories, diabetes, and so on. You will open the way for everyone to have their healthy cake and safely eat it, too!

$$$ ⚒ 🏙

233 LUNCHBOX HOME-COOKED SERVICE

Office workers often have poor lunches because of only half-hour lunch breaks, which is not enough time to order food from a slow-service restaurant with its usual unappetizing menu. Desk-bound executives suffer the same plight. Single men are not into packing their own lunches. Enter you, who prepare delicious home-cooked lunches and deliver them to employees in office buildings. Advertise in the offices that lunches ordered one day by 5:00 PM will be delivered by 11:30 AM the following day. Enclose the next day's menu with each lunch you deliver. Hire a delivery boy. Expect to net $70 to $100 a day.

$ ♿ ⚒ 🏙

234 LUNCH-IN SERVICE

Deliver top-quality sandwiches and other lunch items such as yogurt, juices, and fruit to office personnel such as executives and secretaries too busy to go out for lunch. Stress good-quality ingredients in imaginative combinations at competitive prices, with the convenience you offer as a bonus. Make your deliveries in a picnic basket or some other gimmick with everything done for attractiveness. Set up a route in the downtown business district making deliveries prior to the noon hour.

$

235 MAPLE SYRUP

Everyone likes the yummy flavor of real maple syrup on pancakes. It is possible to make syrup out of sap from lots of other deciduous trees besides the maple. Birch trees also make good syrup. Simply collect the sap from the trees and boil it down until it is thick syrup. Then bottle it and apply your own unique, attractive labels and market it for very good profits. Artificial syrups simply can't match the mouth-watering flavors from nature. Because it is a food product, you must maintain sterile bottling operations.

$

236 NATURAL FOODS BAKERY

If you have a strong belief that people should eat only nutritious fare instead of chemical-laden foods such as white bread and sugar, then this business could be for you. Bake products that are strictly honest, totally nourishing, and overflowing with flavor. To be able to do a business trip and to do something of lasting social value at the same time will bring you unique rewards. People will line up for your carob brownies, your fruit cobblers, or whatever you can stir up while always keeping good health in mind.

$

237 NO-ALCOHOL BAR

There is a large portion of people who will go to no-alcohol bars to find their friends and perhaps some entertainment, and who never drink anything stronger than herbal tea! Some of these people are ex-drinkers. Others want to keep their health. Others have strong religious beliefs and know the dreaded evils of alcohol. Juice drinks and add-ons, such as healthy snack foods, can actually give you a greater profit than a traditional bar! It has been proven! The sheer uniqueness of this undertaking will generate a fortune in free publicity and exposure for you.

$$$ ◣ ᗰᐁ

238 OLD-FASHIONED ICE CREAM PARLOR

Simple formula—get the best tasting ice cream available (make it yourself if necessary), and find the best location for foot traffic available; after investing about $600, settle back to handle real cold cash. If it is choice ice cream, sell it at a premium. Add-on sales possible. Have a gimmick like a player piano (you don't have to pay it to play!) or something similar for best results.

$ ♿ ◣ ᗰᐁᐃ

239 OMELETTE RESTAURANT

Omelette shops are fast becoming the new stars of the $150 billion restaurant scene. The low start-up cost and simplicity of the operation make an omelette shop an ideal first-time business. Highly profitable compared to meat dishes. Average 12 cents input cost retails from $3.50 to $18.00! Experts say that the growth curve is just beginning. Limited-menu restaurants like omelette shops are expected to have the biggest growth in the food-service industry, according to the National Restaurant Association.

$$$ ◣ ᗰᐁ

240 PASTA PLACE

How would you like to create a product for 46 cents and sell it a couple of minutes later for $3.49? Incredible. Pasta shop owners are doing that hundreds of times a week and grossing phenomenal profits. Maintain quality by making it fresh on the premises, add a gourmet touch, serve it in an eye-appealing atmosphere and you will have high repeat business! Keep your menu simple and your atmosphere informal and you will have quick patron turnover. Fifty percent return on investments is common in just the first year!

$$ ◣ ᗰᐁ

241 PEANUTS

Where is the old-fashioned peanut that used to taste and smell so good? It has gone the way of all modern, mass-processed foods. The modern process of roasting peanuts in huge quantities after they have been shelled destroys most of the original flavor. You can experiment with the roasting process itself until you have it fine-tuned. Then market your old-fashioned-tasting peanuts; peanut lovers will line up over and over again to buy some of your by-now-famous goober peas. Your order book will soon be filled.

242 PICKLES

Pickles and relishes made in small batches at home from secret outstanding recipes will sell themselves, especially if they are marketed well with attractive down-on-the-farm labels. Use young, tender cukes and onions and secret home-grown spices. To the relishes add tomatoes, peppers, and so on, until you have assembled mouth-watering products that will bring repeat customers back again and again. Give out free samples and your tasty tidbits will indeed sell themselves.

243 PIZZA

Unlike many specialty foods, pizza is not a fad food. It has become a stable staple in the North American fast-food business. This business can still make a millionaire out of you, if that is your goal in life. New recipe and marketing twists keep surfacing. Nearly everyone loves pizza. Your cost of materials for a $4 pizza will be about $1. This is truly high markup! Set up for home deliveries from your own home, where you make them. Cater to large gatherings if you are so inclined. A double-cheese one, please!

244 PORTABLE RESTAURANT

Many city commuters prefer to eat before they reach home. You can prepare simple gourmet dinners and sell them to commuters as they depart the city in late afternoon. Intercept them with your van or truck before they board their trains or buses or before they take to a freeway. Stress quality nonfrozen foods for repeat customers. Allow a choice of only two or three dinners—this will simplify your preparation and keep overhead low. Keep your prices reasonable and people will look for you every evening if you can keep to a schedule.

245 RURAL RUSTIC DINING

People are heavily into nostalgia today. Reviving the good old days is in fashion. You can open up a fine satisfying business catering to this trend if you have a rustic home in a rural rustic setting. You can advertise and invite people to join with you in your rustic environment for good old-fashioned company and a good old-fashioned delicious home-cooked meal. Wood fireplace, bear skin rug, log house, sipping cider, story telling, singing old-time songs, and so on. All of this and more will have your patrons returning by appointment time and again with their friends and visiting relatives.

$$$ ◣ ▐▛

246 SALADS AND EXERCISE

Slim and trim is in. You can start this very lucrative type of business for as little as 2 to 3 thousand dollars if you are clever. Run a salad bar on ice out front, and out back have a gym for groups exercising to music, showers, and change rooms. After a good workout your clients fill up on a nutritious salad. Schedule your sessions to meet schedules of the participants—noon hours for business people, and so on. Add classes for children and the elderly. Hire enthusiastic leaders who can make it all fun and enjoyment. Avoid expensive exercise equipment.

$$$ ◣ ▐▜

247 SALADS-ONLY LUNCH RESTAURANT

Start with about $3000 and sell only salads and juice drinks. Serve simple cafeteria style with patrons building their own salads from a choice of about 30 ingredients. No expensive chefs or waitresses. A cashier, a busboy, and a prep person can accommodate 400 to 500 customers in a three-hour period, so you can easily control your low labor costs. Produce is bought fresh daily, though some items are reusable the next day. If average, you should show an operating profit the first month!

$$$$ ◣ ▐▜

248 SANDWICH ROUTE

You may be able to establish a profitable sandwich business for less than $40 from the very first day! It has been done. Individually wrap and label sandwiches and place them for sale wherever proprietors are willing to have them. Check food regulations for your area. Deliver daily, collect your share of the money, replace the stale ones with fresh ones. Start out as a spare-time operation at first, if you prefer. Try offering special sandwiches, such as Dagwood Sandwiches and the like.

249 SANDWICH WAGON

There are still plenty of areas where this service is definitely needed. Start up for about $700. Offer nutritious sandwiches, juices, and other wholesome foods. Prepare your food mostly at home in your own kitchen. This will help you buy your own food wholesale. Work construction and factory sites, office buildings, and so on. Have a pleasant, special-sounding horn or signal device to announce to insiders your presence when you drive up.

$$$

250 SASSAFRAS TEA

The sassafras bush grows wild throughout much of North America. You can collect it in the wild and cut off the bark and roots and dry them. It makes a fine spring tonic when taken as a tea. Package it attractively with instructions on why and how to use it. You can sell it in bulk or in tea bags, retail or wholesale. Your main markets will be health food stores and supermarkets.

251 SNACK BAR

It is possible to set up a snack bar for less than $1000. Strive to offer foods that are not only tasty but are also nutritious. Yogurt cones and freshly made vegetable and fruit juices are top foods. Contract out your cooking so you can concentrate on sales. Offer the best quality, the finest, most delicious products available, and you will soon have line-ups. Take the time to secure a good location first. Hire an art student to decorate your place for next to nothing.

$$

252 SNACKS BY PADDLE

Here is a genuinely fun business. You will need a canoe or similar small boat to contain the business. You will then paddle or row your boat-store from customer to customer selling sandwiches, watermelons, sunglasses, suntan lotion, the latest newspapers, and the like. Your customers will be yacht owners, homeowners, and picnickers along lake shores, beach fronts, marinas, and docks. Advertise your presence with an ad on a big sail, or a ship's bell, or something similar.

$$ ◪   �&

253   SOUP RESTAURANT

This business is simplicity at its best. Simply sell a variety of soups during the 11:00 AM to 2:00 PM lunch period every day. Feature three soups of the day, or offer a repertoire of 100 soups to choose from, or whatever you decide. Simply sell items that are inexpensive to prepare and that take little overhead to serve cafeteria-style. Two dollars for a salad and three dollars for a bowl of soup and a roll are about standard. Soup lines can pay quite well!

$$$ ◪   ▲

254   SOYBEAN SPROUTS

Pound for pound, soybeans offer more protein than meat and are twice as easy to digest. Soybean sprouts are especially rich in vitamins and minerals. You can grow them at home and wholesale them to any local supermarket, big or small. First, soak the beans overnight. Then rinse and drain them twice a day for about one week, at which time the sprouts will be ready to sell. The growing sprouts must be kept moist and at a reasonably steady room temperature. Little space is needed. There is good money to be made in this home enterprise.

$ ♿   ◪   ▲

255   SPAGHETTI TAKEOUT

Spaghetti is a complete dinner that is healthier and less fattening than most fast food. A spaghetti takeout home business can rival your local McDonald's for success. Keep hours from about 3:00 PM to 9:00 PM and cater to working mothers and children. Children love spaghetti, if the sauce is mild. You can keep to one menu only of spaghetti with a side salad and a piece of garlic bread. Charge about $2.75 a serving. Serve in styrofoam containers that will keep the meal warm for about half an hour.

$ ◪   ▲

256   SPECIALTY BREAD SHOP

Take advantage of both the nature and the nostalgia trends of today. Patrons will be attracted to your healthy or exotic foreign breads as you sell them in a nostalgic, old-fashioned atmosphere. Delicious sprouted grain breads, which contain nothing but whole grains, are getting more and more people hooked. Don't get so big as a business that you lose the superb quality that is not possible with mass-produced yuck breads.

$$$

257 STUFFED POTATO RESTAURANT

Take a plain old 5-cent potato and stuff it with delicious goodies ranging from cheese to caviar. Sell the Plain-Jane ones from 99 cents on up. Sell the gourmet potatoes for up to $15 a piece in high-class specialty restaurants! Profits are staggering and consumer acceptance has been most encouraging. The market is showing steady gains and appetites.

$$$

258 SUBMARINE SANDWICH SHOP

Here you make a product for about 65 cents and sell it moments later for $2.60 or more! A simple basic operation is easy to set up. Ideal for absentee ownership. Create new kinds of submarine sandwiches and you will subdue much of your competition.

$$$

259 VEGEE PIES

Hot vegee pies from a small storefront can go over big. More and more people are vegetarians. Run a take-out or take-home shop to cut costs (no tables and chairs, and so on). A small, plain shop can do even better than a flashy, expensively equipped chain store. You can start for less than $1000 with used equipment. If local food regulations allow, you may want to begin selling from your own home.

$

260 WILD BERRIES

Nature offers a free gold mine in the form of wild fruit, especially berries, in many parts of North America. They are usually free for the picking. Some driving is often involved in getting to them. You can pick them and preserve them as wild berry jams and jellies. It is well known that wild berries have far superior flavor compared to domestic varieties. Pick and preserve blackberries, raspberries, wild grapes, saskatoons, huckleberries, and so on. Package them in boxed sets. You will sell everything you can produce, so do whatever you can to enhance production!

$ ◪ ▦▐

261 COMPUTERIZED NUTRITION

Few people have a valid understanding of good nutrition. Even many dieticians and nutritionists are out in left field. If you have a solid background in this field and access to your own computer, this home business may be for you. You would simply plan meals and then sell the plans. There are many frustrated working people who would purchase sound meal plans from you on a weekly or monthly basis. You could sell your meal planning to institutions such as nursing homes, hospitals, drop-in centers, schools, and so on. Many pressured chefs would consider the convenience you offer them.

$ ♿ ▦▐

262 FOOD DELIVERY SERVICE

We all know about pizza delivery to your home. There are other fast foods being delivered to homes as well. These delivery services nearly always present unwanted problems to the restaurant managers. Most managers would gladly contract with someone else to do the delivery portion of the business. With a clean compact car, a knowledge of your local streets, and a friendly manner, you can go into the business of making these food deliveries. You may be able to contract with several food firms simultaneously in order to minimize waiting time. Make sure all your deliveries are made promptly.

$$ ◪ ▥

263 PEANUT BUTTER AND JELLY SANDWICHES

You read it right. There are some things that never go out of fashion or demand. This is one of them. In this business, you will need to be near a heavy flow of foot traffic, such as in a mall. Or perhaps you could operate from a vehicle similar to a popcorn wagon. At any rate, you will offer a wide range of these special sandwiches, by offering several different kinds of freshly-made peanut butter to choose from, together with several kinds of jelly, all spread on your own delicious, fresh, homemade bread. Nostalgic people will line up to see if it still sticks to the roof of their mouths.

$$ ◪ ▥

264 **GLOBAL CANDIES**

This is the business of all businesses for sweet profits. In this business you will seek out suppliers of different types of quality candies from all over the world. The more different countries you can get the candy from the better. You then simply sell these candies retail from perhaps your home, if it is quite near the downtown core, or from a small retail space where there is a heavy flow of walk-by traffic. You will then be dealing with a product that sells itself. And best of all, you will be into repeat selling.

$$$$ ♿ ✎ ⌘

⬛⬛⬛⬛║║║HEALTH

265 COUGH REMEDIES

Cough remedies come in many forms—syrups, lozenges, teas, tinctures, and so on. If you are into natural remedies, consider the possibility of combining a variety of them that have been shown to be efficacious for reducing coughing, and then mass-produce the product in a form that can be readily marketed. Rules and regulations may slow you down, but they can't stop you from filling a viable need for the public: nontoxic natural remedies.

$$

266 FIRST-AID KITS

Good medicines do not introduce poisons into the body. Some medicines today produce dangerous side-effects because of their toxic nature. You can learn how to use a variety of good medicines that are free for the taking in nature. These good medicines include simple remedies such as charcoal and pine pitch. You can fashion simple first-aid kits containing these simple remedies and then sell them along with simple instructions to people seeking good, safe medicine.

$$$

267 FOOT MASSAGE

One of the most pleasant experiences possible is a nice foot massage. Try one if you have never had one. It is a simple thing to learn how to do. You can sell simple foot massages in a regular business set up in a tiny office or in your home. Or you may want to work from office to office in a business district. Simply advertise that you will rub one foot for free and the other foot for $4, or whatever you deem is a fair price. Add on foot comfort devices and shoes for extra income.

$

268 HAIRPIECES

Selling hairpieces is an ideal mail-order business if a good catalog is used. Many people have lost their hair or part of it due to burns, disfigurement from accidents, or normal balding. These people need help to restore their appearance in order to obtain decent employment and to have normal social relationships. You can learn to retail hundreds of different hairpieces now available with a minimum of training. This business lends itself to operation from a home if desired.

$$$

269 HEALTH RESORT

North Americans are the wealthiest people on earth. Yet, paradoxically, they are also the most unhealthy people on earth, despite the latest in modern medicine. People simply are slowly killing themselves with wrong habits involving (1) nutrition, (2) exercise, (3) drinking water, (4) getting sunshine, (5) being temperate, (6) breathing clean air deeply, and (7) resting properly. You can open up a simple health resort in which you simply teach people how to regain good health and then go on to maintain it for extending life with a minimum of disease. People are becoming desperate for the hope this simple program will give them.

$$$$$ ◨ ▀▜▛

270 HEALTH TIPS

The majority of people in North America have serious health problems. Hundreds of questionable books are available to point people back to better health. But the only certain way back to good health for most North Americans requires a total lifestyle change—a return to proper nutrition, use of lots of pure drinking water, deep breathing outdoors, good rest, sunlight, temperance, and proper exercise. Anything short of this spells abnormal health. If you understand and practice good health as above, you can become a paid health counselor who helps sick people find the only certain way back to abundant health.

$ ♿ ◨ ▀▜▛

271 HEARING AIDS

The sales of hearing aids are controlled by thorough government regulations in order to protect the unsuspecting public from unscrupulous dealers. You will therefore need to become licensed in order to sell hearing aids, but the effort is well worth it, as it can provide you with an income well above average. You will learn how to test hearing, fit and adjust various hearing devices, provide user instruction, and possibly even make repairs for extra income. Bring in extra customers by holding free hearing clinics and hearing tests in malls and elsewhere.

$$$ ◨ ▀▜▛

272 HOME CONVALESCENT CARE

The high costs of convalescing in a hospital today can create fatal stress. You can set up a business in which you provide professional care for patients, care that enables them to convalesce comfortably in their own private homes at a 60 percent or more savings to them and their insurance companies! You won't be practicing medicine in any sense of the word. Simply collect a list of congenial (perhaps retired) registered nurses and paramedics who are willing to serve in private homes for eight or so hours a day. You collect 30 percent or so as commission for organizing the nursing service.

$$$

273 LANOLIN

Lanolin, or wool fat as it is sometimes called, is the very best skin moisturizing product available for the prevention of chapped hands caused from dishwater, laundering, and so on. It is used as a base in all sorts of commercial hand lotions. Unfortunately, the lanolin is often so diluted in these hand lotions that it is frequently ineffective. You can purchase it cheaply in bulk and sell it in 2-ounce jars for about $8 each. Since it contains no dyes or chemicals, it will actually sell itself. Try it yourself—you are in for a treat!

$$

274 MASSAGE SALON

Massage is quickly taking its rightful place in the area of natural healing, and most people are now aware of its therapeutic benefits. You can take a home study course in scientific massage and then practice on friends and relatives until you feel competent to go public. Set up your own massage salon (or work by appointment in homes) in which you give about six one-hour-long massages a day at about $20 per session. After overhead expenses this can give you a net profit of about $2000 per month. There probably is no more satisfying way to earn that kind of money. Check to see if you need a license to practice in your area.

$$

275 MEDICINAL HERBS

There are many herbs with therapeutic or medicinal value that can be grown profitably in a small garden plot. You can also gather any of them growing in the wild. These include goldenseal, camomile, mullin, sassafras, horehound, snakeroot, and ginseng. There are hundreds more. Several of them sell for $35 a pound or more. Consider selling to laboratories and suppliers by contract. A dealer in crude drugs can quickly advise you which ones are in current high demand and their market worth. Agricultural research stations can advise you more. Check your public library for more information.

$

276 NO-SUN TANNING CENTER

Very modest investment. Very simple operation. A customer goes into an individual booth, disrobes, stands in front of a special ultraviolet light for about ten minutes, gets dressed, walks out with a touch-up to his or her year-round golden tan. And you, the owner, are now about $5 richer, and are ready for the next waiting customer! And most people would much rather spend a few minutes in your cool booth than spend three or four hours in the blistering sun. The no-sweat way to success!

$$$ ♿ ⚲ ⛶

277 NURSING EQUIPMENT RENTALS

You can help make convalescence a less stressful experience for the sick in your community by starting up a very profitable nursing equipment and supply rental business in your own home. You will stock and rent out items such as hospital beds, crutches, traction devices, bed tables, walkers, inhalators, wheelchairs, blood pressure indicators, heating pads, and so on. Keep all your items neatly displayed. Clean and sterilize each item between rentals. Make your service well known in all the surrounding hospitals, clinics, and doctor offices.

$$$$ ⚲ ⛶

278 NUTRITION COUNSELOR

Better nutrition is on nearly everyone's mind in North America. We are quickly finding out that the general diet we have been on is killing us. Most people are looking for better, healthier foods. If you have a desire to help people to better nutrition, you can learn good nutrition and then make a good living sharing this information with others, either through individual counseling sessions or through classes and seminars. Writing good books on nutrition info and recipes would also be an excellent paying way of helping others to save their own lives.

$ ♿ ⚲ ⛶

279 OPTICAL DISCOUNT SHOP

You need no special optical or medical training, but you simply fill prescriptions for lenses and eye frames for clients who have had their eyes examined elsewhere. Offer cut-rate prices along with a variety of plain and stylish frames. Run a showcase of fashions for the eyes. Patients typically pay $80 and up for glasses elsewhere that you sell for as little as $30. Enormous volume will more than make up the difference over time.

$$$$ ♿ ⚲ ⛶

280 PHYSICAL FITNESS CENTER

An estimated 50 million North Americans are overweight, flabby, and out of shape. Ninety percent of the public don't like the way they look, thanks to the influence of TV. You can provide equipment and advice to help people get into shape and stay in shape. With nearly everyone a potential customer, the market will never become saturated. If you are handy, you can make all the inexpensive machines you will ever require and it will be possible to set up right in your own home.

$$$$

281 READING GLASSES

The size of the printing on a printed page helps determine how easy it is to read. Your reading speed is slower if the print is smaller. You can run a nice mail-order business from your home of selling simple reading glasses that magnify the size of print. They are not prescription glasses in any way. Older people with weak eye problems will be your best customers. Advertise nationally for steady solid income.

$

282 REDUCING SALON

Trim and thin is in. Our society puts great stress upon the beauty of a person's figure and face. You can set up a reducing salon in which customers will gladly pay you by the hour to come to your house to rent your exercising and beautifying equipment rather than invest in it themselves. People will not only seek your equipment but they will also come to lean upon your understanding ear and your positive enthusiasm for their reducing projects. You can lease to purchase all your equipment so you won't have to buy it all outright. As your clients reduce, you will grow!

$$$

283 RENT-A-HOT-TUB BUSINESS

Most people can't afford to install a hot tub or spa, costing upwards of $10,000, in their own home. You can capitalize on this situation by offering patrons the chance to unwind with a relaxing soak at hourly rates of $4.50 to $20. Outfit a cozy older home (or whatever) with private hot tubs or spas and rustic woods murals, plenty of plants, and easy listening music. You won't have any trouble filling the tubs, which will in turn fill your savings account!

$$$$

284 STAIRWAY LIFTS/ELEVATORS

Special elevators have been invented and manufactured that allow an ailing person to sit on a chair and push a button and ride either up or down the stairway while simply sitting down. You can purchase these stairway elevator systems wholesale and then proceed to sell them to private homes, businesses, hospitals, and such. You can then install and service them for extra profits. Disabled people would especially benefit with these products in their homes.

$$$ ⬛ ⬛⬛

285 STOP SMOKING CLINIC

A whopping 72 percent of the 42 million smokers in North America have admitted they would like very much to quit smoking! You show patrons the most effective and final method known to help them quit. It includes combining every rational approach available, together with repeated requests for supernatural divine aid. With the latter input, success for both of you is assured!

$ ⬛ ⬛ ⬛⬛

286 STRESS CLINIC

Stress is on everyone's mind these days. Our whole society is wound up and ready to explode. Few people truly know how to destress. You can learn a variety of sound measures that can help people relax and cope with stress. You can work one-on-one in a home business clinic environment to help relieve people of their stress burdens. You will not be preempting the position of medical practitioners; you will simply be sharing with others what you would do if you were in their shoes. Don't diagnose or prescribe—just share.

$ ⬛ ⬛ ⬛⬛

287 VITAMIN STORE

Stores dispensing quality vitamins and minerals and food supplements are experiencing growing pains. No longer is it just little old ladies or health freaks wanting them. The general population is beginning to realize that supermarket food, in general, is robbing them of proper nutrition. Supplements to depleted foods are becoming a must just for survival! "Private label" quality major brands, and triple your income! Add on sound nutritional advice; people today are desperate for it!

$$$$ ⬛ ⬛⬛

288 WATERBEDS

Waterbeds are making tidal waves on the sleeping scene. They offer the ultimate in comfortable sleeping. Back problems disappear almost overnight for many. People pay handsomely for the perfect night's sleep. You can be the one that gets paid! Average annual gross is over $200,000 for many with profits 25 percent to 35 percent of that! Offer custom bedding with leakproof bags, a wide range of furniture styles, and a host of profitable options. Waterbeds are healthy, fun, and heavy money-makers!

$$$ ◪ ▞▜▛

289 WEIGHT CONTROL CLINIC

Make big money by reducing big waistlines. It is easy to see why this is a booming business. Fully 70 percent of North Americans think they are overweight. In today's youth-oriented world, slim is in. You can help people trim down by providing weight loss information resources. About 30 million people each year enter the diet derby spending over half a billion dollars on books, counseling, and diet programs. Expected growth rate of reducing: 12 percent per year on a continuing basis. Put yourself on easy street by taking off pounds!

$$$ ◪ ▜▛

290 WILD HERBS

There are wholesale firms that do nothing but sell bulk orders of herbs. Many of these herbs are grown domestically and are easily harvested. Other of their herbs have to be harvested where they grow in the wild. You can contact these firms and find out which wild herbs they need and in what amounts they need them. Then you can go into the wild and harvest those plants that are available in your area. Then you can dry them and sell them to the firms for good profits. Your overhead will be low.

$ ♿ ◪ ▞▜▛

291 PERSONAL IMAGE CONSULTANT

We all feel good any time we can look in a mirror and see that we look good. If you know how to raise a person's self-image you will also give him or her a real mental lift. In this business you will provide whatever improves the appearance. This will include hair care, manicures, pedicures, perms, facials, tanning, and a host of other special attentions. Simple, encouraging pep-talks are also the order of the day. Quite a bit of training will be required of you unless you are willing to hire on trained help. The services you offer will be far beyond the average hair-care salon.

$$ ▐▜▐▌▐

292 SUN PROTECTION

We are hearing more and more about the dangers of getting too much sunshine on our skin. We hear about the threat of skin cancers, of aging the skin, and so on. A number of good protective agents and items have been developed to ward off too much sunshine. There are various sunscreen products, such as lotions, which are rubbed on the skin. And there are the old standby items such as various broad-brimmed hats which shade the head, face, and neck. You could find and stock up on the best of these products and market them, perhaps even by mail order. It will be a seasonal business, but it can do well.

$$ ♿ ▐▜▐▌▐

293 AMBULANCE CONTRACTOR

In this day of severe government spending restraint and drastic budget cut-backs, ambulance services are coming under the knife as well. If you know the business of how an ambulance service is basically run, you might consider becoming an ambulance contractor in your city or locality. It is also a great idea to extend this service into rural areas, which need the service but can't afford the usual high-end costs. Private ambulance contractors are good at finding ways to keep good service running at minimum cost. In the years ahead, more and more ambulance service will be privatized.

$$$$$ ◤ ▐▜▐▌▐

294 FUNERAL ADVISORY SERVICE

Funerals mean grief. And when people are grief-stricken they are not always in a frame of mind which allows for careful reasoning. This fact has allowed funeral directors who are occasionally unscrupulous to take advantage of the grieving ones. In this business, you become familiar with all the possible funeral home firms, the local funeral bylaws, and all the possible ways a funeral can be conducted in your locality. You then set up in business as an independent, unbiased funeral advisory consultant. Your loyalty is strictly to the grieving parties, and you show them how to obtain their desired funeral at minimum cost to them.

 $ ♿ ◤ ▐▜▐▌▐

295 PAIN RELIEF CONSULTANT

Pain can have a multitude of causes. For example, there are over two hundred known causes of headaches alone. If you have medical, nursing, or even paramedic background, you may qualify to be a pain relief consultant. You will have to check with your local medical authorities to determine what you can legally do and say in this medical field which deals with health. This business might be perfect for you if you are a retired medical doctor. At any rate, you would give people a knowledge of all the possible ways they can obtain relief from any pain they are suffering.

$ ♿ ❮ ▐▜▐

296 STRESS RELIEF CONSULTANT

Most people feel rushed these days. They often complain of being stressed out. It is a very real problem and for many people it is a very serious problem. You don't have to be a medical doctor to legally bring relief to people suffering from this condition. Some background in basic psychology and in counseling or nursing care would steer you toward entry level into this business. Much research has been done in this field which you should become aware of before proceeding. Check your local licensing authorities as to what you will need to have in your resume in order to qualify in this field.

$ ♿ ❮ ▐▜▐

297 HAIR CARE PRODUCTS

Hair care is in big. It seems that nearly every town of any size has more than enough beauty salons these days. All of these businesses need to be supplied and re-supplied with their hair and other care products. From your home, you can open up a business in which you sell these supplies. You stock them at home by the case, and you distribute them, perhaps by using a small van. Try to find the lines of products which are the big sellers. Be ready to extend your business by dealing by mail order, as well.

$$ ▐▜▐

298 DISABILITY CONSULTANT

Many disabled people are never fully advised about the possible disability benefits they can collect. As such, they are often short-changed by the very people who are supposed to be helping them. A disability consultant has thoroughly learned the disability benefit system and is in a position to make full disclosure to the disabled person. Furthermore, the consultant maintains total loyalty to the disabled client. His or her goal is to see to it that the disabled client is completely and fairly taken care of. With the requisite knowledge, a person can establish a decent home business helping the disabled in this manner.

$ ♿   ⚒   👥

299 HOME HEALTH CARE AGENCY

Health care has come full circle. Nursing in particular is shifting out of the expensive institutions such as hospitals and nursing homes, and back into private homes, where it used to be not so many years ago. It is less expensive to hire a practical nurse than it is to hire a registered nurse. By utilizing adequate yet less expensive labor, it is possible to set up and run a home health care business which is profitable not only to you, the owner-operator, but also to the insurance concerns and especially to the patients needing care. You may keep your business small with just yourself providing the care. Or you may hire several others trained to provide the care under your supervision.

$$ ♿   ⚒   👥

300 MEDICAL CLAIMS CONSULTANT

A fair amount of training is required for this business. You must have a good overall knowledge of what goes on in modern medicine. You must also know all the ins and outs of various medical insurance policies and their coverages and limitations. With this knowledge behind your brow it is possible to become your own business by helping both medical practitioners and individual patients with making medical claims and with solving medical claims problems that keep popping up.

$ ♿   ⚒   👥

301 CRAVING CONTROL CONSULTANT

Most of us would be surprised to find out that there are millions of people in our society who have seemingly uncontrollable cravings. There are many kinds of cravings—for food in general, or for certain types of food, for caffeinated products, for nicotine products, for various drugs both legal and illegal, and for a long list of other items which appeal to various unhealthy appetites. Most of these people will readily admit that they are virtual slaves to their cravings. And they will usually admit their frustration at being unable to break free from their enslavement. If you are well versed in the psychology and the physiology of cravings and what is required in order to bring them under control, you could do a great amount of good by selling your services to the desperate people needing this special help.

$ ♿   ⚒   👥

||||||||HORTICULTURE

302 BEDDING PLANTS

Everyone who gardens could easily start their own bedding plants from seed. Few people do this, however, because they don't have the time or the proper place to protect the plants from frost as they grow. Most people prefer to buy their bedding plants ready to set out in the garden. You can build some hothouses or heated greenhouses and grow bedding plants commercially. You will usually be able to sell all you can grow. Grow vegetables and flowers both. Stagger your seeding, as some plants are slow starters while others are faster. Advertise in all the local papers for best results.

$ ▀▜▐▛

303 BENEFICIAL BUGS

More and more people are realizing that insecticides not only kill insects but they can make people deathly sick as well. These same people are willing to buy quantities of good insects that will exterminate the bad bugs without using poisons. You can grow and sell these good insects both locally and by mail order. Some of these insects will include lady-bugs, lacewings, honeydew, and trichogramma. You can offer a free small catalog and free instructions with purchases. You will be helping us all to a safer environment, as well as helping yourself to a good living.

$$ ♿ ⬩ ▀▜▐▛

304 BONSAI (MING) TREE COLLECTING

You can simply dig these dwarf trees from the forest, already naturally bonsaied, and find an immediate market. Collectors abound. Most of these trees sell for $100 to $500. Some go for up to $3500. You can gross $200 to $800 per weekend selling at art shows and flea markets. A tank of gas and a shovel will get you started! The more gnarled and twisted the trees are, the better! You may have to prune the trees into proper shape over a period of time. Strive for an ancient and weathered appearance in the tree. Check your public library for more information.

$$ ♿ ▀▜▐▛

305 CACTUS

Cactus plants are intriguing to everyone. Their variety of shapes and sizes and looks seems endless. You can make a fine living raising and selling them. Purchase seed and grow your own. Make attractive shallow wooden box planters and fill with shallow sand. When your cacti are still small, replant several different kinds of them in an interesting arrangement in a setting of pebbles and sand. These mini-cactus gardens will sell well through florists, department stores, gift stores, and so on.

$ 🦽 ▟▜▛

306 COMPOST

There are innumerable advantages in using organic compost rather than inorganic chemical fertilizers for all kinds of plant growing. Fruits and vegetables have superior taste and nutrition when grown organically. You can make and sell nothing but compost and make a fine living. Arrive at your own special formula, mixing perhaps old alfalfa hay with chicken manure or leaf mold or whatever. Mix it, dry it, pulverize it, package it, label it, and sell it in bulk to nurseries or in smaller packages to homeowners for gardens and potting plants.

$ 🦽 ▟▜▛

307 DRIP IRRIGATION SYSTEMS

Plants grow best if they receive a steady supply of just the right amount of water. Normal watering methods usually supply an excess amount of water at times, alternating with more arid amounts. Drip irrigation systems solve the problem beautifully. You can start a business in which you sell and install these systems; you can operate nicely from your home. These systems require almost no attention once they are in place and working, which nicely frees the owner to be elsewhere. Individual gardeners and commercial operations are fast moving into this labor-saving approach to growing plants.

$$$ ◤ ▟▜▛

308 EARTHWORMS

An earthworm lives for several years and produces about 750 new worms each year; all you have to feed them is garbage! Small propagation boxes or beds stacked up will house them. They will live in a mixture of top soil, leaf mold, grass clippings, oatmeal, old coffee grounds, manure, garbage and organic waste matter, and so on. Keep them lightly moist and at 70°F for best production. They will sell well to gardeners and nurseries as top topsoil builders. Fishermen will of course patronize you for your live bait. Good profits also come from selling breeding stock.

$ 🦽 ▟▜▛

309 EXOTIC PLANTS

With the special know-how required, plus lots of tender loving care, you can establish a very profitable home business raising and selling rare, exotic plants. Most of them will be tropical in origin—banana plants, coffee plants, ginger bushes, tropical ferns, palms, pineapple plants, bonsai trees, and so on. People will drive long distances to buy from you as soon as they find out you exist. Raising a jungle will excite the locals, as well. If your thumb is especially green and you have a keen interest in unusual plants, you will be at home in this home business.

$$$ &   ⚒

310 FLORAL ARRANGING

Arrange flowers in eye-catching arrangements in the comfort of your own home and sell them in attractive pots and vases to department stores, houseware stores, dime stores, and even florist shops. All you need is a supply of artificial flowers and suitable containers. Strive for variety— from porch-sized arrangements to small single flowers in tiny containers. Hire help only on a piecework basis.

$ &   ⚒

311 FLORIST SHOP AT HOME

This business will provide you with one of the most satisfying livings possible. If you enjoy flowers (and who doesn't), then it may be for you. Simply raise your own flowers in your own yard and greenhouse, arrange them in beautiful bouquets and corsages, and sell them out the front door. A bit of floral tape, pipe cleaners, waterproof ribbon, waxed foil, foam bases, and a sign out front and you are on your way. With almost no overhead, you won't have any real competition. You can sell out of your garage or a special small building erected out front.

$ &   ⚒

312 FLOWER TREES

A flower tree can best be described as a hollow vertical object two or three feet in length filled with appropriate soil. Into the sides of the hollow object (the tree) you cut holes of two or three inches in diameter, spaced every six or eight inches. Into these holes you can plant cacti, or trailing plants, or strawberries, or just whatever looks good. The hollow object can be made from old birch trees that have rotted inside, or barrel cacti, which do the same, or other hollow trees, or boards nailed together in a square shape, or whatever. These living flower trees sell well for the few who make them.

$$

313 FUCHSIAS

Most people believe that it is difficult to grow fuchsias, and so they will almost always buy new plants instead of growing them for themselves. Fact is, they are very easy plants to grow from cuttings stuck in warm, light soil with plenty of water and shaded protection from strong sunlight. You can grow them from the plenty of cuttings you can take off of a batch of mature, full-grown plants. Once the cuttings are rooted well, replant them in tiny pots; they will sell well at any nursery. It can be a delightful business selling "Lady's Eardrops," as they are often called.

$

314 GARDEN SALES

It is possible to make a tidy living off of a garden about one acre in size! It is being done by many individuals right now! It requires hard work and a good knowledge of how to fully utilize the ground intensively. This business will provide plenty of top food for your own table. You will also be able to harvest surplus food, which you can peddle door-to-door to earn cash for your other needs. Expand to five acres of garden and net $30,000 a year!

$$

315 GIANT SEEDS

Everyone is attracted by the "world's largest" whatever-it-is. You can obtain seeds from the world's largest plants and simply sell them by mail order through national advertising. Such plants as the world's largest tree, the sequoia or redwood, or the world's largest tomato, or the world's largest pumpkin, or whatever, will sell especially well to thousands of plant curio seekers. Just a couple of seeds in a small envelope packet will sell for $3 dollars or more. A regular postage stamp is all you will need for shipping.

$$

316 GLADS

Gladioli are one of the most popular flowers everywhere. There is a steady demand for them as cut flowers and as bulbs for home gardens.

You can run a very profitable business selling both the flowers and the bulbs. The size of your business will depend only on the amount of space and time you can invest in it. The bulbs multiply quickly year to year. Take up all bulbs each fall and replant in spring. These plants are very hardy and easy to grow, requiring very little care. Market the flowers through florists and market the bulbs door-to-door, or mail order, or in retail outlets.

$$ ♿ 📊

317 GOURDS

Gourds will thrive in nearly every climate in North America. They will grow wherever winter squash and cucumbers grow. You can raise and sell them for a living. You can make them grow in unusual shapes by binding them with tape, bottles, rocks, and so on. You can force them to look like animals to which you can add bead eyes, stick legs, and the like. You can carve, paint, and varnish them. You can use them in utilitarian objects—birdhouses, toys, bowls and dishes, vases, ornaments, and so on. Sell them easily in gift stores, supermarkets, novelty stores. Fun and profit can be combined in this business.

$ ♿ 📊

318 GREEN PLANT SERVICE

The healthy upswing in the popularity of green plants for offices, homes, and businesses has created two new profit-making services—plant rental and plant care. Restaurants, banks, and other businesses use green plants to attract customers. You can be a "plant doctor" or a "plant nanny" with very little investment. Consider putting together a cheap catalog of green plants to show prospective lease accounts. Write up and use simple lease and maintenance agreements. You don't have to be a plant expert to succeed; a good business head will be your greatest strength.

$ ♿ 📊

319 HERB BOXES

Gourmet cooking is such only if it is made from scratch. This includes the herbs used as condiments. You can start a very interesting business in which you grow herbs yourself in a sun porch or greenhouse. Then select the more popular herbs—sage, thyme, parsley, fennel, mint, chives, sweet marjoram, savory, and so on—and replant a plant of each kind into a window box complete with plastic top cover. Sell these to housewives and gourmet cooks directly, or through gourmet food stores, gift shops, and the like. This business has tremendous potential.

$$ ♿ 

320 **HERB GARDENING**

An herb garden will produce green cash. Demand is way ahead of most suppliers for good, savory herbs. Those that are available are very limited in terms of variety. They are usually poorly packaged and are weak and stale. Set up to grow them and sell them—herbs such as dill, sage, chives, parsley, rosemary, summer savory, and so on. Some—sage, mint, chives, thyme, and sweet marjoram, for example—can be grown to full maturity indoors in window boxes. Package them in attractive containers and you will have no trouble selling all you can produce in and around your own home.

$$ ♿ 

321 **HOLLY**

The demand for live holly usually exceeds the supply in most areas of North America every holiday season. It is used in making wreaths and decorative centerpieces. You can raise it and sell it by the bushel basket if you have a hedge of it or a small bit of acreage to devote to growing it. It is an easy plant to grow, and sprigs with berries on them command top prices. You can also grow small holly trees and market them in gallon cans wrapped with pretty metallic foil and ribbon. Supermarkets will retail these well during the holiday season.

$$ ♿   ▮

322 **HORSERADISH**

Horseradish is an herb with a pungent taste and odor all its own. Certain people love to use it as a condiment or relish. You can grow it and sell it for a living. Root cuttings provide new plant starts, as it produces no seed. Dig the roots, clean them, peel them, dice and grate them, mix with apple cider vinegar and salt for preservation and better flavor, bottle the mixture, and apply nice labels. Sell your homemade product in grocery stores and gourmet food stores.

$ ♿

323 HOUSE PLANTS

You will need at least a sun porch or a smaller greenhouse for this business. You should be an enthusiastic floriculturist as well. Begin by purchasing a selection of top-quality bulbs and seedlings from a nursery. Nurture these into mature plants in your greenhouse. Then repot them into attractive ornamental containers. Now you are ready to sell retail from your premises or sell them wholesale to variety stores, supermarkets, and the like. Check around to see what will sell and stick to the better sellers. Try a few rare plants, too.

$ ♿ �

324 LANDSCAPING PLANTS

With nothing but a little seed money this business will just keep right on growing. You can grow nursery plant stock used in landscaping for little investment. Use a new method of growing the plants from seed in flats in your home. Later, transplant them to your backyard and simply nurture them gently with proper amounts of shade, water, fertilizer, and so on, until they reach marketable size. This is a very lucrative type of small-scale farming that can keep you and your family in groceries if all you have is a half-acre or so. Start new seedlings each year.

$$$ ▮▮▮

325 LAWN GRASS

Sod farming is always a lucrative business. There is one type of sod that is head and shoulders above any other; it is called Meyer Zoysia. Since it is seedless, it can be planted only as sod, allowing it to spread. This plant is more resistant to insects, disease, drought, weeds, and crabgrass than any lawn sod known. It stands up especially well to hot weather, hard wear, and poor subsoils. Grow it and sell it in flats or sod rolls. Write the U.S. Dept. of Agriculture in Washington, D.C. for further details on this incredible plant.

$$$$ ▮

326 MANURE

Selling manure will not only get you lots of laughs but it will also get you a decent living. Steer manure is the best all-around fertilizer for lawns, flowers, shrubbery, and gardens. You can contract with a large dairy to buy all their manure by the ton. Dry the manure, pulverize it, and put it into attractive, conveniently sized bags. You can wholesale the product to nurseries, florists, and so on. You can also sell it retail door-to-door, especially in the spring before planting time. New tract-housing developments will buy truckloads for landscaping all the new lawns.

$

327 MUMS

Growing chrysanthemums for a living is definitely possible. These are unusual flowers, as they bloom from August through October, when other flowers are history. They offer long-lasting and brilliantly colored blossoms. You can sell them as cut flowers or as potted plants. Roadside stands love to retail them, as they invariably help attract customers. A few plants can be divided again and again until you have thousands of derived plants. They will multiply like rabbits if you learn how to divide them. Sell them to supermarkets, hardware stores, variety stores, and so on.

$

328 MUSHROOMS

Mushrooms are in greater demand today than ever before. Scientists now believe that the consumption of mushrooms may help to prevent cardiovascular disorders. These delicious little plants are rich in most minerals and vitamins, especially amino acids and the B vitamins. Culturing them requires a low temperature and a high degree of humidity, which you will have to be able to control. You can set up in your basement if you prefer. Growing them is becoming more and more profitable as the market expands.

$$

329 MUTATIONS FOR PROFIT

There are flower societies throughout North America with local chapters in most centers whose members specialize in growing just one type of flower. You can cross-pollinate most flowers and create entirely new flowers, called hybrids. A new variety of flower appears entirely different from either of its parents. These new hybrids can sell for very large sums. You can produce a lot of interest and fun for yourself trying to produce exceptionally fine hybrids both for show and for solid profit.

$

330 NURSERY (PLANTS)

Plants have high commercial value. The profit margin is one of the best anywhere. You can start up a small family-run nursery if all you have is one acre or less of good ground for growing. Build a smaller greenhouse for raising bedding plants; these will sell like hotcakes in the spring. Stock all the more popular plants for landscaping. Small-scale sod farming might be added on. Stock all the accessory items that will sell well—fish fertilizer, seeds, compost, peat moss, tools, hoses, and so on. Keep it family run, so all profits will stay within the family, if possible.

$$ 🚩

331 NUTS

More and more North Americans are realizing that eating meat has very serious drawbacks and that nuts are a superior source of fats and protein in the diet. The prices of nuts—almonds, filberts, cashews, walnuts, pecans, Brazil nuts, and all the others—have climbed steeply in recent years. You can make a full income with a modest-sized nut tree orchard. It is not a demanding business except at harvest time. Government agents can give you full growing particulars as well as successful marketing suggestions.

$$$ 🚩

332 ORCHARD MANAGEMENT

Good orchards result from lots of tender loving care. A well-looked-after orchard will bring in top dollars for its produce. If you have experience and know-how in looking after orchards, you can hire out by contract to manage orchards for clients and get top salaries in the bargain. You can do the work yourself and do very well. Or, you can expand by hiring out others who are well trained in running orchards and receive a cut of their income, making an even bigger income for you.

$ 🚩

333 ORCHIDS

Most North Americans have seen orchid corsages, but unless you travel to Mexico or Hawaii, it is not likely that you will see a real orchid plant. You can learn to raise the orchid plants themselves and sell them to orchid lovers. Your plants will bring in anywhere from $10 to $100, depending on size and variety. Being tropical in origin, orchids need high humidity, mild temperatures, and lots of light. You can raise them in one room of your home devoted to the project. Invest in a selection of seedlings and experiment until you have award winners that are breadwinners.

$ ⬚   ⬚

334 PALM TREES

There is a ready, steady market for growing and selling palm trees. You can grow them from seed indoors and then transplant them out-doors if you live in a milder climate. When they are a foot or more in height they will be ready for marketing. Repot them in metal cans and sell them to nurseries, pricing by size and vigor. Stagger your planting of seeds so you always have a crop ready for sale. This will even out your workload. Before you start up, check your soil, your climate, and your market for suitability, as well as the type or types of palms most in demand.

$ ⬚   ⬚

335 PLANT COLLECTING

Collecting wild plants and selling them to industry can be a very lucrative business. Learn which wild plants in your area of North America have industrial value, and set to work. Florists use a variety of wild plants in making floral arrangements—baby's breath, ferns, pampas grass, cattails, cedar boughs, and so on. Pharmaceutical firms will buy plants such as cascara bark, which is used in laxatives. Woolen mills will purchase dried teasel flowers for use in milling of woolens. The list of possibilities is in the hundreds. Do some research and you will find a job ready-made for you out in nature.

$ ⬚   ⬚   ⬚

336 PLANT SHOP

There is a steady interest in potted plants, and the back-to-nature trend has given it a boost. It is possible to sell them door-to-door if you prepare a colorful prospectus. For less than $1000, you can be well under way.

$ ⬚   ⬚

337 POLLINATION SERVICE

Fruit production can be increased by about 20 percent just by intro-ducing one hive of bees into the orchard for every 40 to 50 fruit trees. You can raise bees and rent the hives out to fruit growers. Before blossom time, visit all the major fruit growers in your area and make contracts for your hive rentals. When blossom time comes, follow your schedule precisely for several weeks, trucking the hives from one client to the next. You can get about 4 clients per hive. Later on, you can also sell the resulting honey for additional profit. Bee pollen can be trapped and sold, as well, as a top health food.

$$ ◣ ▐▛

338 POTTING SOIL

People will pay dearly for convenience when they want potting soil. You can run an excellent business mixing, packaging, and selling potting soil. Mix top soil with sand, pulverized peat moss, and small amounts of fertilizer. Your package is the key item—make it as colorful and attractive as you possibly can. If you can undersell your competition, you can literally do a landslide business.

$ ♿ ▀▜▌▐

339 PRUNING SERVICE

Many, many shrubs, bushes, and trees have been ruined by amateur gardeners who have incorrectly pruned them. You can set up with a small pickup and a tool cart loaded with pruning tools. Drive to a given area, park the truck, take the tool cart out of the truck, and go door-to-door, offering to prune trees, shrubs, and bushes professionally. Most of your work will come in the fall and in the spring. Many repeat customers will come to rely upon your assistance each year. You may also hire out to orchardists, if any are in your area.

$ ♿ ▀▜▌

340 ROADSIDE PRODUCE

A roadside stand selling farm produce can be an excellent business if it is located along a well-traveled highway. Build a simple attractive structure with plenty of space that is easy to close up and secure at the end of each day. You can market all of your surplus veggies and fruits and honey and flowers, and so on. You can also sell items produced from neighboring farms to round out your stock. Sell whatever is in season. Advertise that you will store apples, cabbages, and other such produce into the winter for extended sales months later. You can harvest an excellent income in this business!

$ ♿ ◣ ▀▜▌

341 ROTOTILLING

As an owner and operator of a rototiller, you will have almost unlimited opportunities finding work. You will be preparing gardens for planting, tilling new lawns for seeding, tilling old lawns for reseeding, and so on. Your investment in a good tiller will quickly be recovered. You will charge so that costs of both the machine and your time will be covered. You can add on services of planting gardens and actually seeding lawns if you elect to. Although it is seasonal work, it can provide full-time work if you advertise properly.

$$ ♿ 〽️

342 SAWDUST

Sawdust is usually treated as though it were pure waste. Such is not the case. It is in great demand as a mulch by city gardeners. You can bag it and sell it for mulch. Or you can mix it with used motor oil; this makes an ideal floor-sweeping compound used in janitorial work. It can be pressed into small hard logs or briquettes for burning in stoves and fireplaces. There are many other uses for it. You can usually obtain it for free from nearby sawmills. Regardless of how you recycle it, your investment will be nearly nil, except for your time.

$ 〽️

343 SEED POTATOES

The price of seed potatoes is many times that of regular potatoes. They really sell at premium prices to gardeners. You can grow them and sell them by mail order. Most customers will buy from 5 to 20 pounds per order. You can grow 30 to 40 different varieties and sell them nationally by advertising a free, simple catalog that contains planting instructions. One to two acres of seed potatoes can bring you a very good income.

$ ♿ 〽️

344 SOILLESS GARDENING

Soilless gardening, or hydroponics, has a lot going for it. It does not need irrigation systems or good growing soil. It claims yields from 4 to 10 times the usual yields for space used. Make flat basins or tanks for holding the plant nutrients, which are in solution form. The plants grow on a perforated shelf just above the solution. The plant roots dangle down through the perforations and feed on the solution. Nearly any vegetable or flower can be grown this way. Once set up, it is easy to tend. It is a comparatively easy way to become a farmer without having a farm.

$$ ⬦ ▐▜▐▛

345 SOIL TESTING

More and more people are getting into flower and vegetable gardening. Most people just assume that their soils will be adequate. Poor plant growth shows up too late to allow for corrective measures. The time to correct elements lacking in soil is before planting time. You can provide all gardeners in your area with the vital knowledge they need about their soils for reasonable fees. With some inexpensive soil-testing devices, you can give on-the-spot information gardeners need.

$ ⬦ ▐▜▐▛

346 STRAWBERRIES

A vine-ripened strawberry has to be the most mouth-watering, luscious fruit in the world. You can do very well with strawberries, growing them and selling them with certain precautions. Make sure you choose a variety compatible with your climate and soils. Plant several acres, nurture them properly, and let customers pick their own berries. Supervise their picking and collect payment. People will drive miles on Sundays to pick your berries if you put up a good sign by a well-traveled road.

$$ ▐▛

347 SURVIVAL SEEDS

If nuclear disaster or any number of widespread natural disasters should strike North America, food would become the most important need for survivors. The author believes that a nuclear holocaust would leave survivors. North Americans are not prepared to survive these circumstances. You can sell seeds preserved in vacuum-packed cans, which will last indefinitely, to farsighted people for just such eventualities. Include a good variety of nonhybrid seeds in each can with a list of the different seeds in the can printed on the label. This is a real money-maker.

$$ ⬦ ▐▜▐▛

348 TOPSOIL

You can really clean up with dirt! Locate a large deposit of topsoil out in the country that is sitting idle and is perhaps unusable for some reason.

Buy the soil cheaply. Purchase (or lease) a dump truck and a loader and begin hauling the topsoil into towns, selling it to homeowners for gardens and lawn beds. You can make $150 to $250 a day if conditions are favorable. New subdivisions require a lot of topsoil for landscaping. The key is to find good topsoil at a dirt cheap price to begin with.

$$ 🔨 🏙️

349 TOTEM POLE PLANTERS

No planter will ever be more unusual than this one. Take pictures of real totem poles (the Haida Indian totem poles of British Columbia are among the best) and then find cedar (if you can) or redwood pieces of wood from tree trunks about 10 inches in diameter. Draw your design on the log with felt pen. Then use normal chisels to carve out the features; then paint the pole in authentic colors. Hollow out several openings in the sides and the top of the totem to receive various potted plants, well chosen for effect. Attach to a proper base.

$$ ♿ 🏙️

350 TOWER GARDENS

Necessity mothers invention, especially in raising food. People compressed into tight quarters such as apartment blocks go to special lengths to meet their needs. Some ingenious souls have devised a variety of gardens that rise vertically instead of being spread out horizontally. By using bricks or clay or other materials, they build gardens that stand compactly in corners on decks or patios. They are easy to tend without bending. And they can produce amazingly well. You can manufacture and sell the apparatus necessary for installing these tower gardens for big earnings.

$$ ♿ 🏙️

351 TREE PLANTING

Although it requires real work, tree planting can be a most satisfying and constructive field to get into. It is a matter of cooperating with nature and working in the great outdoors. You can easily hire on to do this work in areas of North America where forests are being replanted. Usual pay is $100 or more a day. Or you can grow bigger and bid for tree-planting contracts with companies and government agencies. In this case, you will organize and supervise crews doing the actual work. In the latter approach, you can earn substantial profits that will allow you to spend leisurely winters in a sunny clime.

$ 🏙️

352 TREE PRUNING SERVICE

A well-pruned fruit or nut tree will put most of its energies into producing fruit or nuts instead of into tree growth. The art and science of pruning trees is quickly and easily learned. With this expertise under your belt, you can do custom tree pruning for a very good living. Many orchardists are getting on in years and are willing to hire a reliable pruner by contract to prune their orchard. Set out to build a good reputation for quality work, and word of mouth will keep you in business season after season with a good income.

$ 🔳

353 TREE REMOVAL

Removing unwanted trees from property can be a risky project unless you have experience doing it. You can put an old pickup and a chainsaw to good use in this business, cutting trees down and then hauling the wood away and selling the wood by the cord to someone else. A day's worth of tree removal is easily worth $120 per man. The logs can then be turned into firewood for $50 to $150 per cord, depending on the kind of wood and whether it is split or not. Advertise in the classified section of your newspaper and it is possible you will have a full-time job within the year.

$$ 🔳 🔳

354 VIOLETS

For anyone with a green thumb and a love of flowers, raising African violets can be an excellent and enjoyable means of making money. You can set up an "indoor greenhouse" using equipment now available to amateurs. Special stands, small plastic pots in trays, and special fluorescent lights will help you raise several hundred of the plants at a time. You can market them in attractive pots, which you may be able to turn out yourself from ceramics, selling them to nurseries, stores, and even private individuals. These are probably the most popular house plant and they are able to sell themselves if properly displayed.

$ ♿ 🔳

355 WATERCRESS

Watercress is in great demand by city housewives as well as by restaurants, as it is one of the choicest ingredients in salads. Most people who have eaten it prefer it to lettuce. If you have access to cool spring water you can grow the cress in water flowing slowly over sand beds you have constructed. In northern areas it will be a seasonal business. It is a perishable product, so refrigeration and quick distribution will be necessary. Supplying direct to end users is best.

$$$

356 WATERMELONS

Watermelons practically sell themselves. You can buy a truckload of them from a farmer who raises them. Park your truck in a convenient stopping place for tourists beside a well-traveled highway. You can set up a large colorful beach umbrella under which you display several prime melons cut open. Set out signs back along the highway in both directions announcing watermelons up ahead. Charge current store prices as they will sell as impulse items without difficulty. You will likely sell out your truckload each day.

$$$

357 WEEKLY FLOWERS

Flowers will boost the spirits of everyone. You can get into this business almost immediately with almost no start-up costs. You simply deliver cut flowers in vases once a week to clients who have subscribed for the deliveries: $4 a week/$16 a month/$200 a year. You use the same type of flower for all of your customers each week to cut your costs. Then each week you deliver a different type of flower for variety's sake. Use mums, roses, carnations, irises, and other long-lasting flower types. Take phone orders at home. Have a colorful brochure describing your service.

$

358 WINTERIZING PLANT SERVICE

Every year homeowners and gardeners throughout North America needlessly lose millions of plants from frost kill. It is not difficult to provide protection to shrubs, bushes, perennials, ornamental trees, and fruit trees, but it does take time and forethought. You can easily learn the simple techniques employed to protect plants from the ravages of winter, and with this knowledge you can hire out to provide this service on a custom basis. Work by phone or simply go door-to-door in the late fall season. Leave your name with florists and nurseries as well.

$$

359 WOODLOT MANAGER

North Americans are beginning to carefully look after woodlots. Some of them are privately owned, others are publicly owned. You may have the abilities and interest needed to become a woodlot manager. You will be exercising good stewardship practices such as thinning trees, selective logging, tree planting, controlling tree pests, monitoring water courses, controlling public access, monitoring wildlife, and so on. For someone with a love of the outdoors it can be a most satisfying job to have. Pay will vary from job to job from being moderate to very good.

$ ♿ ▐▌

360 WEED CONTROL

This is not a weedeater business. Its target is another set of nuisance weeds. Everyone knows about dandelions in lawns, and weeds of all kinds in flower beds and gardens. These are the weeds that can make you decent wages. You will simply sell your service to remove and control these weeds to homeowners door-to-door, either in person or by flyer or display ad. Try to confine your work area to nearby neighborhoods to save time moving about. You can run the business using the latest in herbicides, or you can simply remove all the weeds manually or mechanically. Removing them is the safer method.

$ ▐▌▌

▌▌▌▌▌▌▌HOUSEHOLD

361 CARPET LAYING

Some carpet layers make $4000 a month every month. In most areas of North America this service is heavily in demand. You can learn the trade easily and at your convenience in your home with an inexpensive correspondence course. You will contract with carpet retailers in your area to lay carpets for their customers. A few simple tools are all you will need. A reasonably strong back is needed for only a few minutes each day in this business.

$$ ◣ ▐▌▌▐

362 CARPET RECOLORING

New carpets can cost around $3 per square foot and more. Few people realize that carpets can be redyed for less than one-third of this cost. You can open a business in which you dye old carpets with a special machine and dyes. The dyes are permanent, and they dry immediately without any inconvenience to you or your customers. Complete customer satisfaction is easy. You can work steadily at this business and net about $50,000 a year. Many others are right now proving this money-maker again and again.

$$$ ▐▌▌▐

363 CARPET/UPHOLSTERY CLEANING

Here you can start with a minimal amount of money. Have local newspaper carriers distribute some circulars. Then take bookings by home phone. Rent a carpet- and upholstery-cleaning machine from a local supermarket. Take in an average of $25 an hour! Satisfy your customers, and word of mouth will replace your advertising costs. You will soon be going at it full time and laughing at inflation if you go the extra mile for all your customers.

$$ ▐▌▌▐

364 CHIMNEY SWEEP

No one wants a chimney fire. But with more people using wood stoves, the number of chimney fires is increasing dramatically. You provide clean chimneys and peace of mind for the homeowner. Invest about $500. Skilled sweeps take about $1\frac{1}{2}$ hours per job, doing five to six jobs per day at an average of $40 per job (range of $25 to $75). Many pull in $1000 weekly. This is a wide open market that is growing, and you can work full or part-time. A touch of folklore clothing helps.

$$

365 CHINA REPAIRS

With patience, good manual dexterity, all the broken pieces available, and good glues that are strong and invisible, you can contract to put broken family treasures back together again. China, glass, and lamps can all be put back together carefully if you have all these things working for you. Sometimes you will need to insert substitute pieces of your own devising. Antique dealers will seek out your services. Aim for perfection in your repairs, and word of mouth will talk up additional work for you.

$ ♿

366 CONCRETE REPAIR

Earn your bread without floundering in the nine-to-five rat race. Setting up as a small-scale concrete repair contractor for the price of a trowel and a willingness to work hard can be your ticket for your next loaf! Look around for needed concrete repairs, and then approach the owner and offer her a deal she can't refuse. Check sidewalks, driveways, foundations, and so forth. Start with smaller jobs and work up.

$

367 CONSIGNMENT USED FURNITURE

This is an ideal business for low investment and rapid high return. It is also one of the few recession-proof businesses available. Furniture owners consign their furnishings to you with the selling price agreed to, then you sell the furnishings to a third party. You then keep 30 to 40 percent of the selling price and return the balance to the original owner. All three parties benefit. All you do is display the items consigned to you within your attractive premises.

$ ♿

368 COUNTERTOP REPAIRS

It costs on average about $500 to replace laminate kitchen countertops. These laminate countertops can chip if they receive sharp blows. Instead of costly replacement of damaged units, there are simple methods and techniques of repairing them. You can learn this system of repairs and then go into business for yourself. You can net $50 an hour without much trouble. Work door-to-door. Take out simple small ads. Try circulating flyers on public bulletin boards in your area.

$ ▛▜▟

369 ECONOMY INTERIOR DECORATING

Many people would like to redecorate their home or apartment, but they are quite often perplexed as to how to go about it. You can set up a nifty business in which you merely give advice on how to do a good job of redecorating at minimum cost to your client, who will do all the work herself. Advise on color schemes, furnishing coordination, space utilization, lighting, draperies, plant arrangements, location of best buys, and how-to literature. After a $40 hour of consultation, the rest is up to the client. A truly hassle-free business.

$$ ▛▜▟

370 ENERGY LOSS PREVENTION SERVICE

You can be rewarded well for saving home and building owners thousands of dollars a year. If you know how to retrofit a building with added insulation, caulking, and so on, and possibly even solar conversion systems, this is for you. Get contracts by simply taking infrared pictures of heat loss—tangible proof to the home or building owner that his money is being wasted. It gives you a professional image. A wide open market that is immense and virtually untouched. Many doing this have more business than they can handle.

$$ ♿ ◣ ▛▜▟

371 FLOOR REFINISHING RENTALS

Floor refinishing machines are too expensive to buy for homeowners as they are used only every few years. However, you can buy the machines and rent them out, or do the refinishing work as well. You will need commercial grade disc sanders and a straight sander (for edging), plus a supply of sandpaper. Customers pick them up and return the machines themselves. Add-ons include paint sprayers, ladders, chain saws, rototillers, and many other similar items.

$$$ ♿ ▛▜

372 FURNITURE STRIPPING SERVICE

Two possible ways to proceed in this business are (1) do the hard part for your customer by removing all the old paint, varnish, and so forth for him so he can refinish the piece of furniture at his home, or (2) go on to refinish the work yourself. You can easily begin at home part time with perhaps $30 in start-up costs.

$ ♿ ▐▜▐▐

373 GLASS ETCHING

Etched glass is making a solid comeback in North America. Artistic designs etched or sandblasted into glass panels are fast becoming a favorite decorator item in both homes and businesses. If you are into graphic arts and design, this business would be a natural for you. Sandblasting glass is not at all difficult to master. Like most artists, you may wish to operate on commissions from custom-ordered sales. Make some samples to get yourself underway.

$$ ♿ ▐▜▐▐

374 HOUSEHOLD MACHINE RENTALS

North American homeowners have discovered that the cheapest way to clean their rugs and carpets is to buy a jug of rug shampoo and rent an electric shampooer for a few dollars and go at it. You can make a business of supplying food stores and hardware stores with rental shampooers, floor waxers, and other machines, which these merchants rent out for you. Do your own repairs to cut costs. Your office is in your home. Make collections on sales monthly. You can expand steadily if you like.

$$$$ ♿ ▐▜

375 HOUSE NUMBER CURB PAINTING

Every house has a house number. Many of them are hard to find or see, or are missing altogether. You can start a very profitable specialty business in which you contract with homeowners to paint their house number on the curb in front of their home. People driving by can easily see the number. You can paint it on the spot as you go door-to-door. You can return in a few years to repaint the faded numbers for an additional fee. Check with your city hall for permission to proceed.

$ ♿ 🔧 ▐▜

376 HOUSEWARES SERVICE

With more and more transients in our society wanting to escape costly moving expenses, a new industry is just beginning to develop. You can enter it for minimal investment. Simply stock and rent out standard houseware items such as pots and pans, dishes, cutlery, linens, bed linens, and so forth. You may also want to handle smaller appliances, vacuums, TVs, stereos, and VCRs. Purchase second-hand items or closeout bargains. Contact apartment managers, renting agencies, and real estate firms. Circulate flyers or brochures. Keep everything perfectly clean.

$$$$$ 🦽   🏚

377 INTERIOR DECORATING

With a comprehensive course from a home correspondence school or with adult education courses, you can qualify to be an interior decorator. The business offers flexible hours, a good variety of activities, and a very lucrative return. You will become expert in color, lighting, fabrics, blueprints, traffic flow, patterns, textures, mood, proportions, woods, furnishings, upholstery, draperies, and so on. To be able to decorate a room so that it conveys the mood that the homeowner wishes will be your goal. Because of word of mouth, one job completed well will lead to your next job. Strive for the skillful, personal touch in all you attempt.

$$ 🏚

378 KINDLING

Increasing numbers of people are returning to using wood for heating all or part of their homes. Few of these people have the time or the well-practiced ability to split their own kindling. You can start a business in which you produce and sell packages of kindling. Customers will gladly pay for this convenience item. You can either gang-saw or split your kindling into fine sticks, and you can soak them in pine oil or a similar substance if you want to add on profit. Attractive packages that are easy to handle will sell this product in nearly every retail business.

$ 🦽   🏚

379 LANDSCAPING

Average homeowners are seldom capable of landscaping their home well without some experienced guidance. You can train as a professional landscaper by correspondence course in your own home. You can set up a business to help others with their landscape problems. You will be hired to change a barren plot of ground into areas of natural beauty that will have both practical and aesthetic value for its owner. You may get involved with planning, supervision, consultation service, design, installations, maintenance, and other services for your clients as they try to put nature back where it once was.

$$ ◼▮▊

380 LAWN AND GROUNDS SERVICE

Many men and women work full time and simply do not have the time to look after their lawns and gardens. You can provide them with the required services to keep their lawns and grounds looking smart. Contract on a monthly basis for what is wanted. You spend whatever time is necessary, without watching a clock, to fulfill your part of the contract, going and coming at your convenience. Mowing, weeding, watering, edging, raking leaves, will be the type of light work to be done. Almost everything you take in will be profit!

$ ♿ ◼▮▊

381 MAID SERVICE

This is a low-overhead, easy-to-operate business that can bring in $36,000 a year! Start with pocket money and be willing to organize others, and soon you will be managing a staff of helpers cleaning up for you. Give personal, cheerful, spotless service, and clients will be lining up on a waiting list to obtain your services.

$ ♿ ◼▮▊

382 MENU SERVICE

You can start a business in which you remove the drudgery of meal planning from the lives of working people. You can sell monthly subscriptions to families in which you have complied with a given family's special needs—their likes and dislikes, special diets, regard to budget, family size, and so forth. You sell the monthly menu plans together with weekly shopping lists based on the menu you have assembled. Mail this information with your monthly bill. Faithful subscribers will come to love you and virtually depend on you!

$ ♿ ◼▮▊

383 MICROWAVE COOKING INSTRUCTION

Many new owners of microwave ovens have met with repeated defeat, causing them to abandon their ovens in frustration. This need not be.

You can quickly become an expert on microwave recipes, on correct use of the machine, and on how to adapt normal recipes to microwave cooking. All this information can be sold to classes and individuals and seminars for premium tuition fees. You can demystify the product (or other similar products) and make users of it comfortable with it in two to three hours of intensive teaching and demonstration. Twenty-five dollars per hour per pupil is fair.

$ ♿ ◤ ▚▊▜

384 MOVING SERVICE
Put a second-hand truck or bus together with a stable phone number, plus strong arms and a back to match, and you can become a real mover! You provide a cheap and efficient alternative to high-priced professional movers. Have the customer take responsibility for breakage with his own insurance so that you can avoid high insurance premiums. Call yourself a trucker and not a mover to avoid licensing. Take only the small loads that big outfits find unprofitable, and they will gladly leave you alone. Pay only for your own sweat—avoid hiring others as much as possible.

$ ◤ ▚▊▜

385 NEW NEIGHBORS
Strive to get as many as 15 retail merchants who will agree to pay you to make house calls on new families in your area and acquaint them with the merchants' services! Have a list of services that is well rounded, including food, shelter, transportation, entertainment, and clothing. Also supply civic information such as a free map showing the location of libraries, public pools, bus routes, and so forth. Have coupons or free samples from the merchants to distribute. Keep good records of house calls so that you can collect from the merchants monthly.

$ ♿ ◤ ▚▊▜

386 PINE CONES
Pine cones will burn in a fire with an attractive bright blue flame and a fragrant scent in an open fireplace if properly treated beforehand. Collect truckloads of them and take them home. Then soak them in a solution of copper chloride and water, and allow them to dry thoroughly. Package them in attractive bags of about two dozen. You can sell them directly or by mail order, or you can wholesale them to retailers well

before the holiday season for about $1 per bag. A very good profit can be made, as your overhead is extremely low.

$ ♿

387 PRESERVES, HOMEMADE

Homemade products will never lose their appeal. Homemade jams and jellies are top sellers anywhere. Concentrate on several key factors— procure fruit that is at its peak and tree ripened, put special effort into attractive labels and packaging, and use only excellent and dependable recipes. Choose pretty and unusual glass containers. Freeze fruit that you cannot use right away in order to extend production of your preserves. The first year you will have to advertise, but word of mouth will take over for you.

$ ♿ ◣ ▜▍▛

388 ROOT CELLARS

People who have had root cellars find it difficult to do without them if for some reason they no longer have one. The modern freezer is not a complete replacement for the root cellar. Root cellars can be installed even on larger-sized city lots. They are best built of permanent materials such as cinder blocks for the walls and galvanized metal for the roof. You can set up shop selling and building these very handy food storage units on a custom-order basis for clients. Good steady wages can be made.

$$ ▜▍▛

389 ROTO-ROOTER SERVICE

Plants, especially trees, love to send their roots on penetration missions into your sewer and drainfield lines seeking an easy nutrient and water supply. You can purchase (or rent) an electric roto-rooter device with which you can run a part-time sewer-cleaning service. The machine will quickly pay for itself, and soon, except for mileage, all the profit will be net gain for you. Charge by the hour, including travel time. This can make an ideal second income.

$$ ◣ ▜▍▛

390 RUBBISH REMOVAL

Junk accumulates for everyone, slowly and steadily in millions of basements, attics, and garages. Most of it is fit only for the dump. Most garbage truckers won't handle unusual junk, especially if it needs moving or is bulky. You can manhandle the stuff to the dump in your truck for a fair fee. Part of your income will be derived from valuable items people carelessly throw away. Redeem these for cash at second-hand stores.

391 SAUNA

Having a sauna built into your basement is in fashion. Saunas provide a unique way of cleansing the skin and giving a tonic boost to the entire body. They require building techniques that are quite simple to master. You can pick up this trade and advertise your services for a good healthy living in larger centers.

$$

392 SOLAR SALES AND INSTALLATIONS

We all know that our greatest source of unused energy comes from the sun. Clever individuals all over the continent are setting up to reap inevitable profits from the sky-high possibilities in solar sales, service, and installations. Solar energy products are gaining a solid hold in all markets—consumer, commercial, and industrial. Breakthroughs in solar applications are becoming a regular event and the wise are not waiting to get in on the ground floor.

$$

393 STENCILING

You can become a specialty interior decorator using the idea of stenciling. You can learn how to make your own stencils from stiff heavy paper and how to use them in making custom-made borders on ceilings, floors, staircases, doors, furniture, and walls. Kitchen cabinet doors are also a dandy place for tasteful stencil pictures. Practice, and then make up some samples, business cards, and brochures, and you are in business reviving a wonderful and welcome tradition. You are not likely to find any competition in your area.

$

394 STORAGE EXPERT

Almost all homes are short on storage space. Both new and older homes can use more shelving and closet spaces. Storage space already in place is usually poorly utilized. You can set up a business in which you specialize in storage space. You will be designing, selling, and installing new or better organized storage units throughout homes and even businesses and offices. Collect pictures of clever storage units and methods and put them in a scrapbook to help you sell your services.

$

395 USED CARPET SALES

The recession can only build this market higher and higher. Used carpets are being sought not only for homes, but for hospitals, hotels, motels, schools, restaurants, offices, and banks. Your markups can be 300 percent and more. New carpets are marked up only about 35 percent on average. Start with a small investment and a garage. Collect used carpets, clean them, and sell them. Installing them evenings and weekends is a profitable add-on.

$ 🦽 ▚▐▊

396 VACUUM CLEANER SHOP

Virtually every home has a vacuum cleaner, and from time to time the machines need repairs or replacement. Set up a well-located shop, perhaps in your own home, in which you do the needed repairs or sell new replacement units. A big-ticket item is selling and installing central vacuum systems either in new homes or as retrofits in older homes. Stock parts and bags. Used machines sell well. Start shortly before the holiday season for best results.

$$$ ▚▐▊

397 WALL FABRICS

A new and interesting fashion in home decorating is that of applying fabric coverings to walls. There are many lovely and attractive designs and patterns available for your customers to choose from. Assist your clients in choosing from wholesale catalogs. You will profit from the sales alone. You may also provide the service of applying the fabric to the customer's walls for additional income. You can, with the necessary ability, make a full-time business of selling and applying these fabrics on walls of homes and offices in your area.

$$ ▚

398 WALL MURALS

You can become the most famous artist in your home town almost overnight by getting into this business. Purchase wall murals employing the "paint by number" method. Transfer these to walls, where you then proceed to paint them according to the numbers. They will attract immediate attention and admiration from everyone who sees them in your town's motels, apartments, waiting rooms, banks, and even homes, where they will replace wallpaper with something far more interesting! With no competition likely, your services will be in constant demand!

$$ ♿

399 WALLPRINTING

Wallprinting is a welcome replacement for wallpaper. It gives the same results as wallpaper, but it uses a new technique that allows savings of about 70 percent! Hundreds of different colors and patterns are now available to choose from. Purchase the special printing machine and find proper training, and then set up your own wallprinting business. You can wallprint walls in motels, hotels, business offices, lobbies, bus depots, hospitals, and anywhere else. A full week's work can bring in more than $2000, week after week.

$$ ♿

400 WATER TREATMENT SYSTEMS

Next to air, water is our greatest need. Pure, clean, soft water is a must for good health. However, over half of the drinking water in North America is below acceptable standards. About one-third of all drinking water supplies have been condemned as unpotable by authorities. Yet people are forced to keep using much of it. But now there are wonderful advanced methods and devices available for making any water safe to drink. You can learn quickly how to sell and install these devices and make an excellent living doing so working from your home on your own time.

$$

401 WELL DRILLING

About one-third of the water supply for drinking in North America has been condemned by health authorities as unfit for human consumption. Most of it is surface water that has been polluted. You can get into the domestic well drilling business for under $1000 with a new lighter-duty drilling rig. This machine should easily pay for itself in about six weeks of drilling. After that most of your intake will be clear profit. You will eventually be able to upgrade to a heavier-duty drilling rig with which you can make truly big money fast in more rural areas.

$$

402   WINDOW SHADES

Ordinary window shades usually don't fit into the decor of a room very well. You can go into business making custom-ordered window shades for clients. You can spray glue onto a plain shade and then attach cotton fabrics to match or complement wallpapers and paint schemes. By working at home with nearly no overhead, you can undercut the prices of department stores and interior decorators and still show healthy profits. A bit of advertising will get you under way.

$

403   WOOD SPLITTING

Make yourself a hydraulic wood splitter from used parts, or purchase a good used one. Keep it heavy duty and mount it on big wheels. Tow it from customer to customer, splitting wood by the hour. Ten cords a day will be worth about $150 gross to you. Use a gasoline engine. Keep basic parts on standby so that you won't have any costly breakdowns. Get written interim contracts ahead of time to ward off would-be competition.

$$

404   CREATIVE WINDOW TREATMENTS

Windows are like the eyes of a home. We look through them to see the world outside. A charming window makes an attractive frame around a view of the world outside. There are dozens of things you can do to make any window more becoming. These include special paint schemes, draperies, shades, blinds, decorative hangings, stained glass, mini-pane inserts, shutters, and other tasteful additions. This is a specialty business which requires only minimum training and investment. It is a business which will succeed well with both new and older homes. Your market is as near as the nearest home.

$$

405 VOICE-ACTIVATED HOME AUTOMATION

By using a computer and a special program installed in the computer, it is now possible to automate many of the chores which have been performed manually. You can program the computer to do a wide variety of things: cook your breakfast at a given time in the morning (this includes cooking your eggs as you like them, making fresh coffee, toasting your toast, etc.), turning on and off your automatic lawn sprinkling system, turning on and off your air-conditioner, opening and closing windows, controlling your ventilation in your garden greenhouse, and many other chores. You can run a business in which you sell and install these special home systems.

$$$

406 CUSTOM CLOSETS

Most new home owners are so excited about their new purchase that they fail to realize that the average new home has far too little storage built into it. It takes about six months for this realization to sink in. But by then it is too late to do much about it. So, about this time you arrive at their door with the remedy. You are in business to customize all their closet spaces. You have the expertise and the materials to make every cubic inch of their closets do duty. You install all sorts of shelving and pull-out trays, and bins to fit your client's requirements. All these bins, trays, shelves, and other hardware are readily available at your local building supply. This is a dandy home business and it works well in homes with closets of any vintage.

$

407 HOME COMPUTERS AND SOFTWARE

Life is being computerized for most of us living in North America. One would be hard-pressed to find even a few homes in the middle class that lack a home personal computer. There are millions of them in place and any gaps are quickly being filled in. Their existence makes for a ready market of sales and service. Setting up a modest-size computer retail outlet in even smaller centers is now possible. This type of business can succeed with sales, careful service, and instruction in how to use the more popular software programs.

$$$$

408 NEW HOME INTERIORS

Most new homeowners need some help when it comes to decorating the interior of their new home. Most new owners want to do their new home up right, but they usually lack the skills to do it. With well-rounded training in this special area, it is possible to set up a consulting business in which you provide this service. You can take it one step further by rolling up your sleeves and actually do the painting, the wallpapering, the installation of blinds, the hanging of draperies, the installation of fashion light fixtures, mirrors, and other products required.

$ ▰▮▮

409 KITCHEN TUNE-UPS

There are two rooms in every home which receive lots of wear and tear, especially if there is a large, active family using them. They are the kitchen and the bathroom. From time to time they need a face-lift in order to keep them looking decent. There are many things which can be done relatively cheaply to upgrade any kitchen. Some of these things include new paint, new door and drawer fronts, better drawer glides or rollers, new floor coverings, ceramic tile, new countertops, and similar items. If you are into this line of renovations, you may consider starting a home business in which you supply these kitchen renewal services. It can provide a good living.

$$ ▰▮▮

410 WIRELESS SPEAKERS

In many homes provision has not been made to run stereo speaker systems into all the rooms of the home. During construction, no one thought to run pairs of wires throughout the house for this purpose. Not to worry. A system has now been devised to place speaker pairs in any room of any house without using wires. These special speaker systems can be quickly installed in any room. You can start and run a business in which you sell and install these systems. You can make a profitable and satisfying business out of these unique devices.

$$ ▰▮▮

▐▎▍▋▌HOUSING

411 BARN LUMBER

More and more homeowners are using barn lumber in their homes for
special interior decorating effects, such as wood feature walls in dens
and family rooms. Factories cannot make this lumber. It is made by years
of artistic weathering. You can collect this lumber—the more weather-
beaten the better—and sell it at premium prices. Just treat it gently, as
much of it is fragile. You can usually obtain it free just for dismantling
and removing old buildings, especially in rural areas.

$$ ♿ ▐▜▐▛

412 BEAMS AND POSTS

Lots of owners of custom-built homes desire to have different styles of
open beams installed to enhance the appearance. Some of these beams,
and even posts, are hand-hewn with a broadaxe for a rustic appearance.
These beams present real challenges to carpenters and contractors be-
cause they are not available in building supply stores. You can start a
business of making the beams and posts and delivering them to building
sites. Excellent money is available for this unique product.

$$$ ▐▛

413 HOME INSTALLATIONS SERVICE

Nearly every family frequently purchases items that they then install in
their homes. If you are adept with your hands and have some basic hand
tools, this job may be just the ticket for you. Simply contact building
supply firms and other similar businesses and arrange with them for
you to be available to install any items that customers have purchased
and now need installing. You will be called on to install items such as
curtain rods, baseboards, countertops, cabinets, floor coverings, doors,
light fixtures, plumbing fixtures, mirrors, and the like. You can make a
good living in this job and you will never get bored with all the variety
of things to do.

$$ ▐▜▐▛

414 BUILDING HOUSES

With no working capital of your own you can build houses and sell them,
profiting $30,000 and more a year. Hire yourself out as a laborer while
you help build just one house and study carefully how it is done. You can

then contract to build a custom house for a client who puts the money up front as you proceed. With profits from this house, you can make a down payment on a vacant lot, on which you build another new house. Sell this house for $5000 net profit. Then reinvest in another lot, build a new house, and sell it. Plan to build and sell six houses per year at $5000 net profit each, for a tidy annual income of $30,000. Thousands work this way year after year.

$

415 CABINETS OF ARBORITE AND FORMICA

Arborite, Formica, and similar plastic products offer outstanding durability and beauty when used to surface cabinets of all sorts. It takes special skills to use these products effectively and efficiently, as much precision is required. You can learn these skills in relatively little time. You can then specialize in making custom cabinets using these products. Also learn how to repair cabinets of this type that have been chipped or damaged, for extra income. A few tools will get you into this home business, which has little competition.

$$ ▆▊▐

416 DECKS AND COVERINGS

Most homes never look finished until a deck or decks are in place. Decks, of course, tend to break up the boxy look of a house while adding more value to the house than they actually cost. You can become an expert on decks and deck coverings—in both sales and construction. A good book with sample pictures of different types of decks, railings, and so forth will help considerably as you try to close sales with clients. Strive for complete customer satisfaction so that word of mouth will bring you future sales and work.

$ ◣ ▆▊▐

417 DRYWALL

Drywall is the cheapest way to finish a wall effectively. It can be finished in dozens of different ways. With a short period of training, you can start your own freelance business of installing and finishing drywall. The competition is keen in most areas, but by working from your home you will have a competitive edge. Lower than usual rates will bring you plenty of work.

$

418 FENCES

"Good fences make good neighbors," goes the proverb. There are thousands of different kinds of fences. Regardless of how they are made, it is not long before they need painting or repairs. You might consider going into the fencing business if you are the fix-it type. You can contract to build new fences or repair old ones. You can browse around your neighborhood and spot fences that need repairs. You can then approach the owner and explain how you will fix his or her fence for a fixed fee. You can find good, steady business and work without difficulty in this way.

$ ▰▐▌

419 HOME IMPROVEMENT CONTRACTS

Home improvement loans are the easiest loans to secure from lending institutions. Contact people by phone and sell them on making home improvements they need. Arrange the loan for them, and find a competent home renovator or contractor to take on the project. Your commission will be about 10 percent of the total cost of the project. You will need to advertise your packaged service, perhaps by printed flyers.

$

420 HOME OFFICE MANAGEMENT

Every home needs some sort of an office space in which to keep up with the paperwork of running a home. Families run on red tape just like governments do—appointments, tax records, menu planning, correspondence, bills, banking, and so on. You can open a business in which you build whatever is necessary for your client's needs in a home office— new partition walls, shelves, roll-top desks, or whatever. A scrapbook of pictures showing suggestions will get you additional work. Many businesspeople need home offices as well, as they work mainly from their homes.

$

421 HOUSE PAINTING

Help keep your town or city attractive. House painting offers a good income and many fringe benefits: outdoor work, varied locations, choice of hours, chances to meet new and interesting people, and satisfaction in performing a valuable service. Word of mouth will be your best advertising. Community bulletin boards can help you initially. Work by written contract with all your materials covered by up-front money before you begin.

$$ ⚒ 🏙

422 HOUSE RESTORATIONS

Restoring older houses can be a very rewarding and satisfying business. Many couples are in this business working together and making a good living at the same time. You will need to find a basically solid old house for a cheap price. Then gut it and start on the ceilings and work down to the floor coverings. It is possible to resell a house that has been well restored for a price three times the original purchase price. This business does especially well in recessionary and inflationary times such as we have today.

$$$ ⚒ 🏙

423 KITCHEN CABINETS

Every home has need of good, functional kitchen cabinets. Because they are subjected to so much daily use, after a few years they need repairs or rejuvenation. If you are into cabinet making, this is one area in which good money can be consistently made. Many people are in need of custom cabinets that they cannot buy ready-made. If you can make cabinets, and if you can rejuvenate present units, you are in an enviable position for a steady job with steady income.

$$$ 🏙

424 KITCHEN CABINET REFACING

Popping new doors on old kitchen cabinets is the hottest new home renovation business to come along in years. It saves homeowners two-thirds the cost of new cabinets. Every home more than a few years old is a prospect. Try apartments and condos, also. You don't need an office location, as all your work is performed "on the job." Work out of your home with a small truck or van. This business is easy to start and operate. This is a job computers can't take away from you in the future. There is no end in sight to its bright possibilities.

$$$ 🏙

425 LOG HOUSES

Log houses are more popular than ever before. They are attractive and practical inventions from the past that continue to stand up to modern technology. There are several dozen methods of putting a log house together. Advertise your availability through ads in your area and have a sample of your work to show, if possible. You can make better money in this specialty than a regular carpenter makes because of the special skills required. Finishing off the inside of a log house also requires well-paying skills. One log house built each year will provide adequate income.

426 ROOMING HOUSE

Make a small down payment on an older large house that can be remodeled for about $1000 into five or six rooms for rent. Your profits will more than pay for any overhead and monthly mortgage payments. This is an ideal business for an older person who is still able and desirous of being active with light housekeeping in the rooms.

$$$$

427 SAWMILLING

One-person sawmills can now be bought at very reasonable prices. They are designed so that one person can run them without working overly hard. At least one type uses a band saw unit, which produces little waste sawdust. In this type of business you can produce and sell custom-ordered lumber. If you can find a smaller surface planner, you can turn out specialized types of lumber, such as moldings, which bring in bigger profits than standard-dimension lumber does. All you need is a big backyard in a place where neighbors aren't too close.

$$$

428 STONE SALES

Lots of new homes use stone features in their construction. Stone is used in fireplaces, hearths, wraparound heat shields for wood stoves, floor coverings, entryway designs, outdoor barbecues, and so on. If you can find a source of good rock that has an unusual, attractive appearance and is accessible, you can quarry the rock and sell it. Pile it up on small pallets and load it into your client's pickup with a forklift to make your work easy. Advertise in all your local papers. Charge the going rates.

$$

429 SUSPENDED CEILINGS

Suspended ceilings can be impossible to install for amateurs. Yet just a bit of know-how will make the job not only easy but a joy. Centering the ceiling and leveling it are the key tasks to learn. You can quickly master erecting them and then you can go into business from your home both selling and installing them at less than the going rates for your area. You will find yourself doing big business especially if you can secure one or two major commercial jobs in your first few months.

$$

430 HOME OWNERSHIP FACILITATOR

Prospective homeowners have to jump through many hoops before they ever move into a new home these days. And many hoops turn out to be nonproductive. In this business you simply try to make it as easy as possible for prospective homeowners to move in. You become versed in all aspects of purchasing a home: buying a lot, hiring the right contractor to build, arranging the financing, making house plans, comparing costs of house materials packages, obtaining building permits, setting up utility hook-ups, purchasing construction insurance, and dozens of other items which would harry the new owner. You sell both your ability to shave thousands of dollars off the total home cost, and your ability to cut through red tape.

$ ♿ ꛴꛴꛴

431 STAIRCASES

A fine staircase in a nice home makes a special statement to any visitors to the home. But fine staircases don't come by chance. In fact, most carpenters won't even try to build them, especially if they are made out of natural hardwoods. These type of staircases are in the same league as fine furniture. If you are a master craftsman with wood and understand the intricacies required, especially the mathematical calculations involved, you may consider this specialty business. A very nice living can be had running it. It is highly satisfying work.

$ ꛴꛴꛴

432 BUILDING DEMOLITION

Demolition of smaller buildings is usually a simple matter. But taking apart larger buildings requires special skills and machinery. It is difficult to take apart buildings unless you first study how they were put together in the first place. It is even more difficult to take them apart if they are very close to other standing buildings. It can be a very dangerous undertaking if part or all of the building is undergoing collapse. A great deal of common sense is imperative. If your talents lie in this business, very good money can be made in short order. But make sure you are fully apprised of any potential risks and are fully covered with insurance for any eventualities.

$$ ◧ ▚▜▙

433 CONSTRUCTION ESTIMATION SERVICE

Many building projects run into snags because of projected costs. There are few people who know how to cost out a building project. It requires a thorough knowledge of how a given building is put together. It requires a good knowledge of reading blueprints and the current costs of the variety of materials involved, as well as a knowledge of any possible labor and equipment costs. If you have a thorough background in this field you could set up a business to provide this very valuable service. Good fees working by the hour would be reasonable.

$ ♿ ▚▜▙

434 SKYLIGHTS

Many older-style homes are dreary inside mainly because they lack sufficient lighting through windows. A lot of newer homes, especially those which are energy-efficient, aren't much better. An obvious solution to this problem is to install skylights in the areas of the home that are darker during the daytime. Skylights should be installed only by those skilled at it. Otherwise, leaking around the installation is almost certain. In just a few days of learning, you can become sufficiently versed in how to install the various units you will find available from your local dealers. This specialty home business can provide an excellent living.

$ ▚▜▙

435 GARAGE INTERIORS

Most garage interiors are never finished off. Perhaps because they are low priority items. Or because they too quickly become catch-alls for junk storage. At any rate, it really doesn't cost very much to finish off the inside of a garage. It is usually just a matter of drywall on the walls and ceiling, a bit of window and door casing, perhaps some shelving, and everything painted. And presto, the owners have a garage worthy of the rest of their home. A finished garage can add considerably to the resale value of a home. You don't have to be a highly skilled carpenter to run a garage interior business.

$$

436 MORTGAGE PAYMENT CONSULTANT

Most banks and lending institutions will advise you of all the ins and outs of their own mortgage loans and possible payment plans. But they will be incapable of advising you concerning the details of their competition's loans and possible payment plans. If you learn all there is to learn about all the available mortgage loans in your locality, you can then set yourself up as an independent mortgage loans payment consultant. Your loyalty will not be to any one loaning institution, but it will be strictly toward your paying client. You will be in a position to advise your client of the best possible mortgage loan and the best possible way to pay it off for greatest savings.

$

IIIIIIIIINSTRUCTION

437 ACCENT IN SPEECH SERVICE

Thousands of people are very self-conscious of their speech because it reveals a certain accent that they would like to get rid of. Others, for various reasons, would like to acquire a certain speech accent to use at will. Whatever the case, with some effort you can train yourself to train others how to learn or unlearn a speech accent. Simply use a tape recorder to assist your client in learning or unlearning specific pronunciation patterns. Rote drills and practice sessions will complete the job. Fine hourly fees will be yours. You will need to advertise locally.

$$$ ▐▜▌▐

438 AEROBIC INSTRUCTION

People never exercise properly unless they get their heart beating well and their lungs pumping oxygen to every part of their body for an extended period of time. This sort of exercise includes jogging, skipping, running, hopping, and so on. This type of exercise literally will save the life of anyone who consistently participates in it. At minimum it reduces stress almost instantly. You can run an aerobic exercise center as a business and do remarkably well at it. Add wholesome music and baby-sitting service to enhance business.

$$ ◣ ▐▜▌

439 ASTRONOMY

Looking at the heavens is simply spellbinding, especially through a telescope. The incredible distances and the unimaginable size of most stars is very humbling. More and more people are getting into amateur astronomy because of the various space programs. Special interest and expertise in this field could qualify you to set up a business connected with it. Various approaches come to mind—retail sales of astronomy equipment and books, instruction for those getting under way, an observatory in your home or premises that charges admissions, or fees for renting time with your own private telescope, or even smaller well-built units for renting out to families, and so on.

$$$$ ▐▜▌▐

440 BALLET SCHOOL

If you are good at ballet and can teach it to others, you are qualified to teach others who are attracted to this fine art. You will need a fairly large room and a source of proper music. You may give group lessons, or limit yourself to private lessons. Rates will vary, so see what others are charging in your area, although you may not have any competition. A couple can do especially well in this business in a larger city.

$$

441 CAMP COUNSELOR

A summer spent among children can be an educational, joy-filled experience. It can be sheer fun to talk to eight-year-olds about pollywogs and whatever. You will learn how to move back to the simpler life as you see what is happening out there in the hills, and as you learn to stop and be quiet and think. Be ready to give love to the children there. You will get it all back and then some!

$ 🏔

442 COMPUTER CAMP

Combining the sophistication of the latest computers with the awesome wildness in nature is the secret of a computer camp. The best of nature alongside the best of man's artificial world is an unbeatable combination. Simply organize and run this type of camp. You don't have to know anything about either nature or the computer. You simply hire specialists who can turn well-paying clients, up to 150 in number at a time, onto either one or the other, or better yet, both. A two-week stay can bring in upwards of $1000 per patron.

$$$$ 🏔

443 CRAFTS SCHOOL

If you have access to a large home you can live in half of it and open a crafts school in the other half. You can accept tuition-paying pupils; the tuition will be part of your income. The other part of your income will come from sales of materials used in the various crafts you teach: ceramics, leathercraft, flower making, stained glass, rockhounding, weaving, and so on. Have a useful schedule for classes and lots of display space for crafts materials. Keep regular store hours to enhance sales.

$$ 🏔

444 DOG OBEDIENCE SCHOOL

With an increase of muggings and break-ins, more and more people are equipping themselves with guard dogs. But dogs that have not been properly trained can be problematic. You can easily learn how to train dogs and then sell your training expertise to some of these new guard dog owners for good profits. You will need to like and understand dogs, of course. You can work at home and you can work with a dozen different dogs during the course of the same day. Strive for a high turnover and a solid reputation of well-trained dogs.

445 DRIVING SCHOOL

Auto driving schools do well because graduates from them usually pass the tests and get their licenses easily. This is because the driving school instructor has learned how to drive to the perfect satisfaction of the license test official. You can easily do the same. Find out precisely what is required on the tests and then teach toward the tests. Try it first in your spare time, with a friend as a student, to see if this is for you.

446 ESSAY COACHING

Admission to most colleges today requires the ability to write a reasonably good essay. Writing ability in general is on the decline so there is a lot of room for people able to coach essay writing and term paper writing. If you have the right background, you can run a $15-an-hour operation in your own home, coaching students in these areas. You don't write the essays yourself, but you guide the student through several drafts of each essay until an acceptable work is in hand. You should aim your service at students able to pay for it.

447 FIRST AID INSTRUCTION

Every citizen would do well to update in first aid skills. Everyone would benefit if this were to happen. Many lives are lost because of ignorance in these skills. You can put your abilities and knowledge of first aid to use in making a good living for yourself by offering instruction to groups having interest in first aid for different purposes—industrial first aid, first aid in the home, survival first aid, heart resuscitation first aid, and so on. Keep yourself current and advertise your services to all common interest groups in your area.

$ 🦽 🔨 🏭

448 FOREIGN LANGUAGE SCHOOL

With more and more millions of North Americans traveling abroad as tourists or workers, interest in learning foreign languages increases. A small, successful language school in your home can provide you with a modest, steady income. You may work part time with students coming evenings and weekends. Hire teachers fluent in the common languages. Your ad may say, "Going Abroad? You will have more fun and save more money if you know the language! We offer evening classes in French, German, Italian, Spanish, etc. Contact _____."

$$ ◣ ⚒

449 FREELANCE SUBSTITUTE TEACHER

Here is a teaching position open to those without "proper" credentials. "Side" money comes easy, but a living is possible if you apply yourself to it. Seek and ye shall find. Knock and the door shall be opened unto you. Be ready and open to step temporarily into any teaching position as a substitute. New pupils are always ready to give a strange teacher a "honeymoon period." They will give you the benefit of the doubt. Screw up your courage and apply.

$$ ◣ ⚒

450 GARDENING BY VIDEO

More and more people are learning how to do things for themselves by watching TV video films in their own homes. You can put all your knowledge of gardening on a series of video films and sell the series at a package price to people who are just getting into gardening but are unsure of themselves. A free catalog and national advertising are musts for this business.

$$ ♿ ⚒

451 GOURMET COOKING INSTRUCTION

Gourmet cooking and dining is in. Numerous TV programs show vast audiences how to please their palates more delightfully. If you are well into this activity you can set up a fun business in your own home, teaching others how to become proficient in this delectable field. Gourmet cooking programs on TV tend to hurry things. You can slow things down for your pupils so they can master things as you go along. Adult classes in a local high school home economics room can also be considered as the stoves, counters, and so on, are already in place.

$$ ◣ ⚒

452 HAM RADIO INSTRUCTION

In order to become a ham amateur radio operator, a person has to learn basic radio theory, certain regulations, and Morse code. If you know these things you can put them carefully and methodically on cassette tapes and sell them by mail order to people wanting these skills. Advertise nationally for best response.

453 HOME BUSINESS COUNSELING

Millions of people would like to set up their own independent business in their home in order to make a more satisfactory living. Many of them are hesitant to step out and set up this type of a livelihood for fear of failure. If you have had general experience in setting up your own home business or businesses, you can hang out your shingle or sign and begin advising others of the necessary and the suggested steps to take to optimize their success. As you become more proficient, your counseling fees will naturally increase. Lecture for hire to groups and classes also, if you prefer.

$

454 HOMEMAKING INSTRUCTION

Many young brides, brides-to-be, and even veteran housewives, not to mention husbands, have never had proper home economics training. You can set up a school to teach these household arts in your home. You will present proper nutrition and cooking and budgeting. You will present sewing garments for the whole family. General housekeeping will give you a well-rounded and up-to-date course, which you can present in about 10 or 12 lessons. Limit your enrollment and hold class for different students each night for a full-time, well-paying, and independent income.

$

455 HOME SAFETY COUNSELING

Almost all of industry and commerce is regulated for safety. Special safety experts work full time in every community to assure safe working conditions for staff and employees in every place of work. However, responsibility for safety in the home is left up to individual adults. Every year tens of thousands of needless accidents happen in homes simply because of carelessness and lack of safety consciousness. You can run a business in which you counsel parents on how to make their home as safe as possible. Child-proofing homes could be your specialty.

456 HOME SCHOOLING COUNSELOR

Dissatisfaction with public education is growing at an alarming rate in North America. Every year thousands of parents across the land take their children out of public schools and proceed to either place them in private schools or else set about home schooling them. Public school teachers, more than any other group, are doing this very thing. If you have teaching experience, you can hire your services to parents, assisting them with any advice they might need in getting their children into their own home school. Books to use, methods, curriculum, home schooling associations, and the like will be your stock-in-trade.

$ ♿ ◣ 💹

457 HOMESTEADING SCHOOL

The back-to-the-land movement began in the sixties but it is a phenomenon that has continued steadily since then and shows every sign of quiet continuation. The steady flow of people out of the cities and back to the land presents a problem in that "city slickers" lack the skills and wherewithal to survive well on the land. If you have a good grasp of back-to-the-land requirements and a chunk of good ground, you can start a school in which you charge potential back-to-the-landers tuition to learn how to not only return to the land, but how to stay there successfully.

$$ 💹

458 HORSEMANSHIP

Horses have very small brains in comparison to their body size. It takes a special body of knowledge and skills to handle horses well. This knowledge you may already have. If not, it is not difficult to come by. Once you have it, you can hire yourself out to instruct others on how to properly handle horses—from the finer points on raising and keeping horses to the intricacies of different styles of riding and specialized equipment. Make your services known through horse interest groups, vets, and individual horse owners.

$ 💹

459 HORSE TRAINING

Only a small fraction of people who own and ride horses have adequate knowledge to properly train their own animals. If you are into horses and have the required background in training them, you can sell that expertise and make a good living at it. You will have to know first of all how to break a horse. This business can keep you working full time by itself in most areas. Other jobs that could supplement this one are boarding horses, doing farrier work, and raising specific horse breeds for sale.

$

460 HOUSE BUILDING INSTRUCTION

Your simple ad might read, "Let me save you many thousands of dollars by teaching you how to build your own house." If you relate well to people and if you have up-to-date knowledge and skills for building houses, what is there to keep you from running a business similar to the one suggested in the ad above? More and more people are trying to do things for themselves for self-satisfaction and for saving hard-earned money. You can make upwards of $25 an hour giving out this special kind of valuable information.

$ ♿ ⬛⬛

461 HOBBY SCHOOL

With a handicraft hobby, you can readily make a business of teaching it to others, and it can be quite a profitable enterprise. Whether it is oil painting, candle making, weaving, knitting, leatherwork, pottery, or whatever, you can also sell them the tools and supplies they will need for both the class and afterward. Most North Americans have more leisure time than they know what to do with, and this has given a big boost to the hobby industry.

$$ ♿ ⬛

462 INDUSTRIAL ARTS TUTORING

You can teach industrial arts in the privacy of your own home if you have the expert knowledge and a proper shop set up in which to teach the manual skills. It may be woodworking, welding, blueprint drawing, electrical installations, or whatever. If you proceed with a "low" profile with only one or two pupils at a time, much as a tutor would, then you won't have to forfeit the high costs of setting up a "school" which will need regulating by the authorities. Negotiated tuition fees will be your bread and butter.

$$$ ♿ ⬛

463 KNITTING INSTRUCTION AND SUPPLIES

You can open up a lovely business in your own home if you are a good knitter. With a bit of business acumen you can furnish a comfortable living for yourself. You can teach knitting both to classes and to individual pupils in your home. You may be able to set aside an area or room in your home as well in which you stock knitting supplies for sale— yarns, patterns, needles, and so on. Your pupils will be happy with the substantial discounts you can give them on their supplies. Supplies sales and tuitions will knit you a fun living.

$$ ♿ 🎹

464 MANNERS INSTRUCTION

Good manners are the grease in the machinery of society—they reduce friction. If you have a good background in manners yourself, you can teach others, especially the teen group. You can teach greetings, visiting, conversation, manners in various settings, manners in written letters, notes, and cards, graceful coming and leaving, phone etiquette, and so forth. You can use methods such as role playing and devices such as videotape machines in your schooling. Sizeable tuitions will be willingly paid, especially by the more affluent clients.

$ ♿ 🎹

465 MUSIC SCHOOL

At a music school a student can receive music instruction for a variety of popular instruments, including piano, guitar, violin, flute, and so on. If you can't teach music at all yourself, you can hire instructors that can. Sales of instruments may bring in half of your income. Trading instruments is a common practice for pupil upgrading. Music stores may pay you 10 percent commissions for referrals that lead to instrument purchases. Start small at home if you prefer.

$$ ♿ 🔨 🎹

466 PARENTING INSTRUCTION

Parents are supposed to be parents without knowing how to parent. This is indeed a ludicrous situation. You can run a school for parents in which you teach them how and why to be good parents. You will teach them such things as proper attitudes, proper expectations, proper communications, and so forth. You will teach them how to head off problems before they even develop. You can offer beginner and advanced packages of class sessions. Local professionals handling children and families will want to help promote your business.

$ ♿   ⚒   🏭

467 PENMANSHIP INSTRUCTION

Have you ever wondered how many people have died because illegible prescriptions scrawled by doctors were misunderstood? Besides doctors, there are thousands of other professional and business people whose handwriting can't be read. This lack costs untold millions of dollars daily to the economy. If you have good penmanship you can make a good living training others to write well through classes or special workbooks you publish and market. Help save lives and money for others.

$ ♿   🏭

468 READING CLINIC

Reading is the most important skill that can be learned in school. It is a necessity for success in our society in nearly every field of endeavor. If you have had experience in teaching reading you can set up a business in which you specialize in it. You can work with individuals or smaller classes in your own home. You can work with adults wishing to upgrade, or younger pupils wishing to "catch up," or immigrants who need to learn English so they can fit in. You might also teach better reading skills in comprehension and speed.

$ ♿   🏭

469 REAL ESTATE SCHOOL

It is possible to make a better living teaching real estate at home than can be made by being a real estate agent. You can put your own expertise in real estate to excellent use by converting it into a series of lessons on cassette tapes, which you sell. You can advertise a series of lectures on real estate that you will present. The tuition charge for attending your lecture series will include the cost of your album of lessons on cassette tape. Your pupils can keep the album of tapes for future reference. Real estate agencies will sponsor their own salesmen to attend your school.

$$ ⚒   🏭

470 REMEDIAL INSTRUCTION

Many people are weak in the basic subjects taught in formal schooling. The three Rs are basic to coping with life, and many desire this basic instruction through remedial help. If you have taught the three Rs before, you can set up a school in your own home in which you teach the basics of the three Rs to tuition-paying pupils one-to-one, or in classes. People of all ages will be your clients. Motivation to "hit the books" will be your chief task. Strive for quick and enjoyable results. Give preliminary tests to determine present abilities.

$ ♿ ⚒ ▀▜▐

471 ROPES AND KNOTS

Few people know how to tie knots in ropes to secure loads and other things. You can learn a dozen or more very useful knots and then proceed to teach them to others for a flat fee. You could actually go door-to-door giving an hour of instruction at each home willing to learn how a rope can make their lives easier.

$ ♿ ▀▜▐

472 SAILING INSTRUCTOR

Many North Americans buy power boats instead of sailboats because they think sailing is too mysterious and complicated. You can help erase these misconceptions with your sailing school, teaching would-be sailors how very simple and fun it can be. With a $1500 boat you can average $100 to $150 per day. Supplement the teaching work by selling new and used sailboats on commission in your free time. A net of $45,000 a season is not unrealistic if you are willing to apply yourself in a reasonably good area.

$ ⚒ ▀▜▐

473 SECRETARIAL SCHOOL

For about $400 or so you can start your own home secretarial school. Evening hours are best so students and working people can attend. You will need a rented typewriter and a desk per pupil. You will be teaching typing, shorthand, and transcribing skills, so you will need a blackboard setup and some shorthand and typing textbooks. To succeed always copy the successful, so study how a normal secretarial school operates.

$$ ♿ ⚒ ▀▜

474 SEWING SCHOOL

Many people have never learned to sew. There are many in every community, both men and women, who would like to learn. Some would like to save money by making their own dresses and draperies. Others would like the enjoyment and satisfaction of creating for the fun of it. If you are good at sewing you can do well financially running a sewing school. Make a deal with a sewing machine agency to use their premises, or buy up some good used machines. Have separate classes for beginners and advanced students.

475 SPEECH IMPROVEMENT

Most of us can benefit from learning how to speak better. Certain people who do a lot of public speaking should make special efforts to brush up their speech abilities. These people include job applicants, managing executives, and trial lawyers. You can get into this business with a reasonable background in proper public speaking and with the special help of a videotaping machine. Use the machine to allow your clients to sort out their strengths and weaknesses by seeing themselves as they appear and sound to the public. Fee collection is easy.

476 STOCKS AND BONDS

The stocks and bonds markets are a mystery to about 95 percent of North Americans. Many more people would possibly consider investing in these markets if they understood the possibilities. If you have a background in this area you may consider selling your knowledge and experience to groups or individuals interested in getting into this type of investment. Local evening adult education classes are one possibility. Flyers and/or ads will get those with definite interest to join your classes.

477 TEACHER'S AGENCY

Use a "free" university concept. The student picks a course (e.g., Making Moccasins) and pays, say, $20 for 4 classes. Your agency disburses half of the $20 tuition to the professor (no fixed salary paid). Many teachers and professors make more this way than from their regular jobs. Classes are held wherever the teacher chooses—home, garage, or wherever, and at the teacher's expense. You collect one-half of all tuitions paid. Nifty neat job. Everyone comes off a winner.

478 TEST COACHING

Pressure is increasing for students to get into colleges, especially the best colleges, in order to get into professional programs. Top scores on tests are a must. You can run a business that coaches these serious students on how to score better on standard entrance exams, such as the SAT, GRE, GMAT, and GED. You could also offer other services such as speedreading instruction. You could give personal class instruction, or you could prepare a series of tapes with the test tips recorded and sell these nationally through appropriate advertising.

$ ♿ ⬈ 📶

479 TOUR GUIDE INSTRUCTION

Good tour guides are worth every bit of their hire. They are trained all about travel by air, rail, boat, car, and so on. They have a good working knowledge of history, art, local eccentricities, the environment, local events, handling problems, and dealing with groups of people. You can open up a school in your area that charges students about $10 per hour to learn tour guiding. You must carefully select your students from all applicants for their potential as well as their current backgrounds. There is a very strong demand for competent, efficient, congenial, knowledgeable, trained tour guides.

$ ♿ ⬈ 📶

480 TRADE SCHOOL

You can take your trades and simply pass them on to tuition-paying students. Trade schools help others find jobs. The number of graduates from trade schools has more than tripled in the last 10 years. Disillusioned college grads make up the bulk of this market. Start-up costs are very low. You can work out of your own home, or perhaps work through the adult class program at a local college. Trade your trade for easier living.

$ ♿ ⬈ 📶

481 TUTORING

There are always students who need help in keeping up with their classes. Sometimes they are cramming for tests. Sometimes they are weak in a given subject. Sometimes they get behind because of illness or other problems. If you have taught before or are qualified and proficient as a teacher, you can set up your own tutoring service by simply advertising in your local newspaper. Add on substitute teaching also if you like.

Tutoring is an excellent way to earn money while working at home. Or you may want to make house calls.

$ ♿ ✂ ▶

482 USED CORRESPONDENCE COURSES

The original cost of correspondence courses is just too high for many people. However, many people are willing to purchase these same courses second-hand for reduced prices. You can procure these second-hand correspondence courses quite cheaply from people who have no further use for them and then sell them at a profit to you, and at the same time at a reduced price to new users who want them. You get both your used courses and your customers by advertising to either buy or sell them in national magazines. Prepare a free catalog listing your courses. The response will likely be quite steady.

$$ ♿ ▶

483 PILOT TRAINING

Learning to fly an airplane and obtaining a private pilot's license is more popular than ever here in North America. The sense of freedom experienced in flying smaller aircraft cannot be duplicated on the ground. If you now have, or are able to obtain, an Instructor's Rating, you can proceed to teach other would-be pilots how to realize their dreams. This is a very lucrative business, as it now costs around $2000 and more just to get a private pilot's license. You can buy a less expensive plane and give discount package costs. You will easily find yourself with full-time work.

$$$ ✂ ▶

484 APTITUDE TESTING

Nobody is good for nothing. Everyone has a variety of aptitudes or abilities, even though their abilities may not be developed to a high degree. Many people are at loose ends not knowing what they are really fit to do in life. There are a variety of aptitude tests already developed which can be used for testing nearly all aptitudes or abilities. Obtain these tests, learn how to use them, and then set up your business to test aptitudes. You can work through employment offices or agents, through educational institutions, with personnel officers in larger businesses, or with private individuals. You may have an aptitude aptitude.

$ ♿ ▶

MAIL ORDER

485 CLASSICAL MUSIC BY MAIL ORDER

Classical music is classical simply because it cannot be replaced as the standard for good music. If you are a lover of classical music, you know that it is becoming more and more difficult to have access to it at reasonable prices. You can set up a simple business in your home in which you market reasonably-priced classical music products—records, tapes, CDs, books, and so on—by mail order through a nationally advertised free catalog. Consider calling yourself a classical music club, if it suits you.

$$$$

486 COINS

Coins tend to retain their value even when the value of paper money is losing ground to inflation. Collecting current coinage is a wise practice in these times of a deflating economy. Another wise practice is to collect rare coins with a view to selling them at auction or to other collectors at good profits. Coins containing gold or silver are also highly sought after today. You can become a dealer in the above coins and other coins. Working through mail order with a small price list or catalog you have advertised will extend your possibilities.

$$$

487 FORMULAS BY MAIL ORDER

Just about everybody wants to find a formula for making something from time to time. And it is possible for you to find that special formula and sell it to the party looking for it. This is a very simple but potentially lucrative business. You should have access to a decent public library. You can advertise your service in national magazines. You can sell your formulas by mail order. Your overhead will be nearly nonexistent.

$$

488 HOW-TO BOOKS BY MAIL ORDER

Thousands of books are now in print giving instruction on how to do just about everything under the sun—from how to teach yourself typing to how to dry food for yourself. You name it and there is probably a how-to book about it. You can cash in on these books in the following manner: Simply stock a good basic inventory of these how-to books in your home, and then advertise a free catalog of how-to books in national papers and magazines. Orders will start streaming in steadily in about six weeks from startup.

$$$$

489 LICORICE

Licorice is a one-of-a-kind food treat product. It is so unique, it has no competition. Almost everyone likes its zesty taste. You can open a business in which you specialize in selling licorice products in all shapes and sizes. Upwards of 200 real licorice products are available in North America from various suppliers. Besides licorice for pleasure, people will purchase it for its laxative value or for clearing sinuses or easing sore throats. You can operate by mail order from your home or through a retail outlet, or both.

$$

490 MAIL ORDER

Fortunes are being made every day in mail order. It is one of the most fascinating and profitable of all home businesses. The secret of success in mail order is to choose a product with national appeal that you can sell at a good profit. You may wish to market something you have invented. You can operate this business single-handedly. Imagine opening the mail each day and finding a handful of checks you can cash. Once you have tasted success in mail order your enthusiasm will know no bounds. Try it.

$

491 MAIL ORDER GOURMET FOODS

Truffles, crème de marrons, Irish jams, English muffins. These are just a few of a great variety of foreign gastronomic delicacies that millions of North Americans developed a taste for while touring abroad. But these products can't be found easily here at home, so simply import these gourmet goodies and sell them in the lucrative mail-order market. You will need an attractive catalog, which you send to buyers of gourmet food. Expand with more catalogs. The opportunities are nearly limitless!

$$

492 STAIN REMOVAL SERVICE

This business can be run by phone locally. But you may want to extend this business by working by mail. First, become quite knowledgeable about the subject of stain removal. Libraries have good starting information. Then simply advertise that you will sell information on how to remove any stain. You can start with local advertising and expand into national advertising. You may want to collect your fees via credit cards.

$ ▞▊▐

493 PLASTIC BAGS BY MAIL ORDER
Run this ad in a national magazine and get set for a heavy influx of mail orders. Ad: "Wholesale Direct. Save 40 percent to 50 percent on plastic bags of any size. For storage, trash, freezing, etc. [And your address]." A free catalog or price sheet will boost your sales. You will have to stock a variety of plastic bags so you can provide prompt shipping service.

$$ ♿   ▞▊▐

494 POSTAGE STAMPS
There can be good profit in buying and selling postage stamps by the pound in large unsorted packages from wholesalers. You can carefully and patiently sort these stamps into special categories on approval sheets, which you then resell to mail-order customers. You will be selling these stamps for much more than you originally paid for them. You will be selling mainly to collectors wishing to round out their collections. Advertise your service nationally for best results.

$ ♿   ▞▊▐

495 TRANSLATOR BY MAIL
This is a simple service business you can best run from your home. Advertise nationally or regionally that you will translate letters and various other documents into a desired language from a second language. You will need to be fluent in both languages, of course. This would be an ideal business for someone knowing several common languages well. You can also offer to write letters for clients in specific foreign languages. Businesspeople dealing in import-export will often need this service.

$ ♿   ▞▊▐

496 WALL COVERINGS BY MAIL ORDER
Most people realize that by buying directly from suppliers substantial savings can be made. You can sell wall coverings for an ideal home business. You will stock basic wall coverings in your home. Nationally advertise

your free catalog and samples of wall coverings. Send out shipments to customers by mail order. It is as simple as that.

$$$ &♿; ▟▐▜

497 **WIND CHIMES**

Wind chimes add a special sparkle to a home. There are literally hundreds of different types of them available. Stock a variety of them and then sell them through a free catalog by mail order. You can purchase them from foreign suppliers while traveling abroad and import them for retail. National advertising for your free catalog will send you on your way into a fascinating business. Don't overlook local craftspeople as suppliers.

$$ &♿; ▟▐▜

▐▌▌▌▌▌▐▐MANUFACTURING

498 ARCHERY SUPPLIES MANUFACTURING

Archery is an engaging form of recreation. In recent times it has become quite technologically sophisticated for those who want it that way. Others prefer to leave the technology aside and just stick to the basics of the sport. At any rate, interest in the sport is growing steadily. You can make different kinds of bows and arrows together with quivers and make an agreeable living selling them. Good bows will sell for $300 or more. A basic set of tools for getting into this business will run you about $400.

$$ ♿   ▐▜▐▛

499 BABY PACKS

A baby pack allows a parent to carry a baby about in an intimate yet pleasant manner such that the parent's hands are free at all times. Several good baby packs are already on the market. You may be able to improve on them for styling, comfort, or pricing so that you can set out to make and sell them for an excellent home business. Carefully study other current makes and models and prices before you design your own.

$$ ♿   ▐▜▐▛

500 BROOMS AND BRUSHES MANUFACTURING

Like everything else, the price of brooms and brushes has gone way up. You can make these simple, yet indispensable items and sell them for good money. You can get broomstraw from farmers and turn your own handles on a lathe. Brightly paint the handles and brightly hand stitch the thatchwork with cotton yarn. Make various types of brooms and brushes and label them as being handmade. If you are handicapped, then say so on the label for even better returns. "Handmade by the handicapped" is honest, straightforward advertising. Don't hold back. Go for it.

$$ ♿   ▐▜▐▛

501 BURLWOOD TABLES MANUFACTURING

Grotesque on the outside and unbelievably beautiful on the inside—wood burls! They are usually free for the taking. You can make three or four tables from each burl and they can retail upwards of $600 each! Tree stumps and old pine knots can also be fashioned into lovely collector's items. Join epoxy finishes and well-seasoned wood to create permanent pieces that rate with the best of art.

$ ♿   ▐▜▐▛

142

502 CANOE MANUFACTURING

A fine canoe is truly a work of art. With newly developed methods and materials, canoes can now be made lighter in weight and stronger than ever before. A canoe built of lovely cedar planking encased in transparent and durable epoxy or similar resins will produce a unit at the top of the art worth $2000 and more. It is possible for one person to manufacture one of these prized crafts in less than three weeks. A very good living is possible in this specialized business, working on your own hours in your own home shop.

$$ ♿ ▐▜▐

503 CUSTOM CASE MAKING

Doctors, repairmen, engineers, musicians, electronic equipment dealers, salesmen, photographers, sportsmen, and many others all have something in common—they all need special custom-made storage cases to accommodate their respective tools and products. You can succeed very lucratively at home making these cases and selling them. You will need a few basic hand tools and a few basic supplies and your small home workshop. You will be able to work at your own pace in a creatively rewarding field with little or no competition and a wonderful sense of independence.

$$ ♿ ▐▜▐

504 CUTTING BOARDS

Most cutting boards made of wood will splinter off slivers that will get in the food because of the way the wood grain is exposed. Build cutting boards where only the end grain is exposed—like professional butcher blocks—and the problem is solved! These will outsell the other kind ten to one! They are ideal for cutting meat and bread and for chopping vegetables. Make them right and advertise their decided advantage and you will soon be faced with expansion into a factory!

$ ♿ ▐▜▐

505 DOGHOUSES

If you are into carpentry, you will have sheer fun building doghouses. They give a quick sense of satisfaction as they flow together so quickly and cheaply. You can build prefab kits knocked down for distribution to pet stores, feed stores, building supply firms, and so on. The plain ones sell best and are easiest to make because you can cut the materials for a bunch of them all at once. Work to order, as well, by building replicas of real owners' houses in miniature. Wealthier customers will pay extra for the prestige of the matching houses.

$ & ♿ 〽️

506 ELECTRONIC ASSEMBLING

Japan has an immense advantage in the electronic industry because they have millions of individuals assembling electronic subassemblies by contract right in their own homes, resulting in drastic reduction of overhead for companies. This same approach is now being introduced into North America to make our own electronic industry more competitive. You can do well for yourself if you can get these home contracts from electronic companies. They pay by the piece work. You may also be able to get a job supervising a group of home subassembly operations.

$$ ♿ 〽️

507 FISH LURE MANUFACTURING

You are not a true avid fisherman until you start making your own lures. Some hammer out spinners while others tie flies. If you can carve even a little bit, you can carve out from soft pine a variety of fishing lures, which you can then paint, attach hooks to, and sell wherever the market is active. You can market them in person on display cards, or else retail and wholesale them by mail order, or both. You may find yourself being kept so busy all day every day that you won't be able to find time to ever go fishing again.

$$ ♿ 〽️

508 FLOWER POTS

Potted plants are usually sold in drab-looking, unattractive clay pots. You can double your sales of potted plants by selling them in unusual and attractive pots. Try to purchase these more interesting pots. But better yet, make up your own interesting pots. Example: A chunk of hollow bamboo makes an ideal planter for a tiny plant to grow in. You can create other interesting planters and use them for your plants and expect double profits.

$$ ♿ 〽️

509 FOOD DRYERS

Collect old refrigerators. Convert them into food dryers. Make trays of lumber and hardware screen cloth. Put a screened vent at top with flashing for rain. Cut a hole in the bottom. Heat rises through this hole from a small heating coil or light bulbs placed in the motor compartment below. High capacity, attractive, easy to use units are quickly ready for sale. A good, clean-looking one is worth $200 on average!

$$ & ♪♪♫

510 FORMICA SIGNS

You will need to invest only a couple hundred dollars in this simple business. This formica engraving machine will turn out precision name pins, name plates, and small office signs, which will easily sell themselves as they are available in any color or even in woodgrain patterns. You can buy what few supplies you may need besides, such as pin backs for the name pins, at wholesale prices. Make up a card of samples showing the range of possibilities; this will clinch your sales wherever you go.

$$ & ♪♪♫

511 FORMULA PRODUCTS

Public libraries have books that contain formulas from which small fortunes can be made. Formulas for household cleaners and polishes are typical of these books. You can make one or more of these products, package and label them, and then sell them. Make sure your product or products measure up to your claims for them and repeat sales will sustain your business. You will normally be able to sell at a very high percentage of profit above your actual costs, as the materials you use will usually be inexpensive and easy to obtain.

$$$ & ♪♪♫

512 FURNITURE PREFABS

Retired cabinetmakers will be especially attracted to this business. With power saws and sanders and a home workshop, you can contract to cut only the parts and pieces required for the projects your clients wish to undertake. They will likely be stymied because they have neither the ability nor the tools to begin the project. They bring the plans and necessary wood to you. You precut and sand the pieces. They purchase your work and then assemble and finish the project at their home. The customer saves money and salvages some of his pride.

$$ & ♪♪♫

513 GARDEN HAND TOOLS

With hard times coming, more and more people are getting back into gardening, which will give them a better and a greater supply of needed good food. Good garden hand tools at reasonable prices are lacking in most communities of North America. You can make and sell these products. Or you can import these products from abroad and sell them. National advertising with a free garden hand tool catalog offered together with a sales program through parcel post and special shipping agencies will set you up in a booming home business.

$$$ ▬▮▐

514 GRAIN-RAISING TOOLS

The art and science of growing grains on a small scale is now possible with the right tools. Set up a business producing these badly needed tools, keeping the prices down and the tools simple. See the April 1978 issue of *Organic Gardening* magazine for feature articles on tools and grain growing—an invaluable issue! You may be the "John Deere" of small-scale grain growing in the future!

$$$$ ▬▮▐

515 GREENHOUSE KITS

Greenhouses provide an artificial climate and are capable of fending off raw, natural weather, which can destroy plants. You can make and sell greenhouses in knockdown kit form through national, regional, or even local advertising. The knockdown feature allows for easy shipping and easy off-season storage. There are dozens of possible designs already available, but you may be able to come up with a new ingenious model that has advantages over any competition. Check prices of other models for arriving at your own pricing.

$$$$$ ▬▮▐

516 HOT TUB SALES AND MANUFACTURING

Hot tubs and home spas are one of the hottest health products sweeping the North American continent. There is tremendous interest in them among intellectuals, health addicts, and the well-to-do who are looking for something new. With costs to produce one ranging from $400 to $600 it is easy to see a grand profit potential here. This product is moving so well that no one is bothering to wholesale it. There are just producers and retailers so far!

$$$$$ ◤ ▬▮▐

517 LAP DESKS

Most North Americans are unfamiliar with lap desks. They are simply light weight contraptions that you can place on your lap while seated, which will enable you to write correspondence. Inside a lift lid are pencils, pens, stamps, envelopes, letters to be answered, and so on. You can build attractive lap desks in your home shop and sell them locally. You may want to mass-produce them and sell them wholesale to large national department chains. Try to retail them for best profits for you.

$ ♿ ⛟

518 LAWN ORNAMENTS

Many homeowners wish to draw attention to the beautiful spacious lawns and lush plants surrounding their homes by installing colorful wooden lawn ornaments. Big bullfrogs, Snow White and the Seven Dwarfs, animals of all sorts such as a mother duck followed by her little ones, and the like. These figures are simply attached to a stake, which can be stuck in the ground and later removed for lawn mowing. Patterns abound. Try making your own, too. Plywood, paint, and a weatherproofing finish are all you will need. Make them in winter—sell them in the spring at nurseries.

$ ♿ ⛟

519 LICE-KILLING SCRATCH POSTS

In hot weather young pigs stop eating and growing when they become infected with hog lice. Build special posts as follows: Hollow out a 6″× 6″× 6 foot post to a 2-foot depth. Pour in kerosene crankcase oil mixture, which seeps out through tiny holes drilled to meet the big hole in the center. The mixture soaks into the burlap you have wrapped about the post, which in turn has been covered with chicken wire. Pigs scratch themselves on the wire, get soaked with oil mixture, and the lice expire! Sell them for $50 apiece! You will do better with them than raising pigs!

$ ♿ ⛟

520 LICENSE PLATE FRAMES

You can run a very simple but profitable business manufacturing personalized license plate frames. You purchase the blank frames for about $1 each and then you use silkscreen process to print special, personal, or business messages on the top of the frame. You then market the personalized frames to local merchants such as car dealers, or to clients by mail order for about four dollars per plate or seven dollars per set. You can get into this business at home for less than $100.

$ & 🎹

521 LITTER BAGS

Most litter bags end up as useless litter themselves, simply because they have been poorly designed. Build and market one that has a piece of malleable wire inside that lies flat until it is deployed, in which case it forms a round loop that (1) holds the bag open and makes it thus usable, and (2) becomes a hook or handle that will bend to fasten to the dashboard as desired, or to a bedside table or whatever. Market them in gas stations, tourists stops, motels (as freebies), gift stores, and so on.

$$ & 🎹

522 MARTIN HOUSES

A purple martin will catch and eat about 2000 insects, mostly mosquitos, every day. People who know this fact love to have these natural insect exterminators set up housekeeping beside their own homes. Purple martins love to live in colonies of 30 to 40 pairs. You can easily learn to build special purple martin colony-sized birdhouses, which you can ship knocked down in kit form by mail order. Advertise nationally and you will soon be running an actual factory as the orders begin pouring in.

$ & 🎹

523 METAL CREATIONS

Artists use many different types of metal in their originations. One of the most popular and versatile metals in art work is copper, which can be formed fairly easily into useful objects that sell, such as dishes, boxes, and wastebaskets. Because it is malleable it can readily be formed by bending, hammering, or rolling. Copper items and utensils can be etched or painted with enamels for added value. Once you have practiced well, you may face demands to increase your production.

$ & 🎹

524 MOCCASINS

Moccasins make the best slippers. They are so lightweight, it is easy to forget you have anything on your feet. They go hand in hand with relaxation. You can take an old pair apart and use them for a pattern.

Learn the simple method of hand-stitching them together with leather lacing. Study the variety of ways used to decorate them. You can easily set up to mass-produce them in your home to be marketed during tourist season and holiday seasons. Purchase your leathers and lacings wholesale from larger leather supply firms. Consider advertising nationally.

$ ♿

525 MUSICAL INSTRUMENTS HANDMADE

Mass-produced musical instruments tend to produce music sounding as though it all comes out of a mold. But connoisseurs of fine music expect to hear individual interpretations of works of music performed on musical instruments that offer textures and tones that are unique and somewhat out of the ordinary. You may be into making handmade musical instruments—flutes, guitars, violins, lutes, dulcimers, and so on. You can sell units you make. Or you can buy a variety of these lovely instruments from other craftsmen and proceed to market them retail. This can be a fine home business.

$ ♿

526 NECKTIES FOR SPORTSMEN

This business is a real money-maker and can be duplicated most any-where. Make neckties and sell them. These are special neckties made specifically for sportsmen engaged in specific sports. Your ties will be sewn from plain pure silk in a variety of colors. Using the silkscreen process (which allows for mass production), paint symbols and pictures on the ties for each sport—a sailboat for sailors, a man catching a fish for fishermen, golf clubs, airplanes, and so on. You will net some real winning scores in this business.

$$ ♿

527 PATCHWORK PILLOWCASES

With access to very inexpensive yard-ends of fabrics you can open a home business for producing and selling patchwork pillowcases. You can produce at several levels: (1) the basic slip cover of patchwork, which requires the customer to sew it to size to cover a present pillow, or (2) finished covers, including zippers, to be filled with present pillows, or (3) a complete pillow covered in patchwork. You may want to produce these colonial pillows to order. Advertise in regional or national magazines and expect to be inundated with orders.

$ ♿

528 PHOTO LAMPSHADES

Lampshades can be made to do double duty with this business. You take color photos of the beauties of nature and the historical attractions in your local area. Have these photos blown up to 5″× 7″ or bigger. Lightly wipe mineral oil over the backs of the photos. This will make them semitransparent. Sew the photos to parchment paper lampshades slightly angling and overlapping them as you go. The lamp light will shine through the finished shade, projecting life-like beauty into the photos. Sell them for $12 or more apiece depending on size and market. Tourists and even locals will be proud to buy and display them.

$ ♿ ▐▜▐▌

529 PICTURES ON PLATES

Nearly everyone has seen china plates with pictures on them of special landmarks or historical figures. You can make these plates yourself and sell them for healthy profits. Simply place photographic emulsion on the plate and reproduce a photo of your choice onto the emulsion, using an enlarger. Or you can purchase the plates with emulsion already on them. You can sell plates with personal photos on them, or local tourist monuments or scenery, or local churches, or landmarks, and so on. They will be snapped up by collectors for big profits to you.

$$ ♿ ▐▜▐▌

530 PILLOW MAKING

Start with a sewing machine, some fabric remnants, and some crushed foam stuffing. Make a variety of colorful sofa pillows, decorator pillows, floor pillows, and sell directly to the public, or from your own shop, or wholesale to retailers. Once you get the hang of it you will find that making pillows is quite easy. Soon you will be able to make one in about 10 minutes or so. three or four dollars profit per pillow is common. You may have trouble keeping your business small enough.

$ ♿ ▐▜▐▌

531 PILLOWS, THROW

Throw pillows can be made in hundreds of ways. You can make them very inexpensively by sewing two terrycloth face cloths or two small hand towels back to back, stuffing them with crushed foam or kapok. Use brightly colored terrycloth of contrasting colors so the pillow will have a different color when flipped over. Before sewing the covers together, you may want to fringe out an inch or so of the outer edges. You can support yourself throwing throw pillows together and carefully marketing them. It is being done by others for good profits.

$ [♿]   [▓▓]

532 PINE PILLOWS

This business will be good for those blessed with nostalgia—for the good times past. Simply make small pillows of burlap and trimming, and fill them up with dried needles from any evergreen tree. You can use needles from fir, pine, spruce, or tamarack, but most will prefer the balsam fir. Your pillows will give off a most welcome, spicy, delightful aroma, putting your patrons back in yesteryear surrounded by crisp fresh air and piney woods! Any gift shop will welcome them.

$ [♿]   [▓▓]

533 PLASTIC STAINED GLASS

Light shining through transparent colored material is especially captivating to anyone who can see. Real stained glass is expensive and fragile. Here is a way for you to simulate stained glass and do it very inexpensively. Make an aluminum pan of a given size by simply bending the edges of aluminum foil up carefully. Then arrange tiny plastic colored crystals in the pan to form a design or picture. Then bake your arrangement in your home oven at 400°F and the crystals will melt, forming a connected sheet of plastic, but retaining your design. Presto. Instant "stained glass" that sells!

$ [♿]   [▓▓]

534 POLYESTER CAST CRAFTS

All sorts of craft items can be made by polyester casting. Making decorator lamps on a commercial basis using this method is entirely feasible. Try a couple of them on an experimental basis; then stand back and let your friends and relatives rave when they take in the beauty of your creations. You can turn out about 20 of these lights a week and they will sell for an average of $60 or more. Sell direct or through retailers such as department stores and interior decorators. Any hobby store can direct you to the few materials you will need.

$ [♿]   [▓▓]

535 PORTABLE FURNITURE

More and more people in our society are becoming transient or mobile. Many of these people want furniture that they don't need a moving van for, that they can fold up and move cheaply, in their own car, if need be. You can get into this rapidly growing market in at least two ways: (1) by manufacturing highly portable lightweight furniture, or (2) by retailing this type of furniture. Both ventures can conceivably be run from a home. Consider the possibility of mail-ordering your portable products with a free catalog and national advertising.

$$ & ⬛

536 POTTERY

You can find your fortune by reviving one of the oldest human crafts —the potter's wheel! Set one up in full view of visitors to your workshop, which could be at home. In the summer months, work out on the front porch or sidewalk! Turn out old earthenware items, such as baked bean pots, molasses jugs, pitchers, bowls, jam jars, vases, etc.; the older-looking the better. Display a wide variety of finished items all fired and glazed. Sell the quaintness and handcrafting of your products. They will move well.

$$ & ⬛

537 PUN PLAQUES

Puns, witticisms, proverbs, old sayings, and the like can be turned into a very simple home business that can give you and yours a goodly income. Simply saw out planks of wood to the right sizes and paint the special sayings on them, and then market them by retail or mail order. Simply start collecting wise old sayings and practice lettering with acrylic paints. Your overhead will be especially low. Advertise nationally, offering a free catalog for best returns.

$ & ⬛

538 PUZZLES, WOODEN JIGSAW

Jigsaw puzzle enthusiasts are always on the lookout for novel and unusual jigsaw puzzles. They tire of the cheap, mass-produced, flimsy, cardboard models with uninteresting pictures and poorly fitting pieces. You take $\frac{1}{8}$ inch mahogany plywood panels, find nice artistic prints, glue the prints onto the wood panel with rubber cement, cut out interlocking pieces with your jigsaw, sand well, and package them attractively. Charge $50 or more per puzzle through select sporting goods stores, stationery and gift stores, and even some department stores.

$ & ⬛

539 PYREX GLASS ART

Working with melted glass is a matter of practice, balance, and good timing. In this craft you will be touching two $\frac{1}{2}$ inch pyrex rods together at the hottest point in the flame from an acetylene torch, and then manipulating the molten glass into a given shape. Try all sorts of shapes—vases, animals, boats, planes, people, and so on. Your tiny glass shelf ornaments and replicas will be so endearing, and even exquisite, that you will be able to get a very good price for them in the better gift shops. Set up where people can watch you work when you feel you are ready.

$ ♿ ▐▜▐▛

540 ROLLTOP DESKS

Half the fun of owning a rolltop desk is having a dandy mess sitting on it, and then shutting the mess out of your mind by simply closing the rolltop. You can make these classic desks from yesteryear quite inexpensively and sell them as fast as you can produce them. Good wages can be made doing this. Word of mouth will get you more orders. People are intrigued by them because of the little drawers and nooks and crannies, not to mention the rolltop itself, which mysteriously disappears when open.

$ ▐▜▐▛

541 RUSTIC FURNITURE

If you are frequently outdoors, start collecting all of the interesting, twisted, and gnarled pieces of roots, limbs, trunks, driftwood, and the like, that you can drag home. Put your imagination to work in how to combine these natural works of art into useful, functioning fixtures and furniture to sell—chairs, coffee tables, lamps, benches, stools, and so on. The secret is that each item is unique—one of a kind!

$ ♿ ▐▜▐▛

542 SCENIC PRODUCTS

This business combines two good things to make one excellent thing. Purchase ready-made, inexpensive wooden items such as letter holders, trinket boxes, bookends, small trays, plaques, and so on. Then take scenic color photos that are distinctly from your neck of the woods. Carefully glue these scenic or historical photos onto the wooden articles. Then you might paint by hand a clever border of your choice around the photo. Lastly, cover with a glossy, waterproof finish. Tourists and visitors will happily purchase these articles from gift shops, drugstores, newsstands, and hotel lobbies.

$ 👤 📊

543 SEWING BEACHWEAR

Sewing at home can place you way out in front of the rat race because your overhead is nearly nil. You have an immense advantage before you even begin! You can open up a sewing business in which you create distinctive beachwear accessories—terrycloth robes and throws, sailcloth beachbags and hats, and the like. Better specialty shops for ladies will snatch them up. Prepare samples, and take orders well in advance of the summer beach season. Find which items will sell best and then stick to them.

$ 👤 📊

544 SHAMPOO AND SOAP MANUFACTURING

The ingredients in soaps and shampoos are really quite simple and inexpensive. However, simply price soaps and shampoos and you will quickly see that huge profits are available in this industry, with the right approach. Experiment and you will find that you can make a shampoo or a soap just as good as or better than what you have been buying. Place your products in attractive packaging and you will soon find the profits rolling in, especially if you operate at home with minimal overhead costs.

$ 📊

545 SIGN LETTERS

A senior citizen could have fun and earn extra income with this business. With a jigsaw or a smaller band saw, cut out letters from plywood, masonite, or styrofoam in various sizes and styles. You can get patterns for them from books and pamphlets in your local public library. You can work to order, doing mostly custom jobs. Keep extra letters on hand to fill any rush orders. Sign painters will often willingly buy them from you for their business. House number sets are a great add-on.

$ 👤 📊

546 SPOONS

Wooden spoons come in all shapes and sizes. People never seem to have enough of them in the kitchen. It is easy to make spoons from the right kinds of wood. All you need are a few hand tools. A small band saw will save most of the labor. Make them in a variety of shapes and sizes. Sell them singly or in packaged sets. Sell them retail or wholesale as you prefer. With sound marketing, a steady production of good spoons will certainly bring in a steady income.

$ 🦽

547 STENCILING

You can become a specialty interior decorator using the technique of stenciling. You can learn to make your own stencils from stiff heavy paper and use them in making custom-made borders on ceilings, floors, staircases, doors, furniture, walls, and the like. Kitchen cabinet doors are also a dandy place for tasteful stencil pictures. Practice well, then make up some samples, some business cards, and brochures, and you will be in business reviving a wonderful and welcome tradition. You are not likely to find any competition in your area.

$ 🦽 📊

548 STORE DIRECTORY SYSTEMS

Imagine walking into a large grocery or department store looking for just one or two items. This needle-in-a-haystack problem faces millions of shoppers daily. You can put a stop to it and build a great business by installing a simple computerized directory info center that will instantly tell a customer exactly where to go in a store to find any single item. The industry is only at the idea stage now, but it is ready to explode as soon as you light the fuse.

$$$ 📊

549 STREET SIGNS

People like to have places named after them. You can start a simple money-making business by selling your own line of personalized old-time street signs bearing first names such as Nathan Road, Tad Street, or Keri Boulevard. You will have to track down a supply of metal and someone to help you get into the silkscreen printing process.

$ 🦽 📊

550 STUFFED ANIMAL KITS

This is without question a winning home business. Simply make up simple stuffed animal kits, which customers take home and stuff themselves.

You purchase woolen felt mill ends by the pound through the mail from which you cut out numbers of animal bodies and their contrasting colored tails, tongues, eyes, and ears. Stitch two flat body pieces on your sewing machine, use fabric glue to attach the tails, ears, and so on. Leave a small stuffing hole in body. Staple the flat animal to the sheet of instructions for stuffing. Insert the kit into a clear plastic envelope. Sell anywhere!

$ ♿   👷

551 SUGGESTION BOXES

Good public relations are an absolute must for every business, public or private. Letting people have access to the running of a business by making suggestions will improve public relations every time. Go into business making and selling suggestion boxes. Make them as attractive as possible with a little sign attached that makes a friendly invitation to submit suggestions. Sell by mail order or directly door to door. A tiny home workshop is all you need.

$ ♿   👷

552 SUNDIALS

Sundials have survived from ancient history. People are intrigued by them for a variety of reasons—they have no moving parts, they are silent, they never break down, they are connected to the sun, they are foolproof, and on and on. You can make a variety of these fascinating gems and market them to retailers of all kinds. You can even market them by catalog and mail order, or at gift fairs, or door to door. Attractive units with instructions will make sales a simple lucrative matter.

$$ ♿   👷

553 SWIMMING POOLS

Nearly every family would love to own its own swimming pool. Until recent years pools were made from very heavy and expensive concrete. New technologies have reduced swimming pool costs; they are now within reach of most North American families of today. You can get into this lucrative market in at least three ways: (1) design and make a better line of pools, (2) retail pools, or (3) install and provide follow-up service for pools with a good line of supplies, and so on. There is lots of room for money-making innovations in this growing industry.

$$$$ ◣   👷

554 TEDDY BEARS

Teddy bears are not just for the toddler set. People of all ages are buying them as never before. Collecting bears has become quite serious business, especially for certain adults. You can cash in on this delightful trend by either retailing or manufacturing teddies. A retail shop can offer a multitude of sizes and shapes of teddy bears at prices ranging from $3 to more than $600! You can also stock all sorts of other products dealing with teddy bears—mugs, T-shirts, books, quilts, novelties, calendars, and a lot more. Allow people to handle and cuddle your bears to enhance sales.

$$ ♿ ▆▆▍▐

555 T-SHIRT SHOP

There is a tremendous need for the sale of T-shirts with designs and pictures and sayings that are wholesome. The silent majority will support you well if you enter this business with the idea of displacing the detestable things presently being put on T-shirts. Set out to uplift our society and you, too, will be uplifted. We shall reap what we sew!

$$ ♿ ▆▆▍▐

556 UTILITY TRAILERS MANUFACTURING

Good utility trailers will turn cars into pickup trucks by just hitching them up. These "part-time pickup trucks" are not at all difficult to make. Hundreds of different homemade models exist. You can go into business making these products of convenience and then sell them through nationwide hardware chain stores. Study the possible designs for special features first. Then mass-produce a durable model you know will move well.

$$ ◣ ▆▆▍▐

557 WALL PLAQUES, BLANKS

This is an ideal business for anyone having access to sawmill ends, which are usually used for firewood. Collect 1″× 6″ or 1″× 8″ pieces of pine, cedar, redwood, or whatever is available. Cut these scraps of wood into circles, ovals, rectangles, hexagons, even triangles, and then sand them and put a finished edge with a router on them. Sell them in a variety-pack kit, or in bulk, to individuals, hobby stores, and the like, to be used by people to make their own plaques with quips, photos, pictures, and so on. Your profits can easily exceed 500 percent.

$ ♿ ▆▆▍▐

558 WOOD PRODUCTS

Look through back issues of magazines, or look through big department stores, or look through library books for ideas of wooden things you can build and sell—birdhouses, picnic tables, doghouses, cutting boards, flower boxes, benches, stools, packing cases, cabinets, and so on—thousands of ideas are available, so begin collecting them now. Make whatever you enjoy making and sells. Make samples and secure orders. It is possible to make $1500 or more a month if you apply yourself.

$ ♿ 🏭

559 GOLD ELECTROPLATING

It has been possible to electroplate various metals for years with plating of tin, zinc, copper and other metals. But only recently has a way been discovered to electroplate metal items with a thin covering of gold. You can purchase the device which performs this operation and use it in a home business of your very own. The fees you can collect for just a few items gold-plated each month can buy your groceries.

$$ ♿ 🏭

560 VENDING VEHICLES

There are many people right now thinking about getting into a small business of some kind. Many small businesses require some type of a vending vehicle such as a cart, a trailer, or perhaps even a food truck. You can become a dealer for these vehicles which have already been manufactured. Or you may have the skills to manufacture these vehicles yourself. At any rate, it is possible to make a fine business of selling and servicing these vehicles.

$$$ 🏭

▮▮▮▮▮▮▮ NOVELTIES

561 ARTIFACT SALES

In this business you simply sell individual bricks (or whatever) from famous historic sites, such as bricks or seats from the Ford Theater, or leftover fabric from the "Spirit of St. Louis," and so on. The possibilities are infinite.

$ 🖐 ▮▮▮

562 BABY HANDPRINTS

Parents love to capture memories of their babies before they grow up altogether too fast. You can run a full-time business working out of your home helping parents with this problem. You will contact parents and arrange to make plaster casts of their baby's handprint, or hands and feet prints, which you will then paint and mount as an attractive wall plaque; the proud parents will be happy to buy them for $15 each or more.

$ 🖐 ▮▮▮

563 BALLOON VENDOR

This is not just another get-rich-quick scheme filled with hot air. It really works! Buy balloons (large ones) at about 4 cents apiece, fill them with helium, and sell them for 75 cents or more apiece. Set up your sales at flea markets, fairs, bingos, fund-raising affairs, amusement parks, malls, and so on, and expect to sell upwards of 8000 balloons a month. Five thousand balloons would gross you $3750 a month. Can your bank savings account cope with that?

$ 🖐 ◤ ▮▮▮

564 BUTTON BADGES

Buttons can be made very inexpensively and then sold for large profits to impulse buyers. They can carry photos, sayings, drawings, designs and logos, cartoons, and the like. They are marketed best where crowds of people exist. Displayed on large felt boards, the buttons will attract foot traffic to read them and make purchases. Keep your buttons clever, colorful, and on the light side of life for best success.

$ 🖐 ▮▮▮

565 CANDID KEYCHAIN PHOTOS

Capitalize on the vanity that most sportsmen have. With just basic photography knowledge you can parlay a small $265 investment into a $60,000 profit the first year! All you do is take action color shots of golfers, tennis players, body builders, cross-country skiers, and others engaging in their favorite pastimes (gardeners? chess players?) and sell them keychain slide viewers with their own action photo inside. They will cost you about 15 cents and you can sell them like wildfire for three dollars or more apiece! A dream business no matter how hard you work at it!

$ ♿   ⅢⅠⅢ

566 CANNED SURPRISES

Everyone enjoys suspense and mystery. Simply place all sorts of novelties in tin cans, which you then seal with a regular tin can sealing machine. Whatever will get a wholesome chuckle or a laugh could be canned—dead beetles, neckties, poems, toy novelties—you name it. Label your cans with attractive wording and color. Market them through gift stores, toy stores, novelty shops, and so on. This business would catch on across the continent with national advertising. It could become a highly profitable mail-order business.

$$ ♿   ⅢⅠⅢ

567 COATS OF ARMS

People will often take such pride in their ancestral history that they will pay remarkable prices to get their family name coat-of-arms so they can display it proudly on all their possessions. Others are just curious to see what their family's coat-of-arms looks like. You can start up a business in which you search out and sell family coat-of-arms for a certain fee. You can produce the coats-of-arms emblems by embroidering them and selling them, as well. You could make up quantities of them for common family names, like Smith. Others may have to be custom made. Numbers of people work profitably full-time in this business.

$ ♿   ⅢⅠⅢ

568 CONCESSION RACK MANUFACTURING

Most supermarkets and variety stores have various racks of small items for sale. These racks are often displayed for impulse sales near cash registers. You can make these racks yourself and then sell them to retail outlets. You can purchase small novelty items at very cheap prices and then arrange these items on the display racks made of colored cardboard or plastic. Or you can create your own crafts items, such as pretty wood coat buttons, and arrange racks of them to sell. This is a fine home business that allows you to set up your own schedules.

$$ ♿ ⛪

569 CUSTOM PUZZLES

Nearly anything will sell if it is first personalized in some way. You can make a business of selling personalized puzzles. You take your client's selected photos, then enlarge them, and then transfer them to puzzle boards. Using a puzzle die, you then cut the board, and you can then sell an instant, personalized jigsaw puzzle for very good profits! You can work through mail order or a local photography shop. Make picture puzzles of special local events or landmarks for solid steady profits.

$ ♿ ⛪

570 DOLL CLONES

Imagine a life-size stuffed doll that looks just like you. This hot new idea can be just the right home business you have been looking for. Make custom doll clones for clients; work from good photos supplied of each subject or client. Try to capture his or her body in correct proportions with typical clothes, as well as other features such as skin and eye color, hair, nose, even freckles and warts and moles. The potential market just about matches the world's population, so at $150 or more per clone, you may become a multimillionaire!

$$ ♿ ⛪

571 HISTORIC REPLICAS

Ranchers and city people with ranch-style homes like to decorate both the inside and the outside of their homes with homestead paraphernalia. You can make and sell bona fide reproductions of such objects as heavy wooden yokes, spinning wheels, wagon wheels, buckboard wagons, plows, and so on. Yokes can hang over driveway entrances or support hanging mailboxes. Make your objects authentic in every detail. You should have no problem selling all you can produce at satisfying prices.

$$ ⛪

572 NATIONAL EMBLEMS

Every country has its national emblem. Canada has the maple leaf and the United States has the eagle. Any item you can produce—whether it is a flag or a quilt or a wood carving—can bear your national emblem. It will be in popular demand as a decorator item from one end of your country to the other. They will have patriotic and nationalistic appeal to everyone. Gift stores and businesses catering to tourists will be your best outlets. Try to amalgamate a local product with the national emblem.

$ ♿ ⛰

▌▊▊▌▊▊▊PETS

573 BIRD BOARDING

Many people want their birds well cared for while they are away on vacations. You can devote a part of your home to a boarding house for pet birds of all kinds. Your client will be required to provide the cage, the necessary food, and specific instructions to be followed. You will have little work to do—just feed and water them and keep their cages clean. Some may need flight exercise in a special room. Charge about one dollar per day with five dollars minimum. Advertise in local newspapers. This is an ideal business for a bird lover.

$ ♿ ▐▊▌▐

574 BIRD TALK

Pet birds sell for small fortunes if they have been trained to "talk." Birds, such as parrots, parakeets, and mynah birds, can learn to say certain phrases if they hear them over and over again. You can make up cassette tapes or records that repeat choice phrases over and over again, and then sell your products to pet stores. Phrases like "My name is Clever, what's your's?" or "I am a mynah bird. What's your excuse?" sell well. Have a wide variety to choose from. Contact pet shops and pet supply houses.

$ ♿ ▐▊▌▐

575 BOARDING KENNEL

Advertise "A country motel for dogs and cats." Charge from two dollars to five dollars a day. Provide shelter, spacious runs, clean and attractive premises, and good food. Add on grooming and bathing and other services. Do it right and Rover will want to return first chance he gets. You have to know and love dogs and cats. You should be in a rural setting with at least an acre or two. Some larger boarding kennels net their owners upwards of $30,000 a year!

$$ ▐▊▌▐

576 BUGS

There is a growing market for dehydrated insects that are used as food for pets such as turtles and tropical fish. You can catch tons of bugs in swampy areas by using a special light that attracts them at night and then zaps them dead so they fall into a container. You can then package them after making sure they are well dried, and sell them to pet supply retailers and wholesalers by mail order if you prefer. You will be thinning out the bug population and fattening up your bank account with the same effort.

577 CANARIES

Of all bird pets, canaries are by far the most popular. With their lovely songs, they make such cheerful companions. You can discover that breeding these little songsters can be very profitable if you proceed with a good understanding of what is required. Start with just a few breeding pairs until you get the kinks out. Try to produce colors other than yellow for extra profits—apricot and salmon pink are now available. Color and singing ability will determine each bird's market value. There are special magazines available just for canary breeders.

578 CAT-NIPPERS

Catnip is just another name for catmint, a member of the wild growing mint family. People like it in tea, but cats love to roll and play in it and eat its leaves. You can easily grow the plant yourself. Then dry and crush it and use it as stuffing for toys that you sew for cats and kittens—stuff balls, small cat pillows, and even "mice." These will definitely sell well at pet stores. Advertise regionally or nationally to increase your sales considerably.

$ 🦽 ▓▓

579 CAT SCRATCHING POSTS

Cats love to sharpen their claws, especially on furniture. They can quickly be taught not to do so if they are provided with a cat scratching post. You can build and sell them. Cut up 4″ x 4″ wood stock into 24″ lengths. Attach these to plywood bases from 16″ to 20″ square (or round). Securely attach carpet to the post and the base with glue and staplegun. Sell them in pet stores and home furnishing firms. You can make them on a custom-order basis so that they match the same carpet of the customer's home.

580 CHIPMUNKS

Chipmunks are easily tamed and they make fine entertaining pets for children. You can set up homemade breeding cages in your backyard that allow the animals to dig burrows without escaping. You can purchase your original brood stock from a reliable supplier. After three or more years of developing your animal population and your cages, you can be selling several hundred of them each year in lots of 10 or so for an average of five dollars apiece. They eat simple grains and nuts. Sell to local pet shops and to distant pet shops by mail or air express.

$ ♿ 🏭

581 DOGS BY AIR

If you study ads you will see that there are people from all parts of North America who want to purchase a well-trained dog of a special breed. You can set up a kennel and breed a variety of dogs and train them for special purposes and then sell them through national advertising. You can send the dog to a customer by air freight. Be sure the dogs are properly handled by the airline. You may want to issue a one-month money-back guarantee (less shipping costs), during which the customer and dog will have a trial period. This business will probably surprise you with the demand potential.

$$$ ♿ 🏭

582 EXOTIC PETS

There is big money to be made in selling exotic pets. The more rare or unusual the pet is, the more it is worth. There are hundreds of different pets that you could call exotic. You would have to travel abroad to work your supplier contacts. You would have to know how to handle import/export permits and which animals *legally* cannot be sold. You would have to know how to keep the animals alive and healthy. Marketing would be one of your easier and more pleasant tasks.

$$$ ◀ 🏭

583 PARAKEETS

A fine return on investment can be made by raising and selling parakeets. Advertise monthly in a national bird and pet magazine. From a brood flock of 500 mature birds housed in a proper aviary, you can raise and sell 2500 or more top-quality chicks per year. They sell from $5 each to $20 a brood pair. Parakeet males can be taught to "talk" in as little as two weeks' time. A highly trained talker may bring as much as $300. Strive for fine pedigree and satisfaction guaranteed, and you will have a constant supply of repeat customers, both individuals and retailers.

$

584 PET CEMETERY

There are over 80 million pet cats and dogs in North America and owners spend more than $8 billion on them each year. Less than 1 percent of the 6 million family pets that die each year receive a decent burial. Most of those put to sleep end up as ashes, or soap, or fertilizer, or landfill. You can help solve this problem while providing important peace of mind to owners faced with the loss of a beloved pet—open a pet cemetery where animals can be put to rest with decency and respect. The total market is all but virtually untapped.

$$$

585 PET FOOD SERVICE

People in higher-income brackets and owners of pedigreed pets place much value on the health and welfare of their pets. They wish to protect their investments with the best food available. You can get a vet to design a special dog food formula and one for cats. Then you can mix, cook, package, and sell these products in frozen packages to presold customers. You can attach your own label, or a label bearing the vet's name, which will boost his business as well as yours. Make weekly deliveries as prearranged and bill monthly. Add-ons: leashes, toys, collars, toiletries, worm medicines, vitamins, and so on.

$$$

586 PET HOTEL AND GROOMING SERVICE

This is an incredibly easy way to profit from pet-crazy North Americans who spend millions every year on their dogs and cats! With as little as $200 or so you can set up a pet hotel and grooming service to cash in on this booming market—just about anywhere you might live on this continent. Many providing this service are booked weeks in advance.

$$

587 PET PHOTOS

Pet owners, generally, are unable to take really satisfactory shots of their pets. You can do quite well for yourself in this business if you have a high-speed camera with electronic flash and if you can take good action shots. Pets are difficult subjects to photograph because they don't know what "stand still" or "hold that pose" means. Pet owners will pay you to photograph their darling cats and dogs and even birds. Regularly attend pet shows and make lots of contacts, which you then follow up.

$

588 PET SITTERS

Pets frequently receive poor treatment at kennels. You can set up a good-paying business in which this problem is overcome. Organize a team of people willing to be pet sitters in their homes who will give the client pets a warm, loving, personal stay. Your pet sitters collect half the fees paid to you. They keep up to four pets at a time in their homes. Your fees should be a bit higher than kennels charge because of your superior service. The pet owner supplies all that the pet sitter will use. These include food, medicine, bedding, toys, and so on.

$

589 PET TAXI

In larger centers people need help transporting their pets around the city for a variety of reasons. Working people will hire you to take their pets to the vet, or to another location, or even for a walk. You can set yourself up in business to provide this service of conveying pets around according to specified needs. A home phone and a proper vehicle is all you will need to start up.

$$

590 POODLE GROOMING

Most poodle owners are absolutely convinced that they own the very best poodle in the world; furthermore, their pooch deserves the very aristocratic best available. You can set up a business that caters to such vanity. You can learn how to groom poodles in the many popular styles. Dog show poodles will bring in $50 and more for a professional clipping. You can sell poodle accessories as well—sweaters, special collars, hats, ribbons, perfume, and even sunglasses and colored nail polish. This can be a most lucrative business.

$

591 POODLES

The demand for poodles is greater and more consistent than for other breeds of dogs. Besides being the aristocracy of the dog world, they do make loving pets. They usually bring in goodly prices and they sell quickly. With four poodles you can make around $6000 a year net. You should strive for quality so that word of mouth will do your advertising for you. If you are fond of dogs and have a small kennel possibility, then a serious look should be taken at this business. It can be profitable and lots of fun at the same time.

$$ ▐▜▐▌

592 PUPPY CONSIGNMENTS

Who doesn't love a cute, cuddly puppy? You can open up a business that matches buyers and sellers of puppies. Take puppy litters on consignment. House and feed the puppies in a larger kennel setup. Families will have an interesting and exciting experience visiting your premises, where you will have dozens and dozens of puppies begging to be bought and taken to a good home. Many will leave your store (or home) packing a puppy. You will receive a commission on each sale. Prepare a brochure to give people with litters for sale so they will sell through you. Prepare a second brochure advising proper care of puppies for the buyers.

$ ▐▌

593 DOG POOPER SCOOPER SERVICE

Laugh at this one. But it brings in real bucks. Two young blades in Vancouver, B.C. got masters degrees in Business Administration. But upon graduation, they were unable to find jobs. So they went into partnership in this business they had conceived. They now have a route of going house-to-house scooping up dog poop. You read it right! And they are doing very nicely at the business, thank you! They know each dog on a first-name basis. They charge $5 per five-minute stop! You could add on dog food and other pet supplies. Flyers, a scoop, and a good face mask will launch you into this business.

$ ▐▜▐▌

594 PRIVATE PET CONTROL CONTRACTOR

People living in close quarters with their neighbors often have problems with the neighbors' pets. Noise is sometimes the problem. Other times roaming pets use your yard or flower beds for a toilet. At any rate, local bylaws seldom solve these problems. There are a variety of ingenious methods and ideas which can be used to control these pet problems and to give relief to those being assaulted. Study up on these techniques, learn your local bylaws, send out your flyers, and stand by your phone. You will be surprised how widespread the problem is.

$

595 zoo

You love animals and you know how to take care of them. You live on a larger lot in surburbia or on an acreage in an urban location close to a heavily traveled highway. So you are on your way to setting up your own zoo! You don't want to confine the animals unnecessarily in cages or tight pens, so you give them larger areas to roam in. You might consider having a petting zoo, in which children will enjoy the various creatures you'll keep. You will get permission to put up a huge sign along the highway directing families to come enjoy your animals. You keep your pets and they keep you.

$$$$

▌▌▌▌‖‖PHOTOGRAPHY

596 ACCIDENT PHOTOS

You can collect several hundred dollars for just a few still photos or for a single cassette of video film. You can train and equip yourself so you get to the scene of car and other accidents just about as quickly as the police and ambulance do. Get a scanner radio that monitors all the emergency radio channels. Keep your still and video cameras ready to go immediately to accident scenes. Record the accident as best you can, including names of drivers, insurance companies, and so on. Later, insurance companies and lawyers and individuals may purchase your records to settle claims worth millions of dollars. Newspapers may even buy them.

$$

597 ANTIQUE PHOTO STUDIO

Even if you know nothing at all about photography, you can earn big on the nostalgia craze with this simple winner. Simply take Polaroid photos of couples (or families) dressed in nostalgic costumes and mount them in antique-type picture frames. You can charge nine dollars or more for what costs you 40 cents. And chances are that people will be lined up waiting their turn! Invest about $400 cash and be prepared to gross upwards of $500 or more a day!

$ ♿ ▟▜

598 BABY PICTURES

Every baby is the most beautiful baby in the world to its parents. Good pictures of our children are a lifelong joy providing wonderful memories. Taking pictures of children is the most profitable kind of photography. You, along with your camera, some practice, patience, and know-how, can do well taking baby pictures. Watch birth notices in your local news papers. Show samples of your work to prospects. Offer bargain packages of photos hard to refuse. Ask for a deposit up front with balance paid on delivery. Enclose an order blank and negatives for additional orders, which you will receive in most cases.

$ ♿ ▟▜

599 BIRTHDAY PHOTO ALBUMS

This clever business has built-in repeat sales. Few parents will be able to resist it. Provide a child with a photo album with his name embossed in gold on the cover. Keep the child's birthdate on file. Call the parents each year and have them bring the child in for his or her annual birthday photo. Start at one year old and keep at it each year until the child is grown, if possible. Charge separately, of course, for extra prints of photos. Your repeat business is locked in, but the parents are quite happy with the arrangement.

$$ ▐▜▐▛

600 BUSINESS PHOTOS

Profits in this business are virtually a snap! Spend part of each day taking color photos of storefronts in any city. Concentrate on storefronts that are spiffy and neat, as this suggests pride of ownership. From your best snaps make 8 × 10 glossy enlargements. With these glossies in hand, return to the store owners in turn. Place the photos in their hands and they will not be able to resist your special bargain. You will make a substantial net profit at the same time that the proprietors are sure they have gotten a very reasonable bargain!

$ ♿ ▐▜▐▛

601 BUSINESS PICTURE CALENDARS

This business will be one you will wish you had thought of much earlier. Simply take nice 8 × 10 color photos of business buildings. Then mount the photos in the blank spaces on stock calendar pads, which you purchase wholesale. Store owners will buy these calendars, showing a large lovely picture of their own business, by the hundreds from you to give as inexpensive gifts to their regular customers. For twelve months of the year the customer will be constantly reminded of your client's business. Next year they will sell themselves without fail.

$ ♿ ▐▜▐▛

602 CALENDAR BOOKLETS

Demand commonly outstrips your supply in this business. Photograph twelve special scenes of unusual interest or beauty in your home area. Make these twelve pictures into a little booklet. At the bottom of each picture put the calendar for one month of the year. Print the back cover to accept addressing and mailing. These ideal souvenirs will sell especially well to all tourist and visitor outlets—gift stores, hotels, drug stores, newsstands, info centers, restaurants, and so on. Each year you can start all over again with an interesting batch of new photos.

$$ ♿ ▐▜▐▛

603 COLOR SLIDE SETS

Tourists often visit a particularly attractive location only to find that their camera has packed it in, or the weather is particularly foul, or their schedule won't allow them to visit all the interesting nooks and crannies. You can assist them with their problems. Taking your time in ideal weather and lighting, you can produce sets of quality color slides depicting the highlights of your area (and other areas, too!). Then you can market them in restaurants, gift shops, and so on, in attractive see-through packaging. The tourists will happily have their pictures one way or the other!

$$ ♿ 💹

604 CONSTRUCTION PHOTOS

Take careful photos of the various stages of construction of a given building as each stage is completed. You can hire out to architects and contractors. Show them some samples of your work from other projects—bridges, schools, and so on. Or you can work for new homeowners in the following manner: When you see a new house just under way, start taking photos of each stage until the house is completed. Then, with the whole set of pictures in hand, approach the proud new homeowners and make them a deal they can't resist!

$ ♿ 💹

605 FEATURE PHOTOS

Eccentricity always makes good press. Interesting feature photo stories are easy to find if you have the talent for tracking down unusual characters or people in unusual occupations or predicaments. You will be a free agent as a freelance feature photographer. With well-prepared top-quality samples of your work in hand, show your stuff to local newspaper and magazine editors. If they don't buy, persevere by sending your works to distant editors by mail. Focus on telling stories of unusual human interest and timeless subjects with your camera.

$ ♿ 💹

606 FLOWER PHOTOS

Real flowers will eventually fade into oblivion, but you can capture them at their peak for posterity on film. You can specialize in taking pictures of flowers for clients. Many flower lovers and growers have invested lots of money and time and effort into producing prize flowers. They require professional help in permanently recording what the flower looks like. The recording of true color is a must. Lighting, shadow, and reflection must be just right to get accurate photos. Work contacts in garden clubs, nurseries, florists, and flower shows. Provide only transparencies, as color prints are not color-satisfactory.

$ 🦽 ᵐᵀᶠ

607 MICROFILMING SERVICE

Computers can act as memory banks but they cannot store the actual appearance of valuable documents. Storing valuable records can consume immense amounts of space. Microfilming solves both of these problems. You can start up a microfilming business in which you hire out to banks, lawyers, libraries, larger businesses, auto parts stores, and the like, to microfilm their important documents so they can be stored much more easily and securely. You can rent, rather than buy, a microfilming machine to start up with. Line up some contracts before renting the machine.

$$$ 🦽 ᵐ

608 MINILAB PHOTO FINISHING

You can now set up an incredible new machine that develops high-quality snapshots in less than an hour! High profits are normal. Very few owners of minilabs have much background in photography. The machine is totally computerized, automated, and self-contained. You just feed it films and proper supplies and it will more than feed you!

$$$$ ᵐ

609 MOBILE PHOTO STUDIO

Your camera will pay your way as you travel in this business. You equip your van or camper with a three-sided knock-down "studio" with a fold-up stool for people to pose on and a scenic backdrop curtain. Advertise in advance where you will be and when. Set up your studio beside your van in a parking lot, by beach concessions, at fairs, in village squares, and so on. Take a deposit on all photos and complete the exchange of photos for balance paid COD. Rural areas and towns will give you the best business, since they usually lack this service.

$$$$ 🦽 ᵐᵀᶠ

610 PAPER DOLL PHOTOS

Most everyone has seen the old-fashioned paper dolls made of flat, thin cardboard over which different paper clothes can be hung by bending back some paper tabs to hold them in place. Use your camera to take ordinary pictures of girls and boys. Then you take the negatives and blow them up on your darkroom enlarger until they are life-size. You can then make clothes for the "doll" by either the paper-with-paper-tabs method or by gluing real fabrics to the "doll's" body. Make them for $2 and sell them for $12 or so each. This business will bring fresh air into any community.

$

611   PHOTO AGENT

If it seems it is all outgo and little or no income from your present job, this business will make an earner out of you. Very simply, set yourself up as a one-man picture agency. Submit the best photo works of all your friends who are avid camera buffs to a long list of buyers of quality photos, which will include magazines, trade journals, picture agencies, various publishers, and so on. Your friends agree to pay you a certain commission on all your successful sales of their photos. You help them dispose of their work, and they will help you dispose of your lack of income.

$

612   PHOTO BOOTH

Persuade organizations—lodges, clubs, churches—to let you set up a photo booth at their fairs and bazaars. Split any proceeds with them from sales. You will take photos in your booth using a camera and a nice backdrop. You will also sell pictures taken a few days earlier of, for example, the church choir, the church itself, the church pastor, and so on. You will get future work for weddings, special anniversaries, and the like, from making the booth contacts. Most organizations will welcome the extra funds raised, plus your friendly service.

$$

613   PHOTO COPY SHOP

Millions of businesspeople, homemakers, students, and others cannot afford to purchase copiers. A decent one costs $1500 and more. So these people will stand in line if necessary to rent copier service. Most rental units pay for themselves in short order, leaving steady, easy, almost embarrassing, profits for you. Consider pickup and delivery add-on service, especially for small businesspeople.

$$

614 PHOTOS OF NEW HOMES

People who have just bought a new home are usually too busy moving into the home to take good pictures of the house. They will almost always be glad to pay you for the convenience of having it done for them. Take a number of smaller color prints, which they can then mail to interested friends and relatives at the same time they announce their address change. Later on, they may want you back for interior shots showing the house with its furnishings in place. This is a most pleasant and profitable business. Try the same approach with small businesspeople.

$$ ♿

615 PONY POLAROID PHOTOS

Most city children have never petted a horse before, much less sat on one. Every child identifies with the derring-do cowpoke on his or her cayuse. With a Polaroid camera around your neck you can take your pony (or rent a pony) by trailer into the suburbs and make instant cowboys and cowgirls of all the boys and girls in the waiting lines. They put on your cowboy outfit, chaps and all. Sit them in the saddle and click your Polaroid. Sell the instant picture right there on the spot. It is an immediately profitable business. Little Andy can now show anyone who challenges him that he really is a cowboy!

$ ♿

616 PORTRAIT STUDIO

If you can meet professional standards with professional equipment you can run this business nicely in your very own home. Frames are often more expensive than the portraits, so you may consider promoting your business by offering the public free portraits with the customer paying only for the frame! Check up on current prices charged by the best studios and then undersell them. Display some samples. Consider group discounts for schools.

$ ♿

617 POSTCARD PHOTOS

This approach to photography will pay off almost anywhere. Take top-quality photos of the major tourist attractions in your area and then have a color-engraving firm turn them into picture postcards, which you sell. You can complement the above approach by taking quality photos of all the tourist businesses in your area—gift shops, motels, hotels, restaurants, amusement parks—and convert them to picture postcards, which the owners will purchase from you in sizable volumes. This type of photography is seldom developed to its potential.

$

618 PROMOTIONAL PHOTOS

Businesses are always alert to a better way to promote their image and their products. You and your camera can be that better way. Example: Take pictures of all the various decorated cakes that a given bakery produces, plus pictures of all their other products. Combine these product photos together with other photos of the staff, the operations, and the building itself, and this photo package then can be used in a variety of successful promotions by the owner or manager. Try this program with any number of other similar businesses—boat builders, fitness clubs—whatever!

$

619 PUBLICITY PHOTOS

Advance publicity of coming events is always crucial for their success. Publicity chairmen are usually amateurs who have kindly donated their time. You can keep careful track of future community events and establish close rapport with each publicity chairman, convincing them that you can make their job a whole lot easier if they will hire you to create advance publicity with your camera for the event they are responsible for. Show them samples of your past successes and chances are very good that you will be hired on board to boost both the event and its chairman.

$

620 REAL ESTATE PHOTOS

You have nothing but your time to lose and everything to gain by taking a crack at real estate photography. Good color pictures that are readily available and are attractively presented to prospective clients can be the key to successful sales of homes and businesses and acreages. Extra prints should be available for handling, for window displays, for displays in brochures, and for display advertising in newspapers. Multiple listing photos will bring in even more income. Photos of interiors, especially of feature items like fireplaces, can become sales clinchers.

$

621 SLIDE SETS (35MM)

All you need is a standard 35mm camera to set up this business. You will take a series of slides on a given subject and then offer them for sale as a package to interested buyers. Example: Take pictures of major glaciers and their special features. Then sell the slide sets to colleges teaching courses in glaciology. Just follow this pattern or approach for literally thousands of other possibilities. Publishers, businesses, colleges, and teachers will be prime customers for you. You can work from your home on your own schedule.

$ 🚹 ᛗᛁᚱ

622 SNAPSHOOTING BABY

In this simple business you get paid for practicing your photography skills. You simply arrange with a customer to take a whole roll of film of their baby and to provide the resulting set of snapshots for a set fee. Six-month-old babies are good subjects. Few parents can take even passable pictures of babies because they are always moving. Your investment is very low. You will get good wages, and your work could lead the entire family into your studio for more lucrative work.

$ 🚹 ᛗᛁᚱ

623 SPOT NEWS PHOTOS

This is the most demanding type of photography. You have to be quite good with a camera and you must be willing to "rough it" with your camera in areas that are often very hazardous at all hours of the day or night. You have to be on a first-name basis with all the leaders in charge of crises such as firemen, policemen, ambulance drivers, and so on. You will depend on them for hot tips as to where the action is that you wish to capture on film for your demanding newspaper editor. Emergencies and excitement will be standard fare for you. Your camera must be loaded and ready at all times.

$ ᛗᛁᚱ

624 TINTYPE BIZ

Get started in this nineteenth-century business as up-to-date as today! As a tintypist you have your patrons dress up in authentic nineteenth-century costume, have them pose in front of your big wooden camera, look steadily into the lens for 10 seconds, and have their image recorded on a metal plate. Five minutes later their tintype picture is developed showing them what they might have looked like 100 years ago! Write for info to Elbinger and Sun, 1380 Haslett Road, Haslett, Michigan, 48840.

625 TRICK PHOTO CARDS

With trick photography you can make the most clever holiday greeting cards. Contract with one family at a time to make all the cards they will need. Try to reflect the general lifestyle of the client family in a lighthearted or wholesome way. First, take a group picture of the family. Then cut out just the portion of the picture showing the heads. Take these heads and create the rest of the picture to go on the cards, much as a cartoonist would. For example, if the family likes cross-country skiing you could show the entire family skiing together on just one set of skis. These photo cards will sell themselves for handsome profits.

$ ♿ 📊

626 WEDDING VIDEOS

Portable video recording cameras will put a wedding on TV over and over again. You can contract with prospective brides to film both the wedding and the reception with your video camera. Your approach will capture the formality of the occasion but you won't stop there. You will also capture all the human interest—the tears, the laughter, the joy—of the occasion. Your approach will sell itself if you can let your client view one of your past successful films. Be prepared to work on weekends usually. The rest of the week will be free for other ventures or jobs.

$$ ♿ 📊

627 WINNER PHOTOS (ANIMALS)

Anyone who is the proud owner of a prize winner is always an excellent prospect for a good photographer. Specializing in animal photography, you always manage to show up just when the owner is receiving his trophy or ribbon for his prize-winning animal. Take the right photos, slip into your mobile darkroom, and develop the photos within the hour. Sell the photos to the right client right away, saving mailing and bookwork hassles later on. Work county fairs, dog shows, races, rodeos, horse shows, riding stables, dairy farms, and the like.

$$ ♿ 📊

628 AERIAL PHOTOS

Purchase an older slower-flying rag-bag of a plane that is still licensed to fly, take your good camera and plenty of film, and take pictures of acreages and buildings from the air while flying low and slow. Sell these photos to the owners or builders of the buildings. Owners are quite proud and pleased to buy several pictures from you from different angles. You should contact land developers, surveyors, and so on, as well as owners of large buildings such as hotels, motels, racetracks, condos, and skyscrapers. This business can provide an excellent living.

$$$

629 COMPUTERIZED COLOR PORTRAITS

You have probably seen these businesses before, possibly in a mall stall. Their overhead is small, but their profit can be very sizable, depending upon the walk-by traffic. You will need a computer with a special program in it, together with a special wax thermal printer which prints out the portraits. The entire basic system can be purchased ready to go for about $7000. The daily amount of work involved is about as minimal as you will find. It might be an ideal business for someone who is handicapped. Good on-site advertising is a must.

$$$

630 HIGH SCHOOL VIDEO YEARBOOKS

Those of us who made it through high school will well remember the annual yearbooks we bought which memorialized our work and play with schoolmates. There is a new wrinkle to the annual yearbook. Instead of the laborious collecting of pictures and textual entries gathered together for the printed annuals, you simply pick up a video camera and record all the fun and games, work, and contests during the course of the school year. Then you edit the miles of footage into one video cassette, which may be the most difficult part. Make sure that every student in your class appears in the final video. Then you mass-produce copies from the master and sell them to individual students.

$$$

631 MUGS ON MUGS

This is a clever business to be in. You take pictures of your paying, walk-by clients and, using a computerized process, you take their mug shot photo and place it permanently on a ceramic mug your client chooses from your selection. You can purchase the entire package of hardware and software for about $5000. After that, all you will need will be supplies for photos and the mugs, plus a small stall in a mall where there is lots of walk-by traffic. Mug Mugs by you!

$$

▌▌▌▌▌▌▌▌PRINTING

632 BLANK FORMS
There are dozens of standard forms and certificates that our society uses by the millions. These include birth certificates, baptismal certificates, school diplomas, marriage licenses, wills, awards, and scores of business documents such as tentative real estate agreements, sales contracts, regular bookkeeping forms, and on and on. You can stock all of these forms and many more in your home, and then sell them to people needing them by mail order. Advertise nationally and issue a free list and prices. A copy machine will keep your stock to a minimum and save space.

$$ ♿ �▌l

633 BUSINESS CARD PRINTING
An impressive business card forms a large part of the first impression you make with a prospective client. Everyone wants to make good first impressions, so good business cards simply sell themselves. With a small, inexpensive printing press, you can go into the business of making and selling customized business cards. With good advertising and creative design you can net $100 or more a day working by yourself in your home on your own schedule.

$$ ♿ ▎▌l

634 BUSINESS DIRECTORIES
You can make a living publishing business directories for 10 or 12 smaller towns in your area. Solicit listings and advertising from each town, which the businesses pay you for—this is where your profit will come from. Set up, lay out, and paste up the book until it is camera ready. Have a local printer print and bind the directory. Then fulfill your obligations to the businesses by bulk mailing the directories to all local residents as well as rural box holders near the town. You can make $2000 and more for each of the directories each year.

$$$ ▎▌

635 CATALOG OF CATALOGS
The title of this home business explains itself. Simply collect the names of catalogs and an idea of what they contain, together with an address for obtaining each one. Then publish a master catalog listing the hundreds of other catalogs that you have tracked down. Proceed to market the

master catalog through national advertising. You can expect a steady income right into retirement.

$$ ♿   ▀▀▌▐

636 CATALOGS OF PRESTIGE

Certain groups of people are more inclined to make purchases from catalogs if the catalog has the appearance of appealing only to their select group. You can publish small catalogs listing prestige products for specific affluent groups—for instance, doctors, lawyers, drivers or owners of Mercedes, and so on. You will do best if you can offer a toll-free phone number and credit-card purchasing. Print your free catalogs on good-quality paper and advertise them in prestige magazines.

$$$ ♿   ▀▀▌▐

637 COLLECTION LABELS

The secret of the most successful debt collectors is to allow the debtor to save face in some way. You can help in this process by making pads of gummed labels on which are printed catchy phrases that will appeal to the debtor's sense of humor or conscience so that the debtor will be motivated to pay the debt. Examples include "Did you lose your checkbook?" "Better late than never," "Did the string fall off of your finger?" and "Is your forgettery better than your memory?" Sell these labels wherever businesses need extra help in collecting debts.

$$ ♿   ▀▀▌▐

638 COMPUTER BOOK PUBLISHING

There are thousands of books just waiting to be written. Computers have made the job of writing and publishing books much easier than it used to be. Learn the simplicity of using a computer to write a book, and then publish other books inexpensively for people in your area. The market is just opening up to this new industry and you can easily and inexpensively get into it for a healthy income. Advertise your service of getting manuscripts camera ready for printing.

$$ ♿   ▀▀▌▐

639 CRAFTSPEOPLE GUIDE

The yellow pages contain many names of people and their businesses. However, there are hundreds, if not thousands, of other people in your area with many skills who never make any sort of published list. But the community would thrive if this information entered public print, where everyone has access to it. You can publish such a book for your area. Charge small fees for having people's names and skills listed, and a higher price for a subscription to the book. People in your area will treasure the book because they will be able to find any specialist to get any job done.

$$ ♿   ▥▮▮

640 DISCOUNT COUPON BOOKLETS

These booklets, which you publish and sell, are made up of coupons that advertise discounts for products and services at a number of business firms. Publish the coupon booklet and sell it door-to-door for about five dollars. The total value of the coupons in the booklet can be worth hundreds of dollars if they are all used. Your cost of publishing the cheap booklets will be your only major expense; the rest is almost entirely profit.

$$ ♿   ▥▮▮

641 DISCOUNTS GUIDE

When people change jobs and cities at an ever increasing rate, they are hard-pressed to find stores that offer quality products at reasonable prices. You can publish a directory for your area listing all the bargains and discounts, including the stores where customers can find them. Your best buys directory should be frequently updated. You can market these booklets through larger company offices, hotels, motels, newsstands, bookstores, welcome wagons, and so on. Sales will continue because new people will keep arriving and businesses will keep offering new bargains and products.

$$ ▥

642 DUPLICATING AND MAILING SERVICE

Modern duplicating machines (photocopiers) allow you to run a duplicating service right from your home. Not everyone can purchase one of these machines, so you can contract for smaller and medium runs. You will have little overhead. The machine will pay for itself on a lease-purchase arrangement. You can get sales literature masters from businesses, duplicate them, stuff them into envelopes, and mail them to prospective customers. Businesses will pay well for this service.

$$ ♿   ▥▮▮

643 FREE ADS PAPER

This has tremendous "something for nothing" appeal. Publish a "trader" newspaper that runs classified ads only, for FREE. Newsstand sales of each issue are your source of income. This approach is just the opposite of the weekly or monthly "throwaways" or "shoppers." Consider limiting space available to each person or business placing ads.

$$

644 HAND BOOK BINDING

Hand book binding is fast becoming a lost art. Modern machines can bind 200,000 or more books in a day. If you take up the rare skill of binding books it may take you several days to rebind just one book, but the fees you can charge are astronomical because the volumes you will be working with may be rare, old, cherished editions. You can contract with museums and bigger libraries to rebind their rare volumes. This job will require great patience and skill, but it will also reap substantial financial rewards.

$

645 INSTANT PRINT SHOP

There are lots of customers for instant printing everywhere. Every nearby business, as well as walk-in traffic, buys brochures, resumes, announcements, business ads, flyers, and many other kinds of short-run printing. Substantial subcontracts from high-volume printers are also possible. No great technical skill in printing is necessary. Now, thanks to a new type of camera, anyone with average intelligence can get into this very profitable business with as little as $5000.

$$$

646 MAGNETIC SIGNS

Here is a potential "land office" business for setting up in your home. These are special signs you can easily make. Take various-size Formica-back pieces, glue on letters, and add magnetic tape to the back. You have a new magnetic sign. They are ideal for truckers, salespeople, businesses of all sorts. In an instant they can be attached magnetically to the metal door of any vehicle, and they come off just as quickly. You can take advantage of this convenience with low setup costs.

$$

647 NEIGHBORHOOD NEWSPAPER

A neighborhood newspaper can make money if it is carefully managed. Limit the paper to news only of your local area, and limit circulation accordingly. Solicit advertising only from local businesses. Keep your overhead as simple and inexpensive as possible. Glean news from schools, churches, clubs, pedestrians, and any other strictly local source. Give the first issue away, including the advertising. This is your free sample. In the next issue, charge for the advertising including classified ads. Expect immediate profits.

$$ ▐▜▐▛

648 PRINTING PRESS

Small printing presses are available for small printing projects. You can operate a business in which you take on smaller printing jobs—personal greeting cards, handbills, stationery, letterheads, programs, brochures, and so forth. If the job is bigger than you can handle, simply farm it out. This can begin as a part-time business, but it can easily grow until it becomes a full-time operation.

$$ ♿ ▐▜

649 RUBBER STAMPS

Rubber stamps are used by virtually every business firm in the world—from popcorn stands to IBM, as well as by millions of individuals. A stamp-making machine and a few supplies costing several hundred dollars are all you need to make the stamps. The demand for rubber stamps is high and constant. You will also need a reasonable mechanical aptitude to run the machine as you make the stamps. Your markup will be about 100 percent, and an average stamp can be made in ten minutes and sell for $10 or more. That is $60 an hour!

$ ♿ ▐▜▐▛

650 TYPESETTING BUSINESS

Make $1000 and more a month right from the start by setting up a home typesetting business. Simply rent an IBM composer and make your services known. Quick-print shops often have no desire to handle typesetting work and they will gladly refer customers to you. With average typing speed you can charge around $12 an hour, and customers will return repeatedly.

$$ ♿ ▐▜

651 WILL FORMS

Most people put off making out their wills for a variety of reasons—high lawyer costs, the inconvenience, an inability to face death, or indifference. You can simplify the process immensely by publishing the three different types of legally acceptable will forms and selling them by mail order. Supply a simple instruction sheet and sample wills to ease the task for your customers. Advertise nationally. This unusual business will make a tidy profit for you once your ads reach out.

652 CIRCULARS AND FLYERS

Circulars and flyers are about the least costly way of letting a business make its services or goods known to potential buyers. They are even more effective than the town criers of olden times. The flyer gives the buyer a permanent address he or she can use later to contact the seller. Flyers can bring a seller and a buyer together for a transaction within just minutes. In this business, you would sell flyers to businesses, mostly small businesses, which you would then print and distribute in a variety of ways to potential buyers. Special coupons and offers will ensure results for the flyers. You will be working toward repeat sales.

$$ 🦽 📊

653 GRAPHIC DESIGN

If you are good at graphic design, you will not likely be looking for a job in today's job market. If you are trained in this exciting field, you may give consideration to starting up your own graphic design business. You may work by yourself, or you may hire others to work under your supervision. This work requires a high degree of artistic ability and a high-powered computer with a quality graphics design software program installed. There are dozens of possible types of clients who will gladly purchase your graphics output if you are into top-quality work.

654 APARTMENT AND HOME FINDER

Studies show the typical rental apartment or house in North America becomes vacant every six months. These untold millions of moves open up a lucrative market for apartment and home finding services. Many people don't have either the time or the energy to look for housing themselves. You call sell up-to-date rental lists and additional information matching the special needs or problems of prospective tenants to units available. Minimal start-up costs. There are add-ons such as copy machine rental.

$$ ♿   ⬈   ⛰

655 APARTMENT MANAGER

This can mean free or reduced rent for you and your family in exchange for doing small maintenance jobs, sweeping hallways, taking out the trash, and performing simple repairs such as changing fuses and replacing leaky washers. Rather than paying cash for your shelter, you can work for it directly. You will likely have ample free time in which you can start a side business such as painting, hauling, or whatever you wish.

$ ♿   ⛰

656 BOARDING HOUSE

With a large house you can partition it off in such a way that your family takes up only a small part of it. The rest of the house is turned into a rooming house with the addition of board—food served by you in a cafeteria setting. Providing the public with food and lodging is nothing new. One person who started small and kept on expanding is a fellow named Conrad Hilton.

$$$$$ ⬈   ⛰

657 CONDOMINIUM SERVICE

People moving into condominiums have a large list of problems facing them all at once that they are usually willing to hire a specialist to solve for them. You can be their right-hand special help for good fees. You will arrange installations of their cable TV, telephones, and stereo hookups; moving of household goods; unpacking; and redecoration, including new paint schemes, coordination of furnishings, and interior decor. You can get more clients with a model condo already set up as a demo unit. You will learn to work quickly with a minimum of inconvenience to your clients.

$

658 FLAT FEE REAL ESTATE SERVICE

A threat to traditional realtors! You accept a flat fee to help homeowners sell their homes—without paying the typical 7 percent fee to the broker. Flat fees range from $150 to $1200. All you do is carry out the detail work—writing up documents such as appraisals, helping with financing, and closing and so on. You don't need to waste time driving prospects from house to house. Your services will be much sought after and your profits will reflect this fact!

$$ ♿ 🏠

659 GARDEN PLOTS

Lots of city people would take up gardening if they had both the space and the know-how. If you have some extra acreage, you can ready it for garden planting. Then stake out garden plots and rent them to city people, who can plant them and work them in their spare time. Many would like to raise their own fresh vegetables for themselves and their families. You can give fun prizes for the biggest pumpkins, squash, potatoes, and so forth each year. Many families will be repeat customers year after year. You will make many friends and bring in a pleasing living all at the same time.

$$$$ ♿ 🏠

660 HOMEBUYING DIRECT BULLETIN

In this business you simply publish a real estate listing bulletin for people to use in selling their homes without going through real estate agencies with their exorbitant 7 percent commissions. Contract to advertise a home by displaying its picture and a description for only 1 percent of the selling price. Send out these booklets free to anyone wanting one, and keep careful records of all recipients to enable you to collect your 1 percent later on. You do not sell houses in any way; you leave all the business details to the seller and buyer. In this way you don't infringe upon the real estate profession. You are merely an advertising agency.

$$ ♿ 🏠

661 LOT DEVELOPING

Few people have the ability to pick good building sites, especially if land is steep and hilly. If you have this ability, in addition to access to a smaller bulldozer, you can run a very profitable lot-developing business. You can buy rugged property for next to nothing. Then you can bulldoze good home-building sites with access, often with excellent views, and sell your "new" lots for 20 times or more what you paid for them.

$$$

662 RAW LAND

Country property continues to rise in value if it is within 25 miles of town in an area that is experiencing general overall growth. Many wealthy people with money prefer to live in the country if access to work is reasonable. You can buy raw "country" land for a very small down payment, subdivide it by survey, provide rough access, and then resell the new lots for many times your down payment and purchase price. Tripling your buying price is common. Check with local regulations on subdivisions first.

$$$$$

663 REAL ESTATE AGENCY

If you are a good salesperson with a knowledge of deeds, abstracts, mortgages, and contracts for deeds, you may be well qualified to begin your own real estate agency. Many houses are constantly being bought and sold. The seller usually lists his or her house with an agent, who gets a commission for finding a buyer. The commission on a $60,000 house can run about $4000! You will need a license, a desk (at home if possible), a phone with an answering service or answering machine, and advertising.

$$

664 TOURIST ROOMS

This business could well be called the mini-hotel business. If you have a large home, put up a "tourist rooms" sign on or near it. Charge less than the local motels and hotels do. You can probably live in the same house. Your guests will often return year after year to stay in your clean and comfortable rooms. Many people prefer the quiet atmosphere that a private home offers. This business offers a high rate of return. Your location should be near a major highway where you can be found easily.

$$

665 REFRESH ROOMS

When people are traveling, they miss the comforts of home. They miss a shower and a quiet place to take a nap. Travelers can check into a motel for these comforts, but the high price includes a night's stay, which isn't always wanted. When just a shower and a nap are all travelers want, refresh rooms are the answer. Refresh rooms are small rooms that provide the needed shower and bed for a nap. They can be installed near airport waiting rooms, bus depots, border crossings between countries, and similar places. Renting out refresh rooms can be a good business to be in.

$$$$$

IIIIIIIIRECREATION

666 CANOE RENTALS

Work out of a present active dock area for about 25 percent of your receipts. Locate places frequented by young people. A nice business for a retired person. In the winter you can go "south," taking your canoes with you to Florida. In summer you can cart them all back north into Canada where there are lots of tourists around lakes nearly everywhere.

$$$

667 FISHING IN PRIVATE

If you already own a pond or a lake you can turn it into a very profitable business. Stock it with fish and then charge fishermen for the privilege of fishing in your waters. They will become repeat customers because of the comparative privacy and the good catches. You will need to provide access, parking, drinking water, and toilets. Add on sales with bait sales, refreshment stand sales, fishing equipment, and boat rentals. Charge a flat fee for the day. Provide an area for families to have picnics and other recreation.

$$$$

668 LEISURE COUNSELING

Helping people plan their leisure time is an industry that has just left the launch pad. Helping others shake off boredom can mean big business to you. You will need to know your local area with its possible activities inside out. You then interview clients to find out what specific type of recreation they want to get into. You then provide them with an individualized folio listing everything your area has to offer on the new recreation of their choice—clubs, books, periodicals, other individuals with a similar interest, places, coming events, and so on. You save them lots of time and money and you collect a fine flat fee for your work.

$

669 MINIATURE GOLF

If you are the handy type, you can build and equip a mini-golf course for around $1000. In a good location you can net $2000 or more a month in the course of a six-month outdoor season. Move it indoors during the winter and keep right on going! A setup in an amusement park does well. Devise a mobile setup to maximize sales, so you can move your business to wherever the action is. These can be chained by adding more mini-golf outlets which will expand your living fast.

$$$ 🏔

670 NAVIGATION INSTRUCTION

Sailing a boat from point A to point B across open water out of sight of land is a mystery to most boat captains as well as the public. Many boat owners desire to obtain this special skill for future cruises to avoid getting lost in storms, fog, and so on. If you possess these special navigational skills of celestial and radio navigation you can become an instructor to tuition-paying students who want this special expertise.

$ ♿ 🏔

671 PAY TV STATION

A breakthrough with a new system called MDS (Multi-Point Distribution Service) allows you to set up quickly and very cheaply your own pay TV station. No $7000-per-mile cable to install. No huge sums for decoding equipment and leasing a TV channel. Only those people who have rented a special antenna from you can pick up your signal on their home TV sets. Rent your system to schools or other businesses. Or transmit your own programming. Have your customers prepay so you have free working capital up front.

$$$ ◄ 🏔

672 PICNICS

With perhaps a grove of trees and a flow of creek water you can set up a business of a picnic ground. You will provide the usual amenities of drinking water, toilets, picnic tables, and barbeque pits. You can add on space for archery, badminton, horseshoes, softball, and later perhaps a swimming pool. Charge extra for firewood, ice, the pool, bathhouse, and so on. Charge a flat rate for admission to the grounds. You could later add on pony rides, and the like. In winter you could become a cross-country ski resort with trails, outdoor warming fires, and so on, with flat fee charges also.

$$$$$ 🚩

673 RACQUETBALL

A fast flyer! With a minimum investment of about $10,000 and 1000 members you can gross over $314,000 a year! Expenses are so low that about $220,000 of that amount will be net profit! You will need a city of 25,000 or more to do well at it.

$$$

674 ROLLER SKATE RENTALS

New twist to cut your overhead. Rent a well-swept parking lot. Rent skates for $1.50 per hour or $5 a day out of the back of a truck. The initial cost for the skates will rapidly be paid for by the first few weeks of rentals. Thereafter the return will be unusually high since the skates will be used over and over. Add on other attractions such as food and drink sales. You will be highly visible working outdoors. Obstacle course tournaments are possible.

$$$

675 SAILBOAT TIME-SHARE LEASING

More people would get into sailing if they could only afford it. The average 25-footer costs over $20,000 and used ones are not much less. Enter you with your ability to organize cleverly. Using advance payments from a group of would-be sailors, either lease or buy a boat yourself and then schedule use of the boat among the members of the group. The money you arrange to be left over is yours, some of which you will want to invest in expanding your fleet. Put up all your canvas and reach for it!

$$$

676 SCUBA DIVING

Scuba diving has opened up a whole new world to humankind. The exotic beauty of underwater places such as coral reefs is without compare. But this beauty is not without the accompaniment of potential dangers. Proper training is a must before entering this activity. If you have acquired the expertise needed you can hire out as an instructor, teaching others the potentials, as well as the limitations, of various procedures and pieces of equipment. You may choose to work with individuals or with groups or both. A local swimming pool is a good place to hold classes.

$

677 SKATEBOARD PARK

Skateboards are zooming back again! Set up a park where skateboard "scooters" are challenged to run obstacle courses on their skateboards according to several levels of ability. Similar to a mini-golf course setup. Add on food vending machines and the like. Promote with periodic competitive tournaments, highlighted by an expert demonstrating advanced techniques.

$$$ ⛰

678 SKATING RINK

Ice skating outdoors is possible for most North Americans in much of the winter season. You can flood a level patch of ground and form your own ice rink. You can provide it with extras, such as benches for spectators and for sitting on while putting skates on, night lighting, and so on. You can set up a schedule for different age groups, church groups, hockey teams, all-age open skating, and the like. You will charge appropriate fees for its use and keep the rink up with snow removal. You will be providing wholesome recreation for your area, which will make it worth your while.

$$ ⛰

679 SOCIAL DIRECTOR

Communities hang together because of the things they have or do in common. Many communities in condominium and apartment complexes have hired special social directors who organize various social events— game nights, jogging, hikes, cycling tours, aerobics, bus tours, and so on to attract paying tenants. Companies can boost staff morale and loyalty by hiring social directors to organize company picnics, ball teams, bowling leagues, and so on. You can easily become one of these hired social directors who does a thriving business helping tenants, workers, and others have fun spending their leisure time together.

$ ♿ ⛏ ⛰

680 SPECIAL CAMPS

People used to go to a summer camp just to get back to nature. They still do this, but ever more people are paying well to attend camps that offer specialties that include the following—hockey, tennis, archery, football, baseball, karate, mountain climbing, bicycling, music, "how-to" in just about any field of interest, and so on. The idea of camp for the elderly is just beginning to mushroom. You can retire most of the year yourself after running a specialty camp for a few weeks each year. Give personalized professional service for repeat business.

$$$

681 TALKING BOOK RENTALS

People commuting back and forth to work can "read" a book each week by listening to cassette tapes of the book as they ride back and forth. You can make these tapes yourself after making copyright arrangements with authors/publishers. Then you can either sell these tape sets or rent them out to customers for flat fees. Commuters, housewives, students, blind people, the elderly, and others will be happy to rent your tapes. Consider specializing in a certain type of book for a certain group of readers. A free catalog of your list of titles and prices will boost your sales.

$$

682 TAXIDERMY

Many taxidermists cater to hunters who pay well to have their trophies mounted and preserved. However, taxidermists can easily specialize in other areas, if trophy hunting bothers them. A lover of nature loves to see animal specimens from distant lands as they are preserved in museums. As a trained taxidermist you could thus work for professional naturalists. Or you could mount deceased pet animals for their owners who want them preserved in lifelike mountings. Tanning of hides and the making of fine leathers is just another possibility among many others open to a taxidermist. In this business, overhead is usually low and profits high.

$$

683 TROUT FARM

With a plentiful supply of cold running water and some know-how, you can raise rainbow trout for a living. You will need several different pools—a pool for breeding, one for hatching, one for fingerlings, and one for more mature fish. You feed the fish special commercially prepared pellets. You may sell locally, or you may sell via air freight to distant hotels and restaurants that offer gourmet dishes and are in need of a constant, fresh supply of rainbow trout. You can also charge "fishermen" for the fish they "catch" by the pound!

$$$

684 USED BOAT SALES

New boats are like new cars—very expensive! Used boat sales will do just as well as used car sales. Duck boats, small fishing boats, canoes, sailboats, wind surfers—all used, will be your products. Up to 100 percent profit will be usual. Start small and part-time for extra income, unless you can invest several thousand dollars right from the start. Or sell on consignment. Buy in late fall, sell in spring and summer. Many big marinas started out in just such a manner!

$ ▉▊▌

685 VIDEOCASSETTE RENTALS

The video market is literally exploding. Soon nearly every home in North America will own a videotape recorder. They will soon be as common as TV sets. People will gladly rent first-run movies for $5 or so. A typical movie bought by you at $50 wholesale may gross $2000 the first year! Educational films such as concerts, travelogues, and even golf lessons would be a bonus! With good management and promotion of only wholesome products, this business can mean a good living for you.

$$$ ♿ ▉▊▌

686 VIDEO EVENTS SALES

With a TV video recording camera, you can take video recordings of major events in your community; then, after the event, you can make sales of copies of your video to the people who participated in the event. Watch the community events calendar in your newspaper or on your local TV channels for upcoming events. Events that film well are parades, sports events such as basketball games or track meets, or trade fairs, boat regattas, and so on. Try to get names and addresses from participants before they disperse from the event.

$ ♿ ▉▊▌

687 WAX MUSEUM

The secret of success in wax museums is the lifelikeness of the various figures from history displayed. Most people enjoy history only when it becomes "alive" for them. Wax museums have this ability like nothing else does. If you can combine the ability to work up wax figures with a good grasp of history, you may well consider starting up your own wax museum. You will need access to a flow of tourists or a larger local population. Try to set up next door to other popular landmarks or attractions.

$$$ ♿ ⬛

688 WHOLESOME VIDEO STORE

Cash in on the vacuum caused by current video outlets. Feature a wide range of films for wholesome family viewing, which will include travelogues, animal films, naturalogues, educational nuggets, and so on. You will offer shows to uplift our society out of the pit of suicide it is fast slipping into with all of its filth, sick sex, and incredible violence. You will be paid well for your efforts by the silent majority who are right now waiting for you to lead out!

$$$ ♿ ⬛

689 WINDSURFING SALES AND SCHOOL

It began in Europe and is now sweeping North America as the hottest new sports activity of the century. As a challenging activity that combines both surfing and sailing, it is enjoyed on any body of water, whether river, lake, or ocean. Dealers offering instruction are springing up coast to coast. Challenge, sheer fun, and profitable yet reasonable low prices will make windsurfing, in the long run, the summer counterpart of winter skiing. It can make a fine family business.

$$$ ⬛

690 ALPINE GUIDE

Everywhere you travel in central Europe you will find alpine guides who hire out their services of guiding amateur hikers, flower collectors, photographers, climbers, into the mountain vastnesses. North America has some of the most spectacular outdoor mountainous wilderness to be found anywhere in the world. But we have few alpine guides available. The market is nearly wide open for you to become an alpine guide, especially in the Rocky Mountain region. You can work through hotel and motel managers, through tourist info centers, and the like. If you like the mountains and people, this is an excellent business to get into.

$ ⬛

691 RIVER RAFTING GUIDE

Wild rivers are found in most parts of North America. A float trip down one of these rivers offers the nicest scenery and chances to see wildlife in natural settings. You can train to be a river rafting guide. Once you have your license and a boat you can open up your own float trip business on a river near you. You will need to advertise your trips, nationally if possible. You will do best if you can put together a colorful brochure which describes the highlights of your trips. Strive for a safe record.

$$$

692 ROCK SHOP

You may advertise yourself as a "rockhound emporium" if you like. But chances are you will start in your back yard or in your glassed-in front porch. You must know rocks and the jargon of the trade to succeed. In this business, he who knows not and knows not that he knows not is going to end up on the rocks! Rocks are absorbing things and may well take over your life. Work your gems into other retail outlets, such as drugstores. Set up at fairs and similar events.

$

693 LOCAL FISHING GUIDE

You are the best fisherman or fisherperson in your locality. You know where they are biting, when and how to catch them, and how to get there. All the tricks are yours. You simply put this special, exciting knowledge to work for you. You can do it in person by hiring yourself out to take others to the right fishing hole and show your clients what lures to use. Or you can put all you know together in a printed guide that you sell. Either way, you will create a run on your favorite fishing holes.

$$

694 RV EQUIPMENT STORAGE

Most people living in housing developments are hard-pressed to find space on their small lots to park their various RV vehicles, be they boats, all-terrain vehicles, ski-doos, utility trailers, house trailers, campers, and so on. If you have vacant property of an acre or more out in suburbia or a rural location, you could set up a business in which you fence off an acre or so and rent out spaces for the off-season storage of these vehicles. Flyers placed in mailboxes wherever you see that the problem exists will bring you quick results.

$$$

695 SPEED-PITCHING BOOTH

This business is similar to the baseball batting range. Instead of batting a ball, your paying clients will be trying to measure their pitching performance against such greats as Dizzy Dean and Ty Cobb. They will be pitching a baseball and your speed-pitching booth will be using radar to clock the speed of their throws. You can also set up to measure the accuracy of their pitches through an artificial strike zone. A machine that measures pitching speed is now available on the market. You could possibly combine this business together with the baseball batting range for extra income.

⫼⫼⫼⫼REPAIRS

696 ANTIQUE CLOCK RESTORATIONS

Clock repairmen have the respect of everyone for their expertise. But clock repairmen that specialize in restoring antique clocks, both inside and out, are in a gifted class all by themselves. If you aspire to join this class it will involve your entire lifestyle and years of patient experience. But the end result will be most satisfying and, of course, lucrative. Wealthy owners of disabled antique clocks will track you down from hundreds and even thousands of miles away to pay you whatever it takes to get their basket cases gleaming and ticking happily away again.

$$ ♿ ▓▓▐▐

697 ANTIQUE RESTORATION

Good antiques are always in demand. It takes an expert to recognize, appraise, and restore them. But there are far too few of these experts around. You can train yourself to become one. Give yourself a trial: secure a couple of antiques in junk shops and restore them. See if you have the extreme patience and concern the job demands. You will find that you can resell your restorations to dealers or private individuals for many times what you paid for them when they were still junk!

$ ♿ ▓▓▐▐

698 APPLIANCE REPAIRS

Most households will have at least one appliance break down at least once a year. The broken appliance will need either repairs or replacement. You can run an appliance outlet from your home in which you offer services for either repairs or replacement. You can start small with a small stock of the most common basic repair parts. You may want to work with just small appliances, or with just big appliances, or even both. This is one business that does not depend on fads and fashions. Appliances are here to stay. Steady income is guaranteed in this business.

$$ ♿ ▓▓

699 DIGITAL WATCH REPAIR

Get in on the ground floor without competition; the repair of these watches is currently wide open. Traditional watch repairmen don't understand their workings and usually avoid even looking at them. A repairman working at home can make a tidy living with high profit potential. Necessary start-up costs as little as $300.

$$

700 COUNTERTOP REPAIRS

It costs on average about $500 to replace laminate kitchen countertops. These laminate countertops are subject to chipping if they receive sharp blows. Instead of costly replacement of damaged units, there are simple methods and techniques for repairing them. You can learn this system of repairs and then go into business for yourself. You can net $50 an hour without much trouble. Work door-to-door. Take out simple small ads. Try circulating flyers on public bulletin boards in your area.

$

701 LAWN MOWER MAINTENANCE

Most families own their own lawn mower, and these machines will occasionally need repairs and maintenance. You can operate a repair and maintenance business for them by being on call for emergency breakdowns. Many people have not had much training for possible problems. Make house calls for these problems and pickup, repair, and return machines in distress. Minor repairs can be made on the spot. Run off-season tuneup specials. Country Clubs can become regular customers for you.

$$$

702 OLD TRUNK RESTORATIONS

If you are the patient type that loves old musty-smelling things, this may be for you. Rescue old dilapidated trunks from the dust and cobwebs. Thoroughly recondition them inside and out—hinges, leather harness, finish, reline with quaint quilting. Convert the pitiful into the prized! Then sell them for coffee tables, bookcases, toy boxes, storage for linens and blankets, and so on. It is fascinating to be able to dally in history. This is certainly a profitable line of work.

$

703 ORGAN RESTORATION

Here is an interesting way to cut the moorings and launch out into the deep. Find old pump organs and fully restore them—fix the bellows, which are usually ratched out, refinish the wood, the keys, and actions, and whatever else needs attention. You now have a beautiful old antique organ that will command a beautiful price (if you haven't become too attached to it yourself). Competition is just about nonexistent, so cast off!

$ 🦽 〽️🎹

704 PARKING LOT STRIPING AND MAINTENANCE

This is one of the few legitimate and proven businesses that you can start with little cash and no special abilities and soon become a stable, profitable enterprise. You will be renewing the parking lot stripes, which last on average about two years. You will refill potholes with asphalt and repaint any numbers, names, or parking instructions. You will likely become quite proficient in very short order. Less than $300 for startup.

$ ◤ 〽️

705 PIANO TUNING

There are about 15 million pianos in North America. All of them have to be tuned at intervals—many of them several times a year. You can take a home-study course that will teach you how to tune, repair, and restore most pianos. Tuning can bring you $30 or more each. A good tuner can make upwards of $2000 a month in a large center working full time out of his or her own home. New electronic tuning machines will make the tuning easy by doing your "listening" for you. The new electronic pianos on the market will never satisfy most pianists, who want to play a real piano.

$ 🦽 〽️🎹

706 REWEAVING

Professional reweavers are nearly a thing of the past, simply because the art hasn't been passed on. It pays extremely well. An insurance adjuster would rather pay you $80 to fix a cigarette burn in a davenport than have the entire unit reupholstered for several hundred dollars. You will need good eyesight and a patient manner. You will become so good at this darning method that your repairs will become more and more invisible and a marvel to customers. This is an ideal in-home business.

$ 🦽 〽️

707 SHARPENING SERVICE

It is not uncommon for those who sharpen tools to make a better living than those who use the tools. You can start part-time or go into it full-time if you have assessed your home area and have found it in need of this service. Prepare to sharpen just anything that needs periodic sharpening—saw blades, lawn mower blades, knives, scissors, specialty tools, skates, axes, and so on. You may want to go door-to-door with a mobile service setup. Establish a good reputation for good work at fair prices and you will not want for repeat work.

$ ♿

708 SHAVER REPAIRS

Few people are out there with the expertise, the tools, and the parts to fix disabled electric shavers. You can whip this business up for yourself with some modest preparation. First, get names and addresses of all major manufacturers of electric shavers and order their parts lists. Then stock commonly needed parts for major brands. Get some sample used units from pawn shops and practice taking them apart and putting them back together. With confidence you can then open up shop in your home if desired. Add on sales of new units if desired.

$$ ♿

709 SHOE REPAIRS AT HOME

You can run a successful shoe repair right in your own home, but because people are unlikely to bring many of their shoes to your home, you will need to go get the shoes. You can contract with other retailers located strategically to be your agents for receiving shoes from customers. Provide a sign inviting that shoes be left in each retail outlet agent together with a price list for your various repair services. You pay the agent a 20 percent or so commission on all sales. You pick up and deliver shoes twice a week at each retailer. Within one year you will likely have too much work.

$$ ♿

710 SHOPPING CART REPAIRS

Most shopping centers do not have people who can fix their shopping carts. Sometimes they have a general maintenance man who is supposed to do it when he finds the time, but because of its low priority, it often never gets done. Shopping carts that don't work properly are very annoying and can turn customers away. You can contract with the supermarkets in your area to keep their shopping carts in tip-top repair. Do the major repairs at your home workshop. Have a flat fee schedule of costs made up for store managers and then get your tools ready to go!

711 STOVE REPAIRS

New wood stoves are very expensive. There are still lots of older wood heaters and wood kitchen ranges around, but many of them have burned-out grates or are in need of other repairs. If you know basic metal working, you can set up a business in which you buy these older stoves, make the necessary repairs and improvements, and sell the "new" stove for hefty profits. Stove repair is easily learned. A strong back and tender loving care will be your biggest assets. Fine homes will be proud to house your fine re-creations.

712 SWIMMING POOL SERVICE

It is a bothersome task to clean and service a swimming pool. Most people who can afford a pool will gladly hire someone to service their pool. Often this service is unavailable. You can get in on the ground floor with a pool maintenance service if you live in a smaller town that does not yet have this service. It can be the start of a good-paying business if you can afford to patiently build the business. A bit of pool cleaning equipment and some advertising is all you need to launch out.

713 TELEPHONE SERVICING

Take a short home correspondence course on servicing and trouble-shooting telephones and then proceed to start up your own home boot-strap business that really pays well. Your telephone servicing business will have almost no start-up costs, you will carry almost no inventory, and you will be setting your own hours. Judging by the present exorbitant costs for this kind of service from telephone companies, it is obvious that the phone companies don't want to service phones, so you will be welcomed by all to get into this business.

714 TRACTOR REBUILDING

Like almost everything else, the price of farm tractors has gone out of sight. Many farmers are constantly upgrading their tractors, leaving their older inexpensive units sitting idle. People living on smaller farms or on rural subdivision hobby farms are happy to buy these smaller tractors for good money. You could run a business on searching out these idle tractors, giving them tune-ups and even paint jobs, and then selling them to well-paying customers.

$$$ ▞▌▛

715 TV REPAIR

TV repair continues to be a solidly prosperous business to enter into for an excellent reason—97 percent of homes have at least one TV set; many have two or more. Competition is keen, but there is generally plenty of business for everyone. Start your business in your home. You need a vehicle with which to make house calls. Get proper tools and have access to parts. Advertise. Charging $20 or so an hour is common. Add on new and used sets, plus other up-to-date electronic items. Your business can mushroom fast if you always put the customer first!

$$ ♿ ▞▌▛

716 TUB REFINISHING

There are two main materials used in tub manufacture. Older tubs have porcelain finishes. More modern tubs feature fiberglass resin finishes. Both types of tubs will chip if something heavy impacts them. You can learn the simple techniques of repairing these chips. You can then go door-to-door, if you like, searching out tubs that need your quickie repairs. Earning $20 and more an hour is consistently possible in this business, which has little competition. Work on your own time out of your home.

$ ♿ ▞▌▛

717 TYPEWRITER REPAIR

Every community can use a home typewriter repair service. You can learn this repair service in just a couple of months of effort in a home study course. You can buy used typewriters inexpensively, repair them, and resell them for several times more than you have invested. More and more people are in need of good used typewriters for home use. You will have a good ready market waiting for you in most areas.

$$ ♿ ▞▌

718 VINYL REPAIR

Here is another business where you can make big money by saving others big money! This market is virtually unlimited for repairing and recoloring vinyl products for homes, business and industry, RV equipment, and so on. It is not unusual for a vinyl artist to walk into a used car lot and come away with a thousand dollars or more of business. Many cities are without this service, which you can start for around $500. The need is there. You can easily learn to fill it.

719 EMERGENCY OBSTRUCTED-DRAIN SERVICE

This business is self-explanatory. Who hasn't had a drain back up at one time or another? And doesn't it always happen at the most inconvenient time? In this business you widely advertise that you are on 24-hour call, ready to war against any nasty plugged-up drains. In the meantime, you have armed yourself with all the tools of the trade, which will enable you to unplug any and all drains. Your time on any one job will usually be short, but you will charge a premium because of your willingness to respond quickly and at any time, day or night. You will operate with the mindset of a firefighter.

$

720 FLOOD CLEANUP

Floods don't happen on a regular basis in most localities. But when they do, they can create complete havoc. The local authorities are usually unable to cope with the onslaught of a flood. The ensuing cleanup can take months to correct. You can set up a business in which you respond to the needs of flood victims in the aftermath of a flood. You will contract with insurance companies or individual homeowners or owners of businesses to make things right. You may work by yourself, or you may hire locals to do most of the labor for you. You must know in detail what any given restoration work will involve, and then do it well.

$

721 INSURANCE RESTORATION

In this business you simply find items that have been damaged and that insurance companies want restored to their original condition. It may be any number of things: fences, roof shingles, broken concrete, flood-damaged buildings, smoke-damaged buildings, and the like. You will have to work your contacts who are in the insurance business to find jobs. Sometimes you will get a job just for the asking, but other times you will have to bid on a given job. If you lack knowledge about one aspect of a job, then you can always hire someone with the necessary expertise to help you.

$$

722 PC AND OFFICE MACHINE PREVENTIVE MAINTENANCE

Most personal computers are relatively maintenance free. Not much can go wrong with them under normal use. But problems do occur occasionally. A lot of these problems involve the misuse of cables connecting various devices and the locking up of software programs. If you have the requisite background to deal with these and other common problems of both computers and other office machinery, you can set up a business in which you sell your ability to correct these types of problems. Consider also selling preventive maintenance service contracts for your clients' other office equipment, if you have the know-how.

$$

723 APARTMENT PREPARATION

Rental tenants are often hard on the rental premises. Even when they are not, the normal wear and tear takes its toll. Owners of apartments are usually too busy to bring a given apartment up to standards themselves. If your skills include being able to make simple repairs and to clean and repaint, then you can contract to prepare apartments. The work will normally have to proceed quickly, so there will be a minimum of down time for the apartment. Careful attention to detail will be a must and will lead to additional work of this kind. A few basic hand tools and a set of basic cleaning and repainting tools should get you under way.

$$

724 OUTDOOR EQUIPMENT REPAIR

Pick up some tidy dollars every week to ease today's high cost of living by putting a spare room or space to work. Start your own outdoor equipment repair service. The repair of tents, tarps, sleeping bags, tent trailers, awnings, and other sewed outdoor equipment is a very respectable craft. Paul in the Bible did it!

$

▐▌▌▌▌▐▌▌RETAIL

725 ANIMAL FIGURES SHOP

Animal figures have always sold well, and they continue to do so. The market just keeps booming along. You can start up a gift shop that features only figures of animals. There are literally hundreds of animal figures you can market, from duck decoys to salt and pepper shakers in the form of owls. Since collecting animal figures is here to stay, you will probably never see a downturn in your unique business. You should do well right into your retirement.

$$$ ▐▛

726 ANIMAL WARNING DEVICE

Every year in North America hundreds of people and animals are killed or seriously injured in collisions between cars and larger animals such as deer. This need no longer happen, as a unique device has been invented that scares the animals safely away from roads. The inaudible device installs on any road vehicle. You can retail these simple devices in your area and reap big earnings.

$ ♿ ▐▛

727 ANTIQUE BUSINESS

This is a perennial business to be in, as items are constantly aging into "antiques." Start up with nothing, as a hobbyist, if you like. Learn how to find or buy items for as little as $1/20$ of their real value, or sometimes even for free. As for selling them, you will always have a ready market. Antique auctions are growing in popularity.

$ ♿ ▐▛▐

728 ANTIQUE CLOTHING

Fashion is fickle. It runs in circles. Yesteryear's castoffs are this year's "in" wear. You can cash in on this fact by running an ideal retail business based on it. Purchase sound old clothes, some even dating back into the twenties or earlier, mark them up by a factor of at least three, and then proceed to market them as comeback fashions. The trend toward nostalgia will give you your momentum. These old clothes just keep getting better the older they get. Make sure each piece of clothing is clean and in good repair.

$$$ ♿ ▐▛

729 ARTS AND CRAFTS EXCHANGE

There are many artists and craftsmen in every locality looking for an outlet for their art and crafts. You can open up a very profitable business
at home in which you display all sorts of handmade items. As soon as
you advertise, you will be deluged with people wanting you to sell their
handiwork for them on consignment and commission. You will be ren-
dering a real service to buyers and sellers, not to mention yourself, with
this business. You will have to pick and choose among all the beautiful
items to accept for display unless you have lots of room.

$ ♿ ⬛

730 ART GALLERY

You really don't have to know anything about art to run a pop art gallery
because the public doesn't usually know much about art either. You do
have to know, however, what kind of paintings the man in the street
prefers. Get a good idea of what sells by visiting a commercial gallery
that specializes, like you will, in low-priced paintings of, say, $15 to $75
or so. Go for volume sales and leave expensive paintings to the more
exclusive art galleries.

$$ ♿ ⬛

731 ART PRINTS GALLERY

Open up a small shop specializing in top-quality reproductions of the
works of famous artists. These prints sell for $3 to $20 or more depend-
ing on size, mat, frame, and so on. They sell for decorative purposes,
and also to art-minded students seeking inspiration from the masters.
Picture framing is a must and may be your top source of income. Works
from local artists can also be shown and sold for commissions paid to
you. Small start-up costs to be sure.

$$$ ⬛

732 ART SHOWS PROMOTER

It always pays much better to be the promoter than to be the artist. You
don't have to know very much about art to do well at it either, although
solid knowledge would surely be a strong plus. A couple days a week of
putting on art shows in parking lots can net you a fine living. A $300
start-up is possible. Artists gladly pay $10 a day plus 10 percent of sales
just for a small one-car parking space, because art galleries will exact
from them 20 percent to 50 percent commissions!

 $ ♿ ⚒ ⬛

733 ATHLETIC SHOE SHOP

Not long ago, a pair of tennis shoes was sufficient for most sports. Now, it seems, the only place a tennis shoe is welcome is on the tennis court! Baseball players need spiked shoes, joggers need jogging shoes, and then there are golfing shoes, hiking shoes, skiing boots, and the list goes on and on. It seems that every sport has its own special type of shoe—and people must buy them or face embarrassment in front of their fellow enthusiasts. Slip into a very respectable living by pairing up with this business.

$$$$ ♿ ◤ 〽

734 AUTO PARTS

Auto parts sales are hitting around $80 billion a year in North America. Nearly everyone has a car that sooner or later needs parts. Moderate-size operations can generate steady salaries of $25,000 to $30,000. There is an average of about 5180 cars per parts outlet in North America. These could be your customers out there wearing out car parts and replacing them with your parts. You can add on high margin accessories. Cater to both garages and do-it-yourselfers and you will do yourself well in the bargain.

$$$$$ 〽

735 BABY FURNITURE SHOP

New parents are usually willing to pay premium prices for furniture for their first baby. They want good-quality furniture that will last for several of their children and perhaps even some possible grandchildren. You can run a business that caters to these special needs. You will want to stock durable cribs, carriages, chairs, junior beds, desks, rocking horses, solid toys, wall hangings, bedding, mattresses, pillows, and so on. Check for imported items of excellent quality for your inventory.

$$$$ 〽

736 BACK NUMBER MAGAZINE STORE

Buy used magazines for a few cents a pound and display them on tables and sell them for 10 or more times what you paid for them. Obtain them from janitors of hotels and apartment houses, or from rubbish collectors, who get tons of them. *National Geographic* is a big seller. As your stock builds up you will have even college professors doing research looking for specific issues! Selling price is usually half of the new price.

 $$$ ♿ 〽

737 BACKPACKING STORE

There is no better way to get away from it all than by going backpacking. About 40 million North Americans are regular hikers and backpackers. Operate a shop that specializes in outfitting these modern-day explorers and you can become very busy following the trail to the bank! Expect hefty profit margins averaging 45 percent on clothing, packs, boots, skis, knives, compasses, tents, sleeping bags, and so on. Stock repeat items like special foods for repeat sales. Work out of your basement, if possible, for a fine home business.

$$$$$

738 BARBER SHOP

Learn to snip hair, or else be an absentee partner to a barber. Less than $1000 should get you started with rent, decorating, plumbing, mirrors, signs, clippers, and so on. Advertise with handbills.

$

739 BARGAINS SHOP

When people want to sell something in a hurry, they will sell at only a fraction of the real value. Knowing this and being able to take advantage of it can set you up in a fine booming business in which you will buy anything and everything that you believe you can sell for twice or more what you paid for it. You will scan the classified columns and attend all garage sales and flea markets looking for these rushed sales items. The biggest problem you will have in running your "giant yard sale" business will be to keep stocked up with the bargains for your bargain-hunting customers.

$$

740 BARTER MIDDLEMAN

The recession is really making this job come into its own! Individuals and businesses having cash-flow problems welcome you, the middleman, to arrange for them to exchange either goods or services they produce or sell for vital items they ordinarily must pay cash for. Bartering or horse trading can consume lots of time that most people no longer have. Very efficiently, you arrange the exchanges; both parties benefit, and you get, on average, a 10 percent piece of the action!

$

741 BEACH CONCESSION

Find a popular lake or ocean beach and arrange to set up a concession from which you rent out beach equipment—chairs, umbrellas, floats, swim flippers, beach balls, inner tube floats, canoes, windsurfers, and so on. Add on snacks and juices. Hire a responsible college student to run it for you if you like. This can be a good business for the season. Expansion would require setting up additional concessions at other beaches. Cater to the best-attended beaches.

$$$

742 BICYCLE RENTALS

Bicycling offers the best in exercise, relaxation, and recreation. You can rent them out to the public if you can locate near parks, beaches, colleges, and recreational areas where the topography is fairly flat, so that strenuous exertion is not required. Consider a mobile establishment operating from the back of a truck. Could be a good full-time or part-time job for a retired or semi-retired couple. $10,000 gross a season is entirely possible.

$$$

743 BICYCLE SHOP

The bike boom is not only a matter of increased necessity because of increased fuel costs, but it is also a matter of returning to the simple pleasures of life. Whole families and groups are going biking together. The really big demand is for good bike repair shops. Good repairs will build good repeat business. There is no reason why this business cannot be run in a home successfully if the location is reasonable.

$$

744 BOOK EXCHANGE

You start your Bookateria (or whatever) simply with a stack of flyers put out door-to-door. Offer sound savings for reading enjoyment. Ask people to bring in their books in bags, boxes, or by the bale. Exchange as follows: one book from a patron entitles him to 50 percent off the selling price of one of your books. Your inventory will grow about as fast as you can build new shelving! Stock replaces itself! You will not only be recycling paper, but knowledge and enjoyment as well! Ad: "Bring in two books, get one free."

$

745   BROKER FOR DISTRESSED MERCHANDISE

This is probably North America's least known and possibly most lucrative industry. You can make literal fortunes matching buyers and sellers for distressed merchandise such as smoke-damaged goods, surplus stock, bankrupt goods, repossessions, and so on. As a professional liquidator, you can even make insurance companies and manufacturers your silent partners in potentially super-profitable deals. All you need is enough money to complete your first deal and you are on your way. Buy distressed goods at 10 cents or so on the dollar and then sell them for many times what you paid for them. If you can close a sale before you actually purchase the goods then you can operate without any investment at all, but do be careful of your timing.

$$$ ⬛

746   BUCKLES, BELTS, AND SUSPENDERS

Pants need to be held up. You can retail locally or by mail order colorful suspenders, real leather belts in various sizes and colors, and various buckles that display Western themes, trucker themes, or wildlife scenes, and so on. Big profits are possible if you market your products skillfully.

$$$ ♿ ⬛

747   CAMPING EQUIPMENT KITS

A good home mail-order business is as follows. Start small with perhaps just one good item. Proceed to make and sell kits for do-it-yourselfers to make their own camping gear—sleeping bags, tents, parkas, tarps, pants, shirts, mitts, packsacks, and so on. Several large companies started at home in a small way doing this very thing. The market is nearly wide open to copy their success. Advertise regionally or nationally in top-line sports magazines for best results.

$$$ ♿ ⬛

748   CANDLEMAKING SUPPLIES

One business the author personally worked in started out with one part-time employee. At last count the business had mushroomed until over 60 employees were making, packaging, and shipping candlemaking supplies. You can run your own business of this type quite nicely by mail order from your own home. You will need an attractive catalog listing your various molds, wicks, scents, waxes, and so on. It is a very lucrative business to be in and the market just keeps expanding.

$$ ♿ ▐▜▐▛

749 CANES

There is only one known store in North America that specializes in selling just canes. So competition will be all but nonexistent if you elect to start up your own cane business. You can sell both retail and by mail order from your own home. You will stock all sorts of canes that will range in price from $10 into the thousands for rare antique collector's models. Handmade canes will sell for better prices. Stock the biggest variety that you can afford and advertise nationally for heavy-duty results. A free catalog will help much.

$$$ ♿ ▐▜

750 CHILDREN'S APPAREL STORE

In this business, the new items of clothing you sell will be obsolete in a month or two simply because children grow so fast. These obsolete items need to be replaced every couple of months. This fact will keep your business bustling! A 30 percent profit average means this is a good clean business to be in.

$$$$$ ◣ ▐▜

751 CLOCK SHOP

This is a timely business specializing in selling all kinds of clocks—from $5 tick-tocks to $5000 granddaddies! You should set up a regular retail outlet in a heavy-traffic area for best results. However, you can also run a lower-profile operation successfully right in your own home with good advertising. You can even manufacture a special line of clocks and market them by mail order from your home if desired. Repairs of clocks may or may not interest you. Call yourself the Good Times Clock Shop or some such name.

$$$$$ ◣ ▐▜

752 CLOTHES CONSIGNMENTS

In nearly all dry cleaners you will see signs posted warning patrons that the business will not be responsible for garments that are not called for before 60 days. You can arrange to sell these garments on consignment through your home business in which you advertise that you have "Good Used Dry-Cleaned Clothing for Sale." You will pay the dry cleaners a small percentage of your sales price, plus their dry-cleaning costs or charges. The rest will be your profit from your own "no-investment" home business. Word of mouth will see to future and repeat customers.

$ ♿ ▗

753 COIN-OP LAUNDRY

Self-service laundry has proved itself. This mainstay continues to be a solid profit-making enterprise. Research shows that over 40 percent of apartment dwellers prefer to use nearby laundromats even though their apartment building had coin units on their premises. Laundromats provide large-capacity machines without making people wait, in a social setting like the old village square. Profits are steady and handsome. Add-on services such as vending machines with food, drinks, and games are possible.

$$$$$ ♿ ◢ ▗

754 COLLECTIBLES SHOP

Millions of North Americans are collectors. Many of them have collections that would be worth tens of thousands of dollars if they were put up for sale. No collection is ever really finished—there is always something that can be found that will be an added improvement. You can run a shop in which you cater to collectors specifically. You can sell books and merchandise alike that will assist them with their collection. You could stock items such as salt and pepper shakers, spoons, insulators, barbed wire samples, stamps, and so on. There is very good money to be collected from selling collectibles.

$$$$$ ♿ ▗

755 CONVENIENCE FOOD STORE

Convenience food stores are the fastest-growing industry in North America! People want convenience. Today time is as important as money to the consumer. We value our leisure time and hate to waste time standing in long lines in supermarkets. And unlike supermarket profits of around 2 percent, you will enjoy an average of about 14 percent profit! A good absentee-owner business. Location is the key to success here.

$$$$$ ◢ ▗

756 COOKWARE FOR GOURMETS

The high cost of eating out is bringing people back to the kitchen, and home entertainment has returned in style. Gourmet and ethnic cooking has become a fun hobby for thousands of men and women. Run cooking classes to bolster your sales. Graduates will head for your local gourmet cookware shop in search of exciting new gadgets, cookbooks, and tools with which to satisfy their palates and those of their friends!

$$$$$ 🏠

757 COOKABLES FOR GOURMET CHEFS

This business has close kinship to the above business of Cookware For Gourmets. The two might be run simultaneously in a larger city. In this business you stock all the specialty items gourmet chefs will require for their exotic recipes—the bamboo shoots, the hot chili peppers, the kosher meats, and so on. Keep up with the trends as set on TV cook-along shows.

$$$ 🏠

758 CRAFTS SUPPLIES ON WHEELS

There are many shut-ins and elderly people who love to make crafts and other things with their hands but cannot get out to go shopping for crafts supplies for themselves. You can set up a crafts and hobbies supply service which you run from a van. With this mobile store, you can visit all of these clients with ease, whether they are confined to hospitals, rest homes, mobile parks, or their own home. Service right to the bedside would give you a solid booming business.

$$$$ 🏠

759 COTTON, 100 PERCENT, PRODUCTS BY MAIL ORDER

Synthetic fabrics have caused lots of people lots of problems. Cotton is one of the finest natural products available. You can open up a home business in which you specialize in 100 percent cotton products—pillows, sheets, quilts, mattresses, kitchen items, personal items including underwear, and so on. You can market your products locally, or you can sell by mail order in response to your national ads and free catalogs.

$$$ ♿ 🏠

760 DAY CARE SUPPLIES ON WHEELS

Day care centers are growing by leaps and bounds. From mom-and-pop operations to national chain enterprises, they all have special needs for products and supplies such as glue bottles, art papers, cots for naps, sturdy toys, and so on. You can easily run a business meeting these needs in a larger center. Stock a van with items most needed and set up various routes about the city visiting all day care centers and nurseries. Taking the store to the customers will multiply your potential business many times over.

$$$$

761 DEALERSHIPS

Dealerships are often called manufacturer's representatives. Look for unique articles that you are sure will sell. Contact the manufacturer and get exclusive rights to sell the product in a given region of the country. Then work the region alone, or hire others to help you sell the product or products you have exclusive rights to. You are your own boss. You don't have to sell if you don't want to. You can set up so as to take "overrides" from the salespeople you have hired. Good salesmen do very well in this business.

$

762 ELECTRIC FAN STORE

This venture will thrive on the new trend toward energy conservation. Many new models of efficient, nearly silent fans are now available for exhausting fumes and dead air and for cooling. Specialty fans such as antique ceiling fans will add a fashionable touch. Ceiling fans recirculate warm air, which rises upward, so that furnaces no longer have to run as often. Fan-installing service will be appreciated by many of your patrons.

$$$$

763 ENERGY STORE

There are more than 14,000 energy-saving devices now on the market and more show up every day. A new innovative approach is to sell a wide range of energy-saving devices all under one roof for one-stop convenience. Be ready to teach your customers how to beat energy loss from homes and businesses. Add on the installation of purchased items for extra income. You can set up in your basement.

$$$$

764 EQUIPMENT RENTALS

Wise shoppers know it is better to rent a machine than it is to purchase one if the machine is to be used only infrequently. Nearly every town of any size can use an equipment rental business. You can get into this business just using your garage, where you will rent out all sorts of power tools—table saws, sanders, drills, band saws, torches, paint sprayers, compressors, lawn mowers, cement mixers, hedge trimmers, apple juicers, and so on. Stock hand tools also. Require small deposits, which you later credit toward the rental payment. Keep your machines in good, clean working order. Keep a listing in the yellow pages.

$$$$$　▥

765 EXERCISE CLOTHING

Millions of North Americans are exercising their way back to slim and trim. Before exercising, they put on special clothing. You can get into this special exercise clothing business in at least two ways: (1) through manufacture of the sweat suits and special gear used, or (2) through retail sales of the various types of clothing and footwear worn by people out exercising by jogging, weightlifting, doing aerobics, and so on. New fashions for exercising are constantly coming out, so the market can't become saturated.

$$$$$　▥

766 FABRIC SHOP

Inflation and recession have made women's clothing prices nothing to laugh about. The home-sewing industry is taking off. Open up a discount fabric shop in which you specialize in seconds, irregulars, cuts, and closeouts. You can buy for as little as 10 cents on the dollar. In this manner, large retailers can never compete with you. Record growth is forecast for this type of business in the next decade.

$$$$$　▥

767 FAMILY HAIR SALON

You can take in goodly income by simply making haircutting convenient, reasonably priced, and enjoyable. The whole family can get clipped all at the same time without having appointments ahead. Add on noncost extras to win repeat customers.

$$　▥

768 FLEA MARKET SALES

Imagine $28,000 a year working on weekends only! You can do it easily if you have the right items at the right prices. Average "regular sellers" consistently net $100 and more a day for their trouble. Some consistently earn upwards of $300 every day. Study what will sell best and where you can get it at the lowest price.

$

769 FLOWER SHOP

The flower business is a steady one. People keep right on buying and sending flowers for weddings, births, deaths, or simple "thinking-of-you" gifts. It is no wonder the business perseveres no matter what the rest of the economy is doing. Good location and management are musts. Around $800 can get you started.

$$$$

770 FLOWER STAND

Start an outdoor flower shop for less than $100. Location is the key item here. Find a vacant lot at a very busy intersection. Drive around and around until you are sure you have the right spot. Use your front lawn if you have to. You will be selling cheap cut flowers, those almost ready to be thrown away, by displaying and selling them on a table or stand on a vacant lot. Example: Pick up a quantity of roses for as little as 50 cents a dozen and sell them fast at $2.50 a dozen—a 500 percent profit!

$$

771 FROZEN YOGURT SHOP

An easy way to take advantage of the many looking for quick health foods today. It is catching up with McDonald's! You can even build your own chain if you like. A real ground-floor opening into today's health- and weight-conscious society. Average shops gross about $70,000 and net about 50 percent of that!

$$$$

772 FURNITURE RENTAL STORE

North American society is highly mobile and doesn't want to be tied down. Many would rather rent than buy. Last year over half a million of us furnished our apartments and homes with rented furniture and spent $350 million in the process! Sales are expected to keep climbing. Once you are established, you can spend much of your time in one of your own recliners!

$$$$$ ▐▜▌

773 GARAGE SALE PROMOTER

For a fast infusion of solid, green cash, learn how to promote garage sales for people who want one without suffering the hassles of holding one. Move in and organize, advertise, and stage the entire affair for a base price plus a percentage of all sales. Use your imagination for promotional gimmicks.

$ ♿ ◤ ▐▜▌

774 GOVERNMENT SURPLUS

Many military supplies and pieces of equipment can be converted easily to civilian use. Clothing is a good example. The military frequently disposes of either surplus or moderately used or obsolete equipment and supplies. You can purchase these products for pennies on the dollar and then retail them to the public at enormous profits. A retail outlet is the usual method of marketing them. However, a free catalog and mail-order type of operation works quite well, especially along with national advertising.

$$$$$ ▐▜▌

775 GREETING CARD SHOP

Selling greeting cards is one of the most lucrative markets to be found. The demand just keeps increasing, too. A card shop—handling nothing but cards—can make very good money! Everyone seems to be selling cards, but you will beat all your competition because you will offer the biggest and the most complete selection to choose from. You will need a store, display stands, and a good stock of cards. Your markups are about 100 percent on average! Add-ons of gifts and novelties are naturals.

$$$ ♿ ▐▜▌

776 GROCERIES ON WHEELS

Many rural people are unable, for various reasons, to get to a store at times to stock up on groceries. You can start a mobile supermarket serving outlying areas that will make you a decent living. Purchase an old school bus and rebuild the motor if necessary; rebuild the body with shelves lining both sides and install a freezer, which you plug in at night at home. Put in regular grocery stock. Set up several routes to service once a week on schedule. Charge about 10 percent above regular store prices and you will have a nice, well-earned profit.

$$$$

777 HAMMOCKS

Most of us spend about one-third of our time in bed. More and more people are turning to sleeping in hammocks. Hammocks offer simplicity, low prices, easy storage, a rocking motion that is relaxing, and therapy for many back problems. You can run a business that specializes in selling hammocks. You can get information about importing them from the consulates of hammock-making countries, such as Mexico, Guatemala, the Philippines, and so on. Stock a variety of regular hammocks in all price ranges, and consider swinging or hammock chairs and cribs, as well.

$$$

778 HANDICAPPED RETAIL SHOP

Handicapped persons have special needs that standard retail outlets seldom meet. In a larger center you could set up a business in which you cater to the unusual needs of the handicapped, whether it is clothing or footwear or whatever. You could promote your business through hospitals, rest homes, charitable organizations, and the like. National advertising offering a free catalog for handicapped products could be another approach or an add-on to a retail outlet.

$$$$$

779 HANDICRAFT CO-OP GALLERY

This terrific new business concept violates all the rules. You have no inventory and minimum overhead with an easy 30 percent profit margin! As a take-off on the old flea market idea, this business offers tremendous semipermanent advantages to both buyer and seller. Both artisans and customers alike have the convenience of a nifty store for one-of-a-kind craft items, offering year-round high traffic, high sales, and public exposure. Sublease space in the building you have leased to an artisan for $25 to $75 a month plus 30 percent commission on everything of his you sell. Each lessee stocks his own display, sets his own prices, and provides his own inventory insurance. This job will put many others to work as well!

$$

780 HEALTH FOOD STORE

North Americans are becoming increasingly conscious that we need the best food in order to have the best health. There is a war being waged against junk foods. This phenomenal natural food boom is here to stay. Selected owners of small health food stores are grossing upwards of $300,000 a year with markup of 40 percent to 100 percent on most items. Organically grown produce is a good seller. Bulk foods in bins plus vitamins and minerals will be your major sellers. A soup and sandwich bar can be a valuable add-on. It is a neat way to get your own health foods at substantial savings, too!

$$$$$

781 HEART SHOP

Several shops that sell nothing but heart-shaped products are now doing booming business in several North American locations. You can get in on the ground floor in this business in your home, either retailing or in manufacture of heart-shaped products. Hundreds of heart-shaped items are already available and sou may want to lengthen the list with some of your own creations. The heart is a universal symbol and it will attract impulse buyers like a magnet. You can even go mail order with this business if you wish.

$$$$$

782 HOBBY SHOP

Scale modeling may form the backbone of this enterprise. Whether pastime or passion, it has never been more popular than it is today. Radio-controlled planes, boats, cars, and so on are especially popular and they can be very lucrative for you. You can start small from your home or start up a modest storefront business for upwards of $10,000. This $22 billion-a-year industry has consistently grown for several generations. A huge variety of add-ons are possible.

$$$$

783 HOME BOOKSHOP

You can provide a genuine service to your community by opening up a bookstore in your home, especially if your community lacks one. You can set up in a garage if you like. Shelves and a heated space with adequate lighting is all you really need. Sell both new and used books if you like. You will gross about 40 percent on new book sales and about 100 percent on used books. Try to eliminate all trashy books and keep up a reputation for wholesome books only. Good nonfiction should be your mainstay.

$$ ♿ 🏢

784 HONG KONG TAILORS AGENT

Many people know about the world-famous Hong Kong tailors that can measure a man for a new suit in the morning and have it ready to wear six hours later. Almost no one knows that this same service is available by mail. You can become an agent here in North America for a Hong Kong tailor. Measure patrons for perfect-fit suits that arrive via air express in about three weeks for a total price of about 35 percent of the North American price! Write the American or Canadian Consul, Hong Kong for addresses of Hong Kong tailors. Operate at home by appointment only.

$$ ♿ 🏢

785 HOT DOG AND BURGER STAND

The standard business! Just ask McDonald's! Invest $2000 or so and make a steady respectable living. The trend is to nonmeat meat, which looks and tastes like meat, but is probably a soybean vegetable meat substitute. Cash in on this switch. That way you can offer your patrons better health, plus you can attract the rapidly growing population of vegetarians. Hot dog/burger stands keep good resale value.

$$ ♿ ◀ 🏢

786 HYDROPONICS STORE

Next to air and water, food is our greatest need. A new way of growing food at home that is involving more and more people is hydroponics. In this method no soil is used. Instead, the nutrient chemicals needed by the plants are fed in solution directly to the plants in an indoor environment that is controlled for heat, lighting, air flow, and so on. Quick results are realized and therefore several cash crops a year are possible. You can run a retail outlet that supplies all the needs of families and commercial setups in your area.

$$$$ ♿ ⛰

787 JEANS STORE

Jeans are a type of clothing that has been in style now for many years with no sign of letup in popularity. Jeans made of denim are the mainstay, but denim jackets and other items of denim round out a jeans shop line of products. You can run this type of business from your home in a smaller town. You can offer sewing instruction along with denim fabrics and patterns for do-it-yourselfers, if you like. People of all ages love the rugged durability of their jeans and many people would be lost without them to wear every day.

$$$$$ ♿ ⛰

788 LADIES APPAREL SHOP

Come rain, snow, inflation, depression, or recession, women keep right on buying clothes because fashions keep changing. It is a treadmill situation from which you can make a good living. Buy cheap and sell dear. Consider setting up in the main floor of an older two-story house that has been newly redecorated. Clever merchandising will be vital to success.

$$$$$ ♿ ⛰

789 MATTRESS SHOP

Start an independent sleep shop with all kinds of mattresses—water mattresses, box-spring types, special sizes and densities, therapeutic types, and exotic types such as hammocks! Everyone spends about one-third of every day on a mattress and it is not a habit anyone breaks. Computers won't take this job away from you.

$$$$ ⛰

790 MEN'S CASUAL CLOTHING

Set up as a "dressy-casual" clothing store for men. You eliminate the top end of a heavy expensive suit and sportcoat inventory, and you avoid the too-casual jeans market. You stick to the middle specialty of slacks and dressy sports shirts made of high-quality fabrics. Dress codes are quickly changing toward more relaxed, casual styles, even in business and industry. Dressy-casual is the style of the future. Your profits will always be in style in this middle-of-the-road business.

$$$$

791 NECKTIE STORE

Start with about $1000. Stick strictly to ties—all kinds—and sell them all for the same minimal price. Many other businessmen may think you are going to go broke in a hurry, but you will laugh last! Start in the fall before the big holiday rush. Study another necktie store and see how they operate. It is absolutely necessary that you have a store location on a principal shopping street in the downtown district of a major city. It won't work very well elsewhere.

$$ &

792 ORIENTAL AND PERSIAN RUGS

You may not gross $8000 an hour, or sell a $20,000 inventory of Oriental rugs for close to $48,000 in just six hours, which has been done, but you can do quite well at it if you are only an average dealer. Rugs imported for $110 can go for $1500 and more! You can auction off your goods in a rented hotel room or even hold sales at roadside or at fairs. Auctioning can generate buying frenzy which results in markups of 400 to 500 percent!

$$$$$

793 PAINT AND WALLCOVERING STORE

Stand up to inflation by catering to do-it-yourselfer home redecorators. Build your clientele by actually teaching people how easy it is to fix up their homes, apartments, and even offices. Show them how cheaply it can be done. Use your basement as a sales place in order to cut costs. Go door-to-door with samples.

$$$$$ &

794 PAPERBACK BOOKSHOP

Selling paperback books can become a way of life. There is a certain fascination in running one. In this pleasant occupation you will meet lots of congenial people who share your own tastes in literature. Warning: You may go broke if you sell only the books you personally enjoy. In a bookstore, or any other kind of store, the pressure is always on to give the customers what they want, not what you think they ought to have. Use discretion. Order wholesome titles other successful paperback bookstores order for the most part.

$$$$$ ♿ ⛰

795 PHONE STORE

This business will truly stay on top of inflation. The variety of phones for retail is enormous. Stock a good variety of quality units from basic plain-Jane models to gold-plated antique styles. Add on phone answering machines and other convenience phone accessories for built-in sales. Start in your home with a basic outlay and begin to grow at once.

$$$$ ♿ ⛰

796 POSTERS

Posters say simple things in a big way. They clearly show where our society is today. They are up-to-date mirrors for all of us. Thousands of different posters are presently in print—from the vulgar to the sublime. A larger center can support a retail outlet that specializes in wholesome posters and other complementary products, such as wall murals. Set up your selection of posters on swing boards to save space and thus overhead costs. Good judgment is a must in eliminating posters of questionable value from your selection.

$$ ♿ ⛰

797 PROSPECTOR'S STORE

Gold fever is sweeping the continent and sharp entrepreneurs are cashing in by selling equipment to prospectors hot on the trail of instant riches. You cater to "gold junkies" by selling dredging equipment, maps, books, camping gear, and so on. The United States government predicts that only about 5 percent of the world's gold has been found to date. Those who have been bitten by the gold bug will pay you handsomely for helping them find pay dirt. Potentially a skookum grubstake for you!

$$$ ♿ ⛰

798 PUBLIC WASHROOM CLEANING

There is a need for this service in every community. Not just anyone is willing to provide this service because washrooms can at times be worse than filthy. But with proper protection to you and your body you can literally clean up in this business. You will need strong cleaners and brushes and sponges. Add on sales of paper products, mirrors, repainted walls, and so on, for a real booming business. Call yourself "Washed-up Washrooms" or whatever.

$

799 QUILT SHOP

Quilts have been revived by demand for very good reasons—they combine great beauty with practical function. Prices range from about $100 to $4000 and more. Interior decorators and designers, collectors, homemakers, young couples, and even college students are buying quilts. You can run a quilt shop business selling quilts on consignment. You can add on products for quilters—patterns, lessons, fabrics, and the like. Quilts will brighten and set off any bedroom, sofa, or even walls. You can capitalize plenty on this welcome trend.

$$

800 RELIGIOUS GIFT SHOP

Consumers of many denominations are flocking to inspirational "boutiques" where they can buy music, books, plaques, cards, and Bibles. Bible sales have been increasing about 10 percent annually for the past few years. There is a tremendous hunger in people of all faiths to read more and to understand what they believe and why they believe it. No special experience is necessary here to succeed well.

$$$$

801 REMNANT SHOP AT HOME

The first word that pops into your mind when you say "remnants" is the word "bargains"! You can open up a fabric remnant shop in your home if zoning permits it and if you have ample room. Your overhead will be so low that your selection of remnants will be true bargains for your customers, who will quickly find you in droves with very little advance advertising. Good sources of materials are textile manufacturing mills. Start with a small amount of stock to test your market at first, but be prepared to expand on short notice.

$$ ♿ 🏭

802 ROADSIDE SELLING

People out joyriding in the country love to stop at informal roadside stands and stretch their legs and browse for bargains. You can set up a roadside stand in front of your home along a well-traveled highway and sell year-round whatever you can obtain that you know will sell—original arts and crafts, or food produce of all sorts, which you purchase from neighboring farms. Simply buy cheap and sell dear, or work by consignment. It is important to erect two attractive signs in both directions down the highway to warn drivers in time to stop.

$ ♿ 🔨 🏠

803 SALES BLITZES

In this business, you have to think really big and you have to move very fast. The idea is that you will buy, from a liquidator or a factory or even local merchants, a pile of widgets for pennies on the dollar. Then rent a place with top walk-by traffic for a day or two only. Advertise in every way possible your sale of widgets of the century at unheard-of low prices. Hire lots of help inexpensively to sell to the crowds that will all but overwhelm your sale premises. This proven method has been used to gross more than $500,000 in just one day!

$$$$$ 🔨 🏭

804 SECONDHAND MUSIC

A secondhand music store operates much like a secondhand book store. You can start this business for just a few hundred dollars. Visit auctions, estate sales, and so on, to purchase anything dealing with the music of yesteryear—LPs, 45s, 78s, record players, sheet music, jukeboxes, cassette and other tapes, and so on. Buy for pennies and resell for dollars. Your biggest problem will be in finding new inventory. Very high profit margins can be made in this business.

$$ ♿ 🏭

805 SECONDHAND STORE

With this business you can't lose if you have nothing to start with. Soon you will find you are either on the right track or else out of your mind. What you do is learn how to buy junk from one person and sell it to a neighbor. It is as simple as buy low, sell high. You must get back twice what you give for most items in order to hang on. Look for package deals to buy, such as complete households of furniture—you may stumble onto some valuable antiques that way.

$$$ ▣

806 SERVICE STATION

A number of major oil companies will lease a fully equipped station to you for an initial investment of as little as $1000 and ranging up to $10,000. This debt may be paid off through your profits over a three- to five-year period. Your average income will be about $25,000 or more a year depending on your overhead, location, and your willingness to work. Not all like the longer hours, but you may be the kind of person that will enjoy this kind of work. The oil company will give you detailed instructions on how and how not to run the station. They probably know their business best!

$$$$$ ◤   ▣

807 SHEEPSKIN SEATCOVERS

In Germany, over half of the cars have sheepskin interiors, but it is just now beginning to catch on in North America. They are a luxury for snobs, perhaps, but they are cost-effective insulation for any penny pincher. They are high-class items that offer you low overhead and high margins. Sheepskins are not the one-shot deal many think. Many stores are veterans doing as well after ten or more years as when they started out. With 170 million cars on North American highways, there is an enormous market waiting for you to tap.

$$$ ♿   ▣

808 SHELL SHOP

This business gives you the perfect excuse to vacation in the South Pacific or the Caribbean as a buying trip for beautiful exotic shells! Annual sales can be very impressive. They are the latest collectible and a hot-selling decorative gift item coast to coast. A tiny shop can net an impressive living for you.

$$$ ♿ ▆▆

809 SURVIVAL STORE

A nuclear holocaust? A volcanic eruption? An earthquake? Many possible disasters threaten North Americans, which can in turn be a solid source of income when you open a survival store. You will vend vital basic necessities that would be needed if modern conveniences disappear or are cut off: basic food, tools, medicines, books, and so on. Each new Mt. St. Helens or Three-Mile Island can only boost your sales! Everywhere there are people preparing for cataclysmic disasters.

$$$$ ▆▆▌

810 TOYS OF WORTH SHOP

A shop offering worthwhile toys will be a welcome asset in any community. Worthwhile toys provide harmless fun. They challenge a child's intellect. They are durable and long lasting. They teach nonviolence and avoid excessive competition. They, above all, are not linked to the garbage often sold as toys on TV. You can run a toy shop along these lines and whole families will come to love you for your store. Provide sample toys for children to handle and play with—this will boost your sales immensely. Sponsor story hours for even more sales.

$$$$ ♿ ▆▆

811 TOYS, SECONDHAND

Many parents cannot afford new toys for their children so they will gladly purchase secondhand toys in good repair from your secondhand toy shop. You can purchase secondhand toys very inexpensively from rummage sales, secondhand stores, garage sales, and by advertising for them under the "Wanted" column in your newspaper. Be able to fix up the toys with needed repairs—mending, gluing, sewing, oiling, painting, and so on. During the holiday season your stock will probably not keep up with the demand.

$$ ♿ ▆▆

812 TRACTOR RENTALS

Many people live in small-acreage subdivisions on lots that are too big to landscape without the help of some machinery and yet are too small to justify buying basic machinery such as a tractor. You can set up a business renting out tractors by the hour, with or without you as the operator. The renter provides the fuel. They will have simple jobs to do—scraping, plowing, moving rocks, harrowing, rototilling, and so on. These types of rural subdivisions will provide you with fertile grounds for an eventual full-time, well-paying, independent, home business.

$$$$$ �oı_|ı

813 TRADING POST

Many people would rather barter or trade than buy. You can open up a lucrative trading post, which will allow people to barter their goods for your goods. You will always need, of course, to make a significant gain from each transaction in order to build up your business. Solicit all kinds of discarded items, which you display and sell on consignment only. Thus your start-up costs are nil. Keep accurate up-to-date records of consignments and buyers. Collect 25 percent or more commissions on each sale. Encourage browsing.

$ ♿   ᨧ

814 USED BOOK STORE

The secret here is to deal only in books that have an established track record. Learn what will sell and where to get books at bargain prices. Set up trade-in programs, which will easily give a boost to your profits. Start with about $2000, a love for books, and your independence, and then hang up your sign. Stress wholesome reading matter.

$$$ ♿   ᨧ

815 USED CLOTHING

Set up with $1000 and an attractive storefront. Install clothing racks and hangers, full-length mirrors, and small dressing rooms. Solicit garments door-to-door: "Do you have any clothes you would like to sell?" Accept only garments that are in style and in good condition. Offer only one-third of what you expect to sell the garment for. Acquire a great many garments in a few days. Advertise, too, "Cash for Clothing!" Dry clean all garments. Tag them with size and sales price. Many have gotten rich in this business. A 200 percent markup is standard!

$$ ♿ ᳵ

816 WORK CLOTHING

Most towns of any size can use a retail outlet that specializes in work clothing products. Most of these products are built for rugged wear and durability. Many of them are designed to fend off adverse weather, or for safety in industrial applications. You can start small in this business, in your own home if you prefer. A small investment in a basic inventory of special footwear, pants, shirts, uniforms, raincoats, gloves, stockings, and the like, will see you under way with some basic advertising in place.

$$$$ ♿ ᳵ

817 SHIPPING ROOM SUPPLY

Nearly every business has a shipping room. It is here where various items of merchandise are both shipped and received. It can be any size—from just a desk drawer to a vast warehouse. There is a large array of hand tools, stamps, cutting devices, labeling devices, and so on used in these operations. You can set up a business, preferably in a van, in which you stock all items in general use by these shipping and receiving rooms. You will very quickly learn which items are being used. You then simply drive from business to business selling out-of-stock items. You will also introduce and sell improved devices and supplies. You will have the enjoyment of repeat sales.

$$ ♿ ᳵ

818 CATALOG SHOPPING STORE

Many people realize that they can get the quality goods they want at considerable savings by having the patience to shop through a catalog. Catalogs are expensive for businesses to produce and distribute to each household. Knowing this, you can set up a small retail shop, even in a home in or near the downtown area, in which you have available a wide variety of catalogs covering all types of goods. Your business will be like a giant department store compacted into a small space. You will either sell access to your catalogs, or you will contract to receive commissions from the firms represented by your catalogs. You will also take phone orders. You might extend into local deliveries.

$$ ♿

819 CHINA IMPORTS

China is quickly emerging as a front-runner in the arena of economics. The quantity and quality of Chinese manufactured goods is steadily creeping up on Western-made goods. China is importing increasing numbers of products into North America. You may be interested in becoming a middleperson business that imports items you select into the North American home market. You could also select new products to be made in China and then imported by you into the home market. It is possible to set up your business using financing from silent partners.

$$ ♿

820 AUDIO BOOKSTORE

Hundreds upon hundreds of good books have been professionally read onto cassette tapes. They include the great classics, current novels, good nonfiction, and even the favorites of children. These audio books are especially appreciated by the blind. Millions of people who have long commutes every day listen to audio books in order to use their commuting time productively. Audio books can be sold retail or by mail order. They are seldom ever worn out, so it is possible to recycle them as used audio books. An audio book business can sell both used and new books for good profits.

$$$ ♿

821 COMPACT DISCS ONLY

Compact discs are taking over the lion's share of the recorded music market. They have several advantages over other types of recorded music. They provide less background noise and hiss, much quicker accessibility to a given song, and up to an hour or more of listening time. There are already thousands of titles you could stock in a retail business selling them exclusively. You would need to have a retail space for this business, unless your home is right on the edge of the downtown area. You would have to get permission from the authorities to operate this kind of a business from your home, since there would be a great amount of pedestrian and auto traffic around your premises.

$$$$$ ♿ ◪ ▥

822 DISCOUNT FABRICS

With the economy in a stagnant slump, this business could be a winner in your community. Many people are trying to make ends meet by sewing clothing for themselves and other members of their households. They know that their sewing projects can cost more than ready-made clothing items, unless they can get their fabrics at discount prices. There are a number of ways you could obtain these desired discount fabrics at the lowest wholesale prices, so you could resell them in your own retail business. One way is to purchase factory seconds. Another way is to buy inexpensive import fabrics. Under the right conditions, you could do this retailing out of your home.

$$$$ ◪ ▥

823 ENTREPRENEUR KITS

A person who wants to start up a new business has a maze of problems thrown at him or her all at once. Many who have never experienced these entanglements before get frustrated, at the very least. Others simply give up and go back to an 8-to-5 job. If you know the ropes of how to start up a business, you can put together a kit that will make the job of starting up a new business much easier. Your kit will provide all the direction necessary to lead your client to success. It will be a self-guided tour through the maze of obstacles besetting the new entrepreneur.

$ ♿ ▥

824 BEADS RETAIL

Most items of wear go in and out of fashion from year to year. Few items remain in the marketplace for more than a few months. Beads are one of the exceptions. They have been around since well before the early explorers traded them with natives. They add much color to life when added as decoration to dress. They can be used in an infinite number of patterns limited only by the imagination. Beads are as much in fashion today as they have ever been. There are a few home businesses in North

America that deal only in beads. They continue to do steady business year after year. Beads by mail order do well, too.

$$$

825 COMPUTER RECYCLING

Computers seldom break down or need repairing. They are amazingly durable. But technology marches on, leaving today's computer models obsolete tomorrow. These outdated computers can still be put to good use by people who do not need the latest in high-end computer technology. Homeowners and students could do very nicely with one of these older systems. You can run a business in which you simply buy and resell these older computers. It would be best if you could repair the occasional unit, if needed.

$$$

826 MUSICAL CD GREETING CARDS

This is a clever new product. Musical greeting cards can suit any occasion, such as a birthday or marriage. You can buy them already made, and then you can sell racks of them packaged in bubble-packs to any retailer in the greeting card business. You will probably take on the role of a wholesaler distributing these products.

$$$

▌▌▌▌▌SECURITY

828 BURGLAR ALARM SALES

Help reduce crime and make a good living at the same time. On average, a burglary is committed every eight seconds in North America, 24 hours every day. Every burglary victim and his or her neighbors are prime prospects for burglar alarm sales. Fear is a fantastic sales weapon. You will be able to reduce it with your alarm systems. Most people will pay you well if you can give them greater peace of mind.

$$ ♿ ◤ ▐▬▌

829 BUSINESS RECORDS STORAGE

Governments require businesses to keep their business records for periods from 5 to 20 years. Safe, fireproof storage can be very expensive and wasteful of office space. You can open a business in which you rent out storage for these records. You can erect a fireproof building of concrete and steel in which individual storage compartments are rented out to businesses. It will operate much like bank safe deposit boxes, but on a much larger scale. No fire insurance will be necessary. There will be little, if any, upkeep. You will probably need to attend the building during regular business hours to lightly guard it and provide access.

$$$ ♿ ◤ ▐▜▌

830 CAR STORAGE

For the millions of North Americans living in apartments or other confined areas, storage of large vehicles such as trailers, boats, RVs, and autos poses serious problems. Military personnel serving overseas, tourists away from home, and many others have these same problems. If you own a vacant lot of an acre or more, or if you can lease a similar lot for a reasonable price, you can rent storage space in it for these large vehicles. Two hundred rental spaces at five dollars per unit per month will gross $1000 per month which will be more than enough for groceries.

 $$ ♿ ▐▜▌

831 DETECTIVE

Detectives, or licensed investigators as they prefer to be called, earn their living digging up information that is not public knowledge. They are obliquely called "snoops" for good reason. There are two kinds of snoops: (1) those who perform their work in an upright manner; and (2) the shady, underhanded variety. Unfortunately, many of them fall into the second category. But you can make a living as a detective if you build a reputation based on the first model—the honest upright approach.

$ 🚹 🔨 🏙

832 LOCKSMITHING

Locksmiths have a code of ethics unique in any society. They have to hold a position of public trust that must be kept incorruptible. You may be required to do anything with regard to locks—making key duplicates, changing lock tumblers, picking safe locks, opening locked cars, and so on. You should stock and sell various new locking devices as well as install them. You will find this to be a good year-round business that brings in a stable, secure income.

$$$ 🚹 🔨 🏙

833 MINI WAREHOUSE

Who needs a mini warehouse? Cramped apartment dwellers, homeowners who can no longer park their cars in their own crowded garage, professionals with mountains of records they must keep, and salespeople with sample products, excess inventory, and business forms are just a few examples. Charge an average of 20 to 30 cents per square foot. A low vacancy rate is typical. A new approach converts an existing building into a mini warehouse—this cuts costs drastically. Rural locations cut costs even more. Excellent returns of 35 to 40 percent to the investor.

$$$$ 🚹 🏙

834 PEST CONTROL THAT IS SAFE

Pest control is a multibillion-dollar industry in North America. Unfortunately, it utilizes tons of chemicals that are almost all highly poisonous not only to pests but also to people and to the environment in unrecognized ways. This is quite unnecessary as there are now proven ways to eliminate nearly all pests without using poisons. You can start up a bombshell of a business using *nontoxic* controls for pests that are accessible and available with a bit of research on your part. A nontoxic pest control business will quickly displace the toxic sort in your local area once under way.

$$ 🚹 🔨 🏙

835 SECURITY CHECKING BY PHONE

This business will remind you of a teacher taking the class roll call. You set up with just a phone and a small ad announcing that you will contract to make phone security checks on people needing them—the elderly, the bedridden, the disabled, those who are alone, and many others. Sometimes faraway relatives will hire you to keep track of their loved one. Call at the same prearranged time each day. If there is no answer, try again about 10 minutes later. If there is still no answer, contact the police, or perhaps a designated neighbor to check for the person. Try to have a short, friendly talk with each person every day. This will increase and maintain your clientele.

$ ♿ ⚔ 🏙

836 SECURITY ESCORT SERVICE

Keep a file of names of people trained in self-defense whom you can hire to guard your clients—the elderly, women (especially on college campuses), weaker people, and so forth—who step out at night, perhaps only just for a walk. Your dependable guards give your clients the peace of mind they need to live a more or less normal lifestyle.

$ ♿ ⚔ 🏙

837 SECURITY PATROL SERVICE

The police are unable to cope with runaway crime. You can start a private security patrol for home and business protection. Best markets: upper-middle class and more affluent neighborhoods, high-density well-to-do neighborhoods, small specialty shops, factories, colleges, schools. Watch for special events such as conventions. Look for people who want immediate response in a crisis situation and can afford to buy it. This job has top growth potential. Make crime pay for you!

$ ♿ ⚔ 🏙

838 SELF-DEFENSE SCHOOL

Many people want to be able to protect themselves from criminals, especially in cities. They would like to have the peace of mind that comes from knowing that they possess the ability to embarrass a would-be mugger or robber. You can teach these people methods designed to embarrass without inflicting any real injury to the determined criminal.

$$ ⚔ 🏙

839 TERMITE CONTROL

You can get off to a flying start in this business by engaging in a service contract with customers to control their termite and other household pest problems. Your customers will look upon the service contract as an insurance policy because for an annual fee they will have their home inspected every six months for termites, dry rot, and other pest problems. If any of the contractual problems occur, they will be tended to without additional expense. Rural areas are especially in need of this service.

$$ 🔨 🏭

840 COMPUTER SECURITY

Every computer operation can use add-on security, at least at the minimum level. There is always the threat of someone breaking into the premises where the computers are used. This threat can be reduced with a marking system to identify a computer if it is stolen, a warning placard, and a special cable that locks the computer in place. Internal security to protect various programs and files in the computer from prying eyes can be obtained with a variety of programs already available. Then there is security from the threat of viruses, which can destroy valuable work and programs. You can start a business which covers all these and other threats to both individual and business computer systems.

$ ♿ 🏭

841 AUTO SECURITY CONSULTANT

Car theft is a growing problem, especially in the city. Next to the purchase of a home, a car is the biggest purchase you will probably ever make. The majority of stolen vehicles are either never recovered or are recovered in damaged condition. Most owners of cars are interested in protecting their large investment. You can set up a business that provides this protection. There is a vast array of electronic and mechanical devices that can give this protection. You can sell these items along with information on how to better protect an auto. Most people are unaware of the variety of steps they can take to help themselves.

$$ ♿ 🔨 🏭

842 FIRE PROTECTION CONSULTANT

The best fire protection is fire prevention. It is the knowledge and the means of preventing fire in the first place so that it never happens. Perhaps you have a background as a firefighter or something similar. You can start up a business in which you sell information and various fire prevention devices to both individuals and businesses. You will probably give free examinations of a given home or place of business and determine the weaknesses of the premises in terms of fire protection. You would then suggest and sell solutions to any apparent problem you find.

843 SECURITY CONSULTANT

Nearly everybody and everything you can think of needs security. Homes, businesses, vehicles, valuables, pets, individual people whether old or young, property, personal possessions, and even ideas such as inventions need a minimum level of security. You can educate yourself about minimum levels of security for a wide gamut of items and people. You can then sell this information person-to-person or through various brochures or pamphlets to individuals, families, or businesses.

844 NIGHT WATCHPERSON

When people normally go to sleep at night, it is time for disreputable characters from the underworld to get busy. Night watchpeople are trained to keep an eye on things during dark hours. This service can be contracted by your business. You may want to operate as a solitary person. Or you may want to be a coordinator, hiring other help to do the actual watching. Some night watching requires cruising around in a mobile vehicle, while other assignments require foot patrols or just manning a stationary post. The pay will usually be moderate at best, but it is steady employment.

$ ♿ ■ ▌▌▌

845 SECURITY CONTROL GATES AND FENCING

In high-crime areas of North America, more and more people are moving into sequestered housing developments in which the entire development provides perimeter security. Housing developments are now being built with special fencing around the entire project and with special access gates that are activated by remote control from inside selected automobiles. Then there are condominiums and apartment complexes that have special security doors, and the like. A good business can be made installing and maintaining these specialty security devices.

$$$

846 SHOPLIFTING PREVENTION SERVICE

This business is self-explanatory. You would inventory all or most of the devices that have been developed to help curtail shoplifting in retail stores. You would sell these devices to retailers and install them, perhaps using a van. You could double your business by having on-site training sessions for retail staff on how to stop or reduce shoplifting in their particular retail operation.

$$$

847 WINDOW SECURITY SYSTEMS

Most people install respectable locking devices on their doors. But often they fail to install similar sound locking devices on all of their windows. Villains know this and take advantage of it. The majority of breaking and entering is done through poorly secured windows. You can start a home business in which you supply proper locking devices and other security items specifically for windows. In most cases, the buyer will want you to install them as well. Free installation could be your best selling point.

$$

848 CRIME PREVENTION DEVICES

Inventors keep coming up with new products designed to combat rising crime. Not all cities and areas of North America are infested with crime yet, but many are. You can run a solid business built around the inventory and sale of the leading brands and types of products that help private individuals and even businesses protect themselves from crime. You can market these wares door-to-door, or you can sell display racks of your merchandise to key stores in each suburb or smaller town. Check most magazines for ads about these products.

$$$

849 SECURITY ENGRAVING

Breaking and entering crime is soaring out of control. It is very difficult to stop it. One of the best methods of controlling it so far is to have potential victims engrave all their valuables with a special engraving tool. Each valuable is engraved with the name and address of the rightful owner. Warning placards are then posted on windows of the home warning possible thieves of the marked valuables. Police then have a chance to return a stolen item to its proper owner when it turns up in a pawn shop or elsewhere. You can inexpensively set up a small home business in which you simply go door-to-door engraving the valuables of your clients for decent fees.

$$ ◤ ᴹᵀᴵ

▌▐▐▐▐▐▐SEWING

850 CLOTHES REPAIR AND ALTERATION

You can make fairly good wages in this home business. Contact launderers, dry cleaners, clothes shops, and fabric stores and advertise your services. Give them lists of typical repairs and alterations and their respective costs. You can repair rips, take in or let out waists, shorten or lengthen hems, and so on. There is a shortage of skilled people in this trade.

$ ♿ ▀▀▌

851 CROCHETING

Machines are doing more and more sewing and needlework for today's markets. However, crocheting is a delicate skill and art that humans still dominate. You can enhance your livelihood if you specialize in what you choose to crochet. Roses in all colors sell well by mail. Afghans are probably the best sellers, and they command incredible prices. Much work, art, and money goes into each one. Exquisitely crocheted baby clothes will collect top prices as well. Advertise or crochet to order.

$ ♿ ▀▀▌

852 CUFFS

Men's trousers of the finer type are always sold unhemmed. You can contact men's clothing shops and form an agreement in which you hem or cuff all the trousers they sell. Offer 12-hour service. Pick them up near closing time, hem them, and then have them returned near opening time the next morning. You can hem them by blind stitching them on a sewing machine. You can easily do 30 pair a day at $2.50 or more per pair for a comfortable living.

$ ♿ ▀▀▌

853 CURTAINS, CUSTOM

Drapery firms are generally not interested in producing and installing curtains. This seems odd, but nevertheless it is true. Many windows are odd-size and will not accept ready-made curtains. You can develop a good business making curtains to order. You will find very little competition in this personalized business. You must be able to sew and have some interest and ability in interior decorating. Prepare a scrapbook of suggestion pictures to show, as well as sample fabrics. Advertise by flyer, in fabric stores, with interior decorators, and so forth.

$ ♿ �▮

854 CUSTOM PATTERNS

Commercial clothing patterns do not usually fit properly because they are designed for an average body, which few people have. You can develop a money-making custom pattern business in which you design several basic patterns that can be adapted or tailored easily to fit any figure. Stick to three or four basic designs per garment type and keep everything as simple as possible so that all the pattern pieces are interchangeable regardless of the proportions of a given figure. Home sewers will love you. You can expand your sales easily through national advertising.

$ ♿ ▮▮▮▮

855 DRAPERY STUDIO

The demand for drapes is high and constant, not just for homes and apartments, but for offices, restaurants, and other business places as well. A great deal of money can be made in this business. You can work with fabric brought in by the customer, or you can supply both the fabric and the required labor. Installing the finished drapes can bring in extra income. Cut expenses by working from your home.

$$ ▮▮▮▮

856 DRESS MAKING

Because of the high cost of ready-made dresses, plus generally unsatisfactory mass-production results, the current demand for good dressmaking service remains very high. Use modern fabrics, styles, methods, and labor-saving attachments for sewing machines. You will have consistent workload and income in this business. Working independently and at home will give you advantages over any competition. Thread up your needle and fly at it.

$ ♿ ▮▮▮▮

857 EMBROIDERY PAINTING

Beautiful embroidered-looking items can be made without using the old-fashioned needle and thread method. A new method uses tubes of textile paints, which are now available for use on tea towels, pillow cases, aprons, mats, scarves, and so forth. These paints are extremely fast drying and easy to use. Embroidery-painted articles can be washed by hand, and they resist fading. Many colors are available. You can make various embroidery-painted items and sell them at craft fairs, gift stores, and even department stores. The supplies you will need are readily available in craft stores.

$ ♿ 🏭

858 HOSIERY MENDING

You can make good spending money by starting a service in which you repair expensive support hose prescribed by doctors for patients with certain leg problems, such as some overweight people or those with varicose veins. You can easily learn how to mend these items. Your clients will be grateful as they will save money. Inform doctors and physiotherapists of your service and they will refer people needing your services.

$ ♿ 🏭

859 KNITTING

The secret of knitting for a living is to search out the local needs and tastes in an area and then cater to them. It is usually better to make articles to specific custom orders than it is to invest in premade articles and then hope to sell them. Knit unusual pullover sweaters in bright colors and attractive patterns with mittens to match. Knit baby bonnets and booties, sweaters, ponchos, pillow covers, afghans, and scarves. Sell to gift shops and interior decorating studios. You can make a good living if you can click your needles just right.

$ ♿ 🏭

860 NEEDLEPOINT

Needlepoint is a modified form of embroidery. You can easily make extra income with it by working to order. Work colorful tapestry yarns into designs of your choice (or your clients') using canvas or similar fabric as the background. These works of art can then be mounted on the backs and seats of dining room chairs, benches, or stools, or framed and hung, or made into pillows with fabric backing. Many, many other items can be made profitably using needlepoint with a smattering of imagination.

$ ♿ 🏭

861 NEEDLEWORK PICTURES

This business will single you out as being clever! Collect smaller remnants of drapery materials on which are repeated designs or pictures of birds, flowers, scenery, and so on. Then cut out these pictures and designs singly; leave some square-shaped background material attached. Carefully embroider or emboss the animal or design, using extra thicknesses of bulky backing material behind the picture. Frame the finished picture. Handsome profits are in store for you, regardless of where you choose to sell these works of art!

$ ♿   ▛▜

862 SEWING ALTERATIONS

Most clothing is manufactured for the average person. Unfortunately almost nobody is average, so ill-fitting clothing is very common. You can keep yourself steadily employed by becoming a professional dressmaker and alteration specialist for hard-to-fit people. Advertise your services at the local TOPS club, fabric stores, and so on. Collect patterns specially designed in hard-to-fit sizes. Soon your reputation will spread by word of mouth until you have a healthy backlog of work.

$ ♿   ▛▜

863 SEWING ARTISTS' CLOTHING

Most would-be artists would like to do everything just right. You can assist them in your area by sewing at home and selling the traditional garments worn by artists. Aprons will sell, but real smocks will sell even better—give them class with sloppy sleeves elasticized at the wrist, big palette-shaped pockets, and so forth. Set off the smock with a beret to match. These outfits have such unusual appeal that they will soon make you a famous artist!

$ ♿   ▛▜

864 SEWING DANCE COSTUMES

Children taking dance lessons need proper costumes in order to succeed. Ready-made costumes are often too expensive, ill-fitting, and of substandard construction. You can take up the slack in this market by custom tailoring these needed items on a custom-order basis. Visit various dance schools; many of them will happily have you make the costumes for their students as required. You will be able to reuse your patterns repeatedly. You are likely to have no competition in this business. Specialize and you will do well.

$

865 SEWING DOLLS' CLOTHES

Dolls' clothes have become nearly as expensive as real children's clothes. Few people can afford them. You may want to move into this lucrative business because of this fact. Using your own sewing machine at home, make doll clothes (to fit standard dolls) that are not only less expensive but also of superior quality. Sew a big inventory throughout the year and market them at the beginning of the big holiday rush. They will all sell. You may also have advance orders. You will have better pricing because you won't have middle management and will have low overhead.

$

866 SEWING EXCHANGE

Accept all kinds of home-sewn articles for sale on consignment into your home. You display the goods on shelves and tables. Browsers and sellers and buyers stop by and chat with you while they do their thing. You collect 30 percent commissions on all sales. No overhead to speak of— no inventory—very little work once set up. You have put many in the community happily to work. Best of all, everyone involved benefits!

$

867 SEWING FOR BRIDES-TO-BE

You can make an excellent profit while providing a tremendous saving to the couple and their parents. With reasonable experience and ability you can make wedding gowns as well as gowns for bridesmaids, maids of honor, and flower girls. You can easily compete with custom dealers in wedding apparel because you can work in your home, where your overhead is almost nonexistent. Your personal service will be much appreciated. Send letters and brochures to prospective brides. After one or two weddings, word of mouth will keep you quite busy!

$

868 SEWING MACHINE REPAIRS

The recession has made owning a sewing machine a must for many people. To be able to mend clothing and to make new clothing can save hundreds of dollars each year for larger families on tight budgets. You can learn to repair sewing machines easily if you are mechanically inclined. You can set up your own repair business operated from your home. Contact sewing machine retailers, fabric shops, and so on for work referrals. A small continuous ad in a local paper will help build a steady clientele. Consider a sideline of selling new units as well.

$ & ▀▜▛

869 SEWING/MENDING

It would probably be nearly impossible to find a person who doesn't have some clothes that need mending. Many men and women, for one reason or another, do not or cannot mend their own clothes. Traveling salespeople can benefit from this service. Simply advertise to mend clothes—rips, tears, hemlines, edges, and so on. Leave advertising at dry cleaners and laundries. Put a sign in front of your home. This is a good business to run.

$ & ▀▜▛

870 SEWING (MOBILE) ALTERATIONS

By taking the horse to water there is a far better chance that it will drink! Employ this principle by taking your alteration business right to the doorstep of the customers. Equip a van with lighting, ventilation, sewing machine, worktables, shelves for thread, and so forth. Circulate flyers in advance telling customers where your mobile alterations van will be parked and when. Keep to your schedule and route and you will have made a steady job for yourself. Best of all, there is almost no overhead except for upkeep on the van and sewing machine! Almost everything you earn will be net profit!

$$ ▀▜▛

871 SEWING ON EMBLEMS

This may seem on the surface to be an unlikely business to get into, but it can keep you quite profitably occupied. Work in your home attaching felt letters, names, and emblems to sweaters, sport shirts and jackets, and club uniforms. Some will be attached by machine, whereas others will need to be sewn on by hand. Work through the firms retailing the uniforms, sweaters, and so on, giving them a percentage of your earnings in exchange for giving you referrals. Word of mouth will stack up more orders for you as you proceed.

$ ♿

872 SEWING SOUVENIRS

Souvenirs sell best if they are lightweight, easily packed for travel, region specific, and reasonably inexpensive. A good souvenir sewing business that you can operate involves taking a number of different felt and cloth appliqués and sewing them onto towels, mats, and so forth. These appliqués should reflect the landmarks of the region in which you live. Follow the souvenir guidelines above in sewing any souvenirs, and you can be successful. Be prepared to build up your inventory of souvenirs well in advance of the tourist season for your area.

$ ♿

873 SEWING STUFFED TOYS

This home business will go wherever you live in North America. Everyone loves original stuffed toys with facial expressions that are cute, unique, and adorable. You can make them and sell them in an unusual way. You approach another retailer, for example, a pizza restaurant, and have the manager there purchase your stuffed toys. She then issues coupons to her customers with each pizza purchase. When the customer has accumulated a certain amount in sales coupons, he redeems them with the pizza manager for a stuffed toy of his choice. Pizza sales will increase by at least 20 percent and your business will blossom, too.

$ ♿

874 SEWING UNIFORMS

Many bigger businesses require their employees to wear uniforms while at work. It helps convey an image of orderliness and cohesiveness to the public when all the employees are dressed alike. You can capitalize on this with your sewing machine. Contract with proprietors to produce their uniforms. Solicit orders from restaurants, fast food shops, and beauty parlors. You will be essentially using the same pattern over and over, which will make things easier for you. You may have to hire a helper soon to help you with the less demanding stitching.

$ ♿

875 SEWING WORK ITEMS

Using heavy fabrics, like denim, you can establish a business of quality, hand-sewn work items that will give everyone connected with them great satisfaction. You can turn out a line of his-and-hers barbecue and cookout aprons and work aprons for the carpentry shop and the garden, that have big pockets for tools, cooking mitts, and gardening gloves, and with matching knee pads for kneeling. Buy your fabrics off season. Balance style with utility. Be ready to move fast with this business.

$

876 SHIRTS (CUSTOM MADE)

Professional and business men and women, to whom clothes are quite important, will pay high prices for well-fitting, finely tailored dress shirts. Many people cannot purchase shirts that have the right combination of collar size and sleeve length to fit them properly. You can do considerable business making custom-made shirts. Contact professional people in your area, advertising your services. Also contact dry cleaners and tailor shops. You will soon have all the business you can handle and be making a good income at it.

$

877 SLIPCOVERS, CUSTOM

This is a fine home business opportunity. Slipcovers are in constant demand. You can find plenty of customers, for example, motels, hotels, apartment houses, offices, and waiting rooms, that will purchase tailor-made slipcovers from you to protect their furniture. There are dozens of ways to find customers. Word of mouth is always best, so strive for top-quality workmanship. You will find constant demand for your service; this field is almost unlimited. You may quickly reach the point where you will have to turn work away or hire additional help.

$

878 WESTERN CLOTHING

About 60 percent of North Americans wear some form of Western gear on a daily basis, if only jeans. Jeans alone bring in an average of 45 percent gross profit. City people, especially, go for Western gear for added status.

$

879 WOOL WORKS

Wool is a unique product that has never been threatened with replacement by man-made synthetic fibers. Wool is the only fabric that will keep you warm, even if it is soaking wet. The reason for this is that wool is the only fabric that dries from the inside out. You can base an entire retail operation upon products made from 100 percent wool. Virgin wool (wool from the first shearing) products are choice for softness, and they virtually sell themselves. Handmade woolen products can be included for extra sales. Custom-knitted woolen goods can also be a major source of income in this business.

$$

▌▌▌▌‖‖‖SPECIAL SERVICES

880 ACCIDENT INVESTIGATOR

Accidents can happen anywhere to anyone. You can become an accident investigator and claims adjuster through home study. Thousands of businesses have need for accident investigation and adjustment. Many insurance firms cannot afford to maintain full-time investigators everywhere, so you can contract your services to a number of these insurance companies operating in your area. This home business offers you lifetime financial security, your independence, respect from your community, and interesting adventures.

$$$ ◤ ▐▜▌▛

881 ADVICE CONSULTANT

No matter who you are, you probably have certain specialized expertise that you can sell. There are literally hundreds of possible fields. Example: One young man specializes in reducing phone bills and he makes a good living just doing this. Example: A given product consultant becomes intimate with every product's capabilities and performances. He sees them in a variety of environments and applications. Most of all, unlike a salesman, he is not biased. He is able to match a company's needs with the most suitable product on the market. Everyone involved benefits.

$ ♿ ◤ ▐▜▌▛

882 AGENT

Some lawyers charge $200 an hour and more if you hire them to be your agent for even simple projects. If you are bondable and have a trustworthy reputation you can set yourself up in business as an open-ended agent for hire. Advertise yourself as such. Others will hire you at reasonable rates to be their agent for a multitude of reasons. You will be required to substitute for them according to their specific needs, which they will advise you of when they hire you.

$$ ♿ ◤ ▐▜

883 SELF-GUIDING TOURS

All of us need to be guided from time to time. We may be a tourist in a new location and need directions and background information about the area. Or we may need information about the environment and the flora and fauna as we hike along a special nature path. There are numerous possibilities in your area that will lend themselves to self-guiding tours.

First, carefully research your topic, and then either publish in booklets or record on cassette tapes the highlights of your research. The tape or booklet will lead or guide your clients along the tour step by step, providing rich detailed information each step of the way. You will market your tapes or booklets through motels, restaurants, and similar outlets.

884 BLIND SERVICES

You can contract to act as an assistant to blind people by contacting various agencies in your area. Check with social service agencies, societies for the blind, churches, fraternal organizations, schools and colleges, and so on. You may want to specialize in just reading to the blind. Blind students especially require this service. A good reading voice is an asset. You will make many lifetime fast friends and at the same time make a satisfying living.

$

885 BOOKFINDING

Avid readers and book collectors are often frustrated because, with their limited abilities or time, they are unable to find rare or out-of-print books. You can run a successful bookfinding service from your home. If you are an avid reader yourself, you will enjoy trying to help other readers. You will be using your library and various journals of the book trade. To entice clients, advertise nationally in the *Saturday Evening Review of Literature*. This can be a very rewarding business in terms of both new friends and income.

$

886 BOOKKEEPER TO GO

A traveling bookkeeping business will have no problem winning new customers. Your client's records will never have to leave the premises when he or she hires your expert care. You provide your customer with a set of daily record forms on which daily entries are made concerning any and all cash flow. One day each month, as scheduled, drive to your customer's place of business in your van, which is fully equipped inside with all the apparatus a bookkeeper requires. You pick up the customer's records for the month and in a few minutes you have a profit-and-loss statement ready for him, plus your monthly bill. Then you are off to your next customer. And so on.

$

887 BOOKKEEPING

Bookkeeping services do have a high profit potential. Most small firms are not capable or desirous of doing their own bookkeeping, especially in view of the complications imposed by a jungle of tax regulations. Operate at home by mail if you like. You will need a filing cabinet, proper forms, and stationery. Around $300 will see you on your way. Earning $15 to $20 an hour is common. Advertise your services by flyer to prospective clients. Go easy or you could immediately overload yourself with work.

$

888 BOOKS ON WHEELS

With a love for people, books, and the great outdoors, you may be just the person to run this business in your locality. Simply set up and run a bookmobile. Many rural people do not have access to public library books so they will be more than happy to have your rental library service. Renovate an old schoolbus or a trailer with all the shelves you can build into it. Buy boxfuls of books from the Salvation Army, thrift stores, and so on. Sort them well, placing index cards in each for borrowing. Set up a monthly schedule, which you carefully keep as you visit every hamlet and farmhouse for miles around. People will love you and your fine service.

$$$

889 BUILDING MAINTENANCE SERVICE

Contract by the hour or by the month to take care of any maintenance problems a given building might have. Expect to work at a variety of tasks, including plumbing, heating, lighting, painting, floor coverings, window and door problems, lock and key problems, and so on. A jack-of-all-trades ability will serve you well. Several continuing contracts will keep you independent and nicely fed!

$

890 BUSINESS OPPORTUNITIES OPPORTUNITY

Most readers will have seen the classified ads section titled "Business Opportunities." You can make money from this money-maker. Collect several hundred of these Business Opportunity addresses. Then put an ad in the same section of the paper which reads, "Hire me to send your name to over 300 business opportunities addresses" for a specified fee. Clients will send you your fees and you will forward batches of names and addresses to the 300 business opportunities. This saves each of your clients 300 stamps and envelopes for your package service.

$ ♿ 〽️

891 BUYER-SELLER FINDER

If you have a mind that retains factual information like an encyclopedia, this business may be for you. You work two ways: (1) you contract for a fee to find a buyer for a seller of a product, no matter what the product might be, and (2) you contract for a fee to find a seller of a product that your client wishes to find and purchase. A library will help you with the product manufacturer information. Advertise that you will find anything under the sun and then prepare to apply yourself like a leech to a rock!

$ ♿ 〽️

892 CHAIN SAW JOBS

Chain saws are too expensive to purchase unless the owners are able to put them to frequent use. Many homeowners, people with summer cabins, and others need things done with chain saws only on an occasional basis. Many of these same people are unable to operate a chain saw safely. If you are an accomplished chain saw operator, you can hire out to clients to do chain sawing jobs for them by the hour. Advertise in your local paper under the Services column.

$ 〽️

893 CHRISTMAS TREES AND ORNAMENTS

Here is a business without the hassles of a year-round business that only operates two to four months a year and can net an entire year's snug income! The holiday season retail boom offers a fun and lucrative business. Offer trees, decorations, and a setup service where you (and possibly your helpers) hire out to decorate trees and homes for busy people!

$ ♿ 〽️

894 CHAUFFEUR FOR THE ELDERLY

This business will boom in an area where there are lots of retired people. All you need to be is a friendly person and a good driver. Advertise that you will drive elderly people about on business, or for pleasure, and that you will act as their personal escort. If you find it necessary to use your own car, which will happen about half of the time, then charge mileage as well as an hourly rate. You may be besieged with replies from clients anxious to pay you for taking joy rides with them!

895 COLLECTION AGENCY

The total debt load of North Americans is approaching several trillion dollars! Credit cards greatly fuel the situation. Because of this, collection agencies are thriving in small towns as well as in bigger cities. In a nutshell, you get accounts from retailers, professionals, and others who have given up hope of collecting bad debts. Then you follow prescribed methods mixed with ingenious thinking to collect on those debts. You earn a commission of 30 percent to 50 percent on any money you catch up with and collect!

$ 🦽 🔨 📊

896 COLLEGE SCHOLARSHIP SEARCH SERVICE

College attendance costs are becoming more and more prohibitive. Students are reluctant to take out expensive loans for good reasons. Few students know of the various scholarships, grants, bursaries, and so on, that are already available and just waiting for students to apply for. You can run a business in which you track down the various free monies available to a given student. You then sell this information for set fees or commissions. Students will welcome your help and you will welcome your well-earned fees.

$ 🦽 📊

897 COMPUTER CONSULTANT SERVICE

Most businesspeople now realize that their business, big or small, can really begin to hum if a computer is brought on board. You can put your broad knowledge of computers to profitable use by learning how to match the computer needs of clients with the computer products already available. Computer consultation will be a multibillion-dollar industry by 1990. Today is the time to move into this exploding field if you are so trained and inclined. Good computer system designers are currently earning $90 and more an hour.

898 DATING SERVICE–2 APPROACHES

1) By computer: Install and service computers programmed with matchmaking and dating services at a multitude of locations. Higher investment, but excellent profit on large volume.

2) Provide personal service, one-to-one intimate counseling to anyone searching for his/her "soul mate." Very low investment. Women, especially, want to escape the demeaning "meat-market" approach of many singles bars. So you provide a high-quality screening approach. Singles are increasing rapidly, so the future of this job can only grow.

$ &   ☖

899 DAY NURSERY

In this business you contract to provide child-care service in your home for the children of working mothers or single parents. You may need to remodel somewhat to provide a larger combination classroom-indoor playroom. The backyard may need proper fencing to allow for outside play. Garage sales will provide you with sleeping cots, chairs, tables, toys, and playground equipment at low cost. Advertise and accept children from two to six years of age at about $50 to $100 per five-day week. Provide two recesses and a hot lunch at noon. Check out the appropriate licensing requirements in your area before starting up. Check out public liability insurance also.

$$ ◤   ☖

900 DO-IT-YOURSELF WOODSHOP

Many people would fix up their own household items if they just had a workplace and the proper tools with which to fix them. You can turn your garage or basement shop into extra cash by renting it and your tools to do-it-yourselfers, thus allowing them to bring their woodworking repairs and other projects into your shop to complete properly. You charge separately for each tool or workbench used. Add on sales of your assistance, wood finishes, screws, and so on. You will normally be simply standing by, giving expert advice and making good friends.

$$$$ &   ▚

901 ECONOMIZING

Everyone is usually eager to save money. There are thousands of known ways to stretch money and make it last longer. You can easily become an expert in this area by reading books and articles on the subject. Then you can sell your valuable information in one of several ways. Evening adult classes or seminars will bring in good tuitions. Writing a book on saving money should sell well in these hard times. Try showing industry and business where they can save big bucks for even bigger earnings.

$

902 ELDERLY CARETAKING

Most senior citizens do not look forward to spending their last years in lonely, inferior rest homes. Many of them would dearly love to live in a private home where they would feel welcome and secure. If you have a spare room and you have the friendly patience required, you can hire out your service and premises to one or more of the elderly, who will pay a handsome price to become part of your family. A small ad will likely inundate you with prospective clients. Screen them carefully to ease your workload.

$$$

903 ELDERLY DAY CARE

Many elderly people would not have to be placed in rest homes if they could just have part-time day-care attention five days a week from about eight to five. You could run this type of business if you are qualified to do so. You would pick up the clients each day and look after their physical, emotional, social, and mental needs during the day and then return them to their family's home toward late afternoon. You would need to hire helpers who are qualified and sensitive and caring. A registered nurse on staff would likely be required by law.

$$

904 ELDERLY EMPLOYMENT

Millions of elderly people are receiving old-age benefits and pensions of various kinds. But many of them want or need to keep working at least part time. Perhaps their pensions are insufficient or perhaps they want to remain more active. Whatever the reason, you can work full-time as your own boss at home, finding part-time jobs for the elderly seeking them in your locality. You need only advertise continually with a small ad asking for the jobs and the workers. From then on you simply match them up for a reasonable fee.

$$

905 ELECTRICITY ALTERNATE SYSTEMS

Electricity is one of the key ingredients in modern life. We have all become so dependent on it that we would be lost without it. Most people are in a position to consider switching over to a free source of electricity such as solar, or wind generation, or small hydro generation. You can become an expert at designing, selling, and installing these systems to people interested in opting out of the North American grid. Many people will pay well for help in setting up their own independent electrical system.

$$$

906 ELECTROPLATING

You can apply a metallic coating to any object or piece of material by simply immersing the object in a solution of a chosen metal into which a low voltage of electricity is introduced by an electrode. With proper metallic solutions and methods you can cover anything from a butterfly to an engine part. The cost of materials and equipment is very low while your margin of profits will be unusually high. You can operate the whole business in a small room. It is a very simple business from which you can make your entire livelihood.

$$ ♿   ▀▜▐

907 EMPLOYMENT AGENCY

No inventory necessary. No sales tax to collect. No special experience necessary. With a very modest investment this prestigious business can be yours. The average private agency places more than one applicant each day. At a $250 average placement fee, that is about $90,000 gross each year! Good jobs are seldom advertised in a newspaper but are placed with an agency which will screen and interview applicants, thus saving employers time and money. You become the agent for the employer. Everyone benefits in this approach. A small computer would be your right-hand helper!

$ ♿   ◤   ▀▜▐

908 ERRANDS ABOUT TOWN

In every town, businesses need errands run for them. Often the business people are too busy or tied down to run the errand themselves. You can set up an errand-running business with just your present pair of shoes. Contact all the businesses for your service and you will soon be posting letters for clients, getting snacks or lunches for them, making bank deposits for them, and so on. If you can arrange to work in conjunction with a small phone-answering service, you will be able to double your business. Charge for each errand according to the time it will take.

$ 🏃   🏙

909 FAMILY BOOKKEEPING SERVICE

Businesses have always hired someone to do their bookkeeping for them. Individual people and families are beginning to hire bookkeepers to keep their personal and household finances in good up-to-date order. You can easily learn to provide this type of bookkeeping service and make a good living doing it for those willing to pay to have it done. You will arrange all of their financial needs—paying bills, file receipts, reconcile bank accounts and checkbooks, enter expenses in a ledger, and so on. Be mobile so you can work right in their home twice monthly.

$ 🏃

910 FAMILY TREES

Everyone has natural curiosity about the history of his or her ancestors. But few people have the long days and weeks to spend patiently tracking down the record of their ancestry. You can research family names and then sell your findings for a nominal fee to thousands of other people with the same names you have researched. Send postcards announcing your research on a specific name and its cost to people having the same name listed in telephone directories. The response will likely overwhelm you. With a copy machine you can easily keep up with orders for specific family trees.

$ 🏃   🏙

911 FESTIVE DECORATING

Good festive decorations will always get the festive occasion off to a flying start by setting a proper mood. Whether it is to be just a private birthday party or a huge gala convention in a hall, many groups and individuals are too busy nowadays or too inexperienced to arrange the decorations required for the occasion. You can set up a special business in which you cater to clients' needs to have special decorations installed and removed. There is good money to be made in this convenience service. Strive for low overhead. There is almost no competition in this field.

$$

912 FINANCIER

Financiers often help finance small business ventures run by able and ambitious men who lack capital. They do not lend the money; rather, they invest the money as a silent partner, probably not taking part in the operation of the business. If the enterprise succeeds, the financier collects his agreed share of the profits without lifting a finger—and his profits may continue to roll in for a lifetime. If, on the other hand, the business fails, the financier loses his investment. It is legitimate gambling. But think of the men who invested a few dollars in an ambitious young man named Henry Ford!

$$$$$

913 FINDER SERVICE

Nearly everyone alive is looking for something. You can advertise nationally that, for a fee, you will find whatever people are looking for. You will need a retainer fee plus authority to charge long-distance calls to your client. You will need good common sense, much patience, and as much perseverance. Just do the finding of the special things being looked for, and then let your client do the actual buying of the item. This treasure hunting business can become one of the most enjoyable and lucrative in any area anywhere on the continent.

$

914 FLOWER SERVICE

Freshly cut flowers will add a delightful perfume and a certain graciousness to any office or business that serves the public. You can set up a business to supply the flowers they need. First arrange with a flower wholesaler to supply you with freshly cut flowers of the less expensive types (avoid orchids, roses, etc.). Arrange these flowers with a bit of greenery into attractive bouquets and then deliver them to your clients on a weekly basis. Sell to photo shops, small businesses, hair salons, and so on. Keep your prices reasonable, but work toward a 100 percent net profit.

$

915 FOREIGN FINDER

Many wealthy people from places such as Japan, Hong Kong, Germany, Arab countries, and so on, have extra money sloshing around in their portfolios these days. They are looking for good solid investments here in

North America. You can be a purchasing agent for several of these people, helping them to purchase whatever it is they want to invest in. You will make commissions off of each purchase. The commission amounts will need to be negotiated.

$$

916 FUND RAISING

If you have been gifted with a friendly, outgoing personality and have the ability to sell ideas, not products, to people, this business may well be for you. You will be raising funds for all sorts of organizations, both private and public, and you will be paid a good percentage (usually 20 percent) of every dollar you collect in pledges and donations. Be sure you have been hired by an organization that has confirmed integrity; otherwise, your business can suffer badly. Contact all organizations in your area and advise them of your professional services. Present evidence of past successes.

$

917 GIFT WRAPPING

A gift is always extra special if it is wrapped in a pleasing manner. There must be thousands of different ways of wrapping gifts up. You can open up a business in which you simply specialize in wrapping gifts according to the tastes of your customers. A small location in a very busy mall prior to the big holiday seasons would bring in the best returns. Strive for efficiency, low overhead, and reasonable rates, for volume sales. You could operate in your home if you are in a good convenient location for shoppers.

$

918 GUN REPAIR

Customers will gladly travel hundreds of miles to find a good gunsmith. Gun collecting is growing in popularity. If you are into guns, especially gun collecting, you probably already know something about gun repair and antique gun restoration. This is a fine business to get into and it is one which you can easily run from within your own home. Contact gun collectors, sports shops, hunting associations, and even police officers for referral business. Add on instruction in safe handling of guns for extra income.

$$

919   HAIRCUTS AT HOME

Haircutting is a well-paying business, especially if you operate in your home where overhead is minimal. Learn the trade from a school or in an on-the-job training program and then strike out on your own so you will be the one collecting the profits. You can be on call to go cut the hair of hospital or rest home patients for extra income. Advertise good work at better prices and this will keep you in steady income. Hair keeps growing year-round, so your business should never suffer from a recession.

$ ♿   🏙

920   HANDYMAN

Variety is the spice of life, especially if you can find it in your job. This one has variety and a lot more. If you are the handy type that enjoys and is able to fix most anything, you will want to go for this job. Throw your many small tools into your van or pickup and go door-to-door offering to fix anything except broken hearts. You will be a winner—a well-paid winner. Within just a stone's throw of your own home there is a wealth of work waiting for you. No two jobs will ever be alike. Repeat customers will start saving up their repair projects for you.

$ ♿   🏙

921   HOME DELIVERIES

You can contract with several businesses in your area to make home deliveries for them. Contact drug stores, restaurants, quick-food shops, dry cleaners, florists, bakeries, independent food stores, caterers, and so on. Route your deliveries to save time and mileage as much as possible. Be on call with a mobile phone in your delivery vehicle for much added business. Charge by the mile or by the delivery or by the time spent. You can become full time if you have enough businesses using your service.

$$ 🏙

922   HOMEMAKING SERVICE

This business can begin part time for extra income, but it can grow into full time in larger centers. Collect names of people who will hire out to do jobs connected with homemaking—cooking, washing, ironing, cleaning—by advertising for said names. You then run a second ad announcing that you can provide people to perform these services. Your ad might say, "Need quick help? Home work performed on quick notice by reliable people. Phone _____." Charge the workers a percentage of the pay they receive. This plan works. Many use it with good results.

$ ♿

923 HOME SECRETARY

Many small businessmen and women cannot afford full-time or even part-time secretaries. You can make the rounds of all offices and leave your business card, which promotes your willingness to compose, type, and post "spot" letters. You can emphasize that you are as close as a telephone call away. Many people are not good at composing business letters. Small businesses, such as garages, magazine stores, appliance repair stores, corner groceries, and the like, all need this type of service more often than one might think.

$ ♿

924 HOSPITAL HAIR CARE

The morale of a long-term hospital patient simply skyrockets from receiving a simple hair trim and a shampoo and perhaps a simple scalp rub. You can set up and run this business with just a very few dollars. Work through the hospital board and administration. Giving shampoos to a person prone in bed is easy after a bit of practice. With two or more hospitals per week you will have a full-time job on your hands. Relatives of the bedridden will love you for the way it gives a real lift to their loved ones.

$ ♿ ▦

925 HOSPITALITY PLUS

Most people want to fill their leisure time just getting out to see what is going on. You can set up a fine business of showing both visitors and locals what your town and area are really like. You will need a comfortable passenger van, a phone with answering service, a few brochures distributed to hotels and so on, and a chauffeur's license. You can have special tours for special groups. Examples: zoo trips for children, or night-life trips for couples. You will provide doorstep-to-doorstep transportation and information service for your clients.

$$ ♿

926 HOUSEKEEPING

A good housekeeper is worth his/her weight in choice goodies. It is probably the oldest respectable profession and remains so even today. You will find opportunities for housekeeping in any community of any size. More and more dual-career couples will be looking for good housekeepers. You may be able to work for up to five customers per week, which will give you a steady respectable income and still allow you time to do your own housekeeping.

$

927 HOUSE SITTING

Hire out your bonded services as a temporary house caretaker while the owners are away vacationing. For a reasonable fee you live in the home and look after it just as the owners would—mowing the lawn, looking after any pets, watering the lawn and all plants, answering the phone, forwarding mail, and mending clothes, perhaps. Your being fully bonded and of responsible reputation will allow the owners to leave in full confidence and peace of mind. Word will spread fast among wealthy people and your services will be well booked.

$

928 IMPORT/EXPORT BROKER

You don't have to invest one cent in this business. You don't buy anything. You don't manufacture anything. You don't own any trucks or ships. You need no facilities other than an office, which can be in your home. Firms all over the world are losing out, simply because they don't understand the workings of international trade. This is where you come in. You show them how it is done—you make the contacts—you take care of all the details. You arrange shipping, communications, licensing, bonding, banking, and so on. In the end you collect your one percent to five percent of quoted price of goods, which can be a fortune! And your clients love you and pay you because you get rid of their headaches and bring them profits!

$

929 LAUNDRY FOR FINERY

Many garments and household articles cannot be safely sent out to a normal laundry without risking damage to them. You can start up a simple home laundry in which you provide the safe, special care in laundering the items required—sweaters, knitted blouses and skirts and suits, down garments, special draperies, and so on. Even though your prices may be above average, you will be deluged with work when your reputation for careful workmanship and excellent results is established. Little extra equipment will be required from normal laundering facilities.

$$

930 LAWN MOWER SHARPENING

Few people realize that this is a multimillion-dollar industry. There are tens of millions of lawn mowers that all need sharpening at least once a year. Charge $8 to $12 for the service. Because this work is seasonal you can keep yourself busy by going door-to-door and offering 20 percent (or so) off the regular price by having it done in the off-season. Most customers will take advantage of the bargain. Add on lawnmower tune-ups.

$$

931 LECTURER

Organizations and groups are always looking for interesting programs to present to their members. You can become a popular, well-paid, informal speaker for such groups as lodges, PTAs, women's clubs, and the like, if you know how to appear well and speak well in public. Circulate a letter to all the groups in your area explaining your service of giving interesting and informative talks on topics of their choosing. Book reviews on assigned topics could be part of your approach. Groups will pay well if you can help them to be better informed and at the same time entertain them.

$

932 LEFT-HANDED SHOP

Forty-five million North Americans are left-handed. These people all struggle to survive in the world designed for right-handers. There are about two hundred products that are designed for the left-handed. You can stock these items and sell them for 100 percent and more markup. You can sell both by retail and by mail order from your own home. You can run the business completely by yourself. Your biggest problem will be finding suppliers of lefty products. You will have little if any competition.

$$$

933 LIBRARY RENTALS

Rental libraries used to be very common businesses. When cheap paperbacks appeared, these businesses all folded. Paperbacks are no longer cheap, so rental libraries are back, doing good business. Set the library up in another retail business such as a drugstore. The merchant will gladly rent the books out for you, because (1) he gets one-third of the take, (2) he has a potential customer in his store, and (3) he has the same potential customer back in his store when the book is returned!

$$ ♿ ⌂

934 LIMOUSINE SERVICE

People are beginning to use limousine service for special occasions like weddings, proms, and birthday parties. Corporations are using them more and more for business purposes. You can start up a limousine service of your own, inexpensively, by leasing a unit or by buying a good used one. They rent at upwards of $30 per hour. You should strive for the luxury image with excellent, prompt service, a good clean waxed car, special uniform, and so on. Solicit clients with direct mailings of your brochures. If you like fine people, fine cars, and fine driving, this is for you.

$$$ ♿ ◤ ⌂

935 LINGERIE SHOP

Many women are desirous of clothing items that make them feel more feminine—fancy slips, satin knickers, lacy camisoles, and silk stockings. The market for nontraditional lingerie is steadily growing. Add on exercise wear, and the like. This business can be profitably run from the front of a well-located home.

$$$ ♿ ⌂

936 LOADING ZONE SIGNS

Most businesses require loading and unloading zones by their buildings to facilitate the shipping and receiving of merchandise via trucking. Cities issue permits for these zones. The businesses then must paint the signs designating these zones. You can contract to paint these signs, using stencils, and repaint them as required with individual businesses. They are seldom interested or equipped to do the special job themselves. In a larger city you can work full time providing just this one specialty, and at the same time make a good living.

$ ♿ ▙

937 MODELING AGENCY

This business thrives on human vanity. Gather together and keep on handy file the phone numbers and photographs of a great variety of models of all types, of both sexes, and of all ages. When an advertising agency calls you, you supply them with any kind of model that is required. Your model agency may get 20 percent or more of the model's fee. Good money can be made if your business is in a larger city.

$ ♿ ▙

938 MONEY BROKER

Few, if any, businesses offer more prestige, power, and high earning potential than the money brokerage business. Businesspeople, farmers, and homeowners need money for building projects, expansion, and startups. They will gladly pay you large finder fees, from 2 percent to 10 percent, to locate money for them so they can avoid banks and traditional loan sources. For you, start-up costs and overhead expenses are all but nil. Ideal for the ambitious or retirees.

$ ♿ ▙▌

939 MUSIC LESSONS FOR BEGINNERS

Lots of youngsters and even adults would like to play a musical instrument. But for many of these people, their desire is just a fleeting one. If you are a good amateur pianist you can give lessons to beginners only. They can find out how serious they are in the meantime. They can also use this experience in music to branch out into another instrument. You will not charge the rates of the more professional teachers, thus saving your clients money. Your students can easily move up to more advanced teachers if required.

$ ♿ ▙▌

940 NATURAL CHILDBIRTHING

Ninety-nine percent of all humans who ever lived came into this world through natural childbirth without the intervention of modern obstetrical childbirth procedures and gimmicks. The results of natural childbirth are far superior to the common North American approach, which treats childbirth as though it were a disease. Midwifery is frowned on and even repressed by most North American medical dispensers. However, in most areas of the continent, it is slowly gaining justified ground. You can become a paid counselor to those couples seeking help for natural childbearing in many areas of North America. Check your local area for legalities.

$$

941 NEWSCLIPPING AGENT

Many people are looking for news about themselves, or news about their products, and they are willing to pay for it. Subscribe to all newspapers and magazines published in your area and begin reading, clipping, and filing. Contact prospective clients such as politicians, manufacturers, special personalities, leading sports people, and so on. Charge each client a flat fee for maintaining a listing with you and an additional fee for each clipping you send to him. In a year's time you may find you will need to hire an assistant.

$

942 NOTARY PUBLIC

You can supplement your income by performing the services of a notary public. You obtain the seal and license to become one usually upon the recommendation of two resident lawyers in active practice in your area. (This can vary from place to place, so check it out.) You will be administering oaths, witnessing signatures to leases, deeds, bills of sale, and so on, for which you can charge a small fee. Advertise with a sign in the front window of your home. Add on service of typing or retyping documents in conjunction with your notary work for extra income.

$$

943 OFFICE EQUIPMENT RENTALS

This business can be built slowly but surely if you have little money to invest initially. You can start with just one piece of office equipment—let's say it is a secondhand typewriter. Rent the typewriter out for a day, a week, or whatever. With these profits you invest in a second machine. Keep this up until in about two or three years you will have dozens of pieces of office equipment being rented out. Rent out calculators, adding machines, and the like. Nearly all you bring in will be clear profit. Two or three years patiently invested in this manner will give you a full-time salary eventually.

$$$$ ♿ 🏙

944 PACKAGE WRAPPING SERVICE

Lots of people are either unable or unwilling to wrap their own packages for gift-giving or for shipping away. There is a steady demand for this service in any center of any size. You can provide this service in your own home. A few supplies—scissors, tapes, twines, labels, various papers, ribbons—are necessary. Advertise your location and existence and people will return for help again and again.

$ ♿ 🏙

945 PAPER RECYCLER

Next time you see a scruffy-looking character rummaging through trash bins for old newspapers and cardboard boxes, don't feel sorry for him. Chances are, he drives a better car than yours and lives in a nicer subdivision. Chances are he is making a fortune off what others are throwing away. He gathers wastepaper and cardboard and sells it by the ton to recycling plants—used newsprint at about $50 per ton, cardboard at $75 per ton, and high-grade office paper at $110 per ton! The money is there. Just get an old pickup, line up your contracts and customers, and begin your collection route. Newsprint for greenprint!

$ ♿ 🏙

946 PICTURE FRAMING SHOP, DO-IT-YOURSELF

North Americans are on an art-buying binge unrivaled in recent history. Custom framing shops abound, but they are expensive. A do-it-yourself framing shop is set up so your customers can make their own frames and save 40 percent and more. They select from different molding patterns and matte colors and put their own frames together for the fun of it. Most parts of the continent are wide open and the demand vastly exceeds the supply of available shops. If you have been living in a cold-water flat, get ready to move up with this one!

$$$ ♿ 🏙

947 PLASTICS RECYCLING

Since plastics are made from petrochemicals (oil), it is obvious that as oil becomes more scarce and thus more expensive, more and still more attention will be given to the recovery of waste plastic. Already the average plastics recycler collects thousands of pounds of scrap plastics a month, and then sells them at prices from 15 to 35 cents a pound to reprocessors or manufacturers netting hefty profits. The potential for visionary marketers who get into this business now has got to be phenomenal!

$ ♿ 🏙

948 PR SUGGESTIONS SALES

This business operates on the "Suggestion Box" principle. Every business needs to have good public relations in order to succeed. Business leaders spend sizable portions of their budgets annually to build better public relations. You can become an expert in identifying areas in which any given business falls short in maintaining good public relations. You can make a list of areas of needed improvements together with a list of suggested solutions and sell these lists to various businesses, companies, factories, corporations, and so on. Do well with the first submission for repeat sales in the future.

$ ♿ 🏙

949 RAGS TO RICHES

Thrift stores, the Salvation Army, and other businesses receive tons of discarded clothing every year. Much of it is unfit for further use and ends up in the dump. You can usually have it free for just hauling it away. Cut up this clothing into wipe rags, launder them, and dry them at home, bale them and sell them on a route that includes janitor supply shops, garages, machine shops, printing shops, and so on. You may soon need more laundry equipment as your business grows.

$ ♿ 🏙

950 RED TAPE CUTTING SERVICE

Is there a person alive who isn't sick of the piles of bureaucratic red tape? You can quickly master a fine-paying business based on this predicament. Set up a tiny office, perhaps in your own home, with a phone. You then proceed to obtain clients who pay you for coping with the red tape problem they have. Work by flat fee or by the hour. Jobs you will be doing for clients will involve birth certificates, permits of all sorts, various licenses, passports, registrations, special sensitive information, and whatever red tape problems are entrusted to you.

$ [♿]   [▲]

951 REMAIL SERVICE

Some people do well at remail service as an extra-income business. Advertise your remail service at the regional or national level. For a multitude of reasons, people will pay you to remail their letters for them so they will be postmarked from your city or town. They sometimes want it done as a joke to their friends. Sometimes they have it done because they don't want their whereabouts known. Sometimes they are on vacation and need help. It is an old business that can work for you. Copy the wording of other ads for your ad. Start up with $100 or less.

$ [♿]

952 REMINDER SERVICE

Most people have a forgettery which is much better than their memory. Busy people especially fall prey to this ailment. You can set up a reminder service. Contact everyone in the phone book and individuals will subscribe to your service. They supply you with all pertinent data—family names, addresses, phone numbers, things and dates to be reminded of, etc. Keep an excellent file (perhaps on your personal computer) which will remind you to remind your clients as the year progresses of the special things they want to remember. Charge an initial subscription fee, plus $1 for each phone call made during the year. Bill the client each quarter.

$ [♿]

953 ROOMMATE FINDER

With the cost of rents rising far faster than wages, the new trend of "doubling up," of joining with a roommate to cut the rent in half, is catching on very fast. With a small computer and a phone answering service you can begin this business right away in your own home. Make up and then use simple "seeker" and "finder" agreement forms. Expect much of your business from college students just before school begins in the fall. Elderly persons on fixed pensions will also welcome this valuable service.

$ [♿]   [▲]

954 SCRAP METAL

Almost all metal eventually becomes scrap metal. With an older truck you can begin a thriving scrap metal business. Size up the markets where you can sell it and for what prices. Acquaint yourself with the various common metals—zinc, iron, steel, cast aluminum, lead, bronze, copper, and so on, so you can identify them instantly. Canvass your area and collect as you go. Often you will get tons of it free just for removing it. A hydraulic hoist will often be necessary for loading and unloading.

$ ▰▰▰

955 SEMINAR PROMOTER

People will pay you handsomely to learn how to do something easier, better, cheaper, faster, more efficiently, or more profitably. Arrange top-name speakers on any conceivable subject, as people delight in getting their info "straight from the horse's mouth"; offer the chance to ask questions afterwards. Add on sales of cassette tapes and typed transcripts to people who can't attend the session. It is not uncommon for seminars to net $50,000 for a three-day series!

$$$ ◣ ▰

956 SHOPPING SERVICE

Many people are just too busy to shop for themselves. You can begin a shoppers' service business on just a shoestring budget from your home. You will be buying lists of groceries for people who are working full time, or gifts for businesspeople to give to others, special items for housebound elderly, and others. You may be hired to buy special deli foods for a special dinner. Just keep careful records, study where the bargains are, know your clients' needs, be congenial, and charge from $12 to $15 per hour for your time and mileage.

$ ♿ ▰

957 SHOPPERS' TRANSIT

In this business, you provide all the services you would expect from a taxicab plus a lot more. Pick up your clients at their homes and drive them to the various places they wish to go shopping. You will help the client with any additional help required—perhaps he needs someone to wheel him around in a wheelchair, or perhaps she needs special errands run, or perhaps he needs someone to carry bundles and packages for him, and so on. Then you take him or her safely back home. Your constant ready services and attention to detail will give you business that taxis will never touch.

$$

958 SMALL BUSINESS CONSULTING

Sit at home and do this business! You can give advice to amateur small businesspeople by mail. You, perhaps a former businessperson now retired, can contract to pass along some of your knowledge and experience to other small businesspeople who need it. You can dispense both general and specific information, except legal advice. Don't use form letters at all. Work for a personal touch. Charge a flat fee for a package of services available. Guarantee satisfaction or money back. You may find this undertaking both pleasant and profitable.

$ ♿ ■

959 SNOW REMOVAL

The weather is always fickle, so this business is at the mercy of the weather. You can get into this business for the price of a snow shovel, which you can use on roof shoveling or walkways. Or you may want to invest about $1000 in a snow blower to use on walkways, driveways, and medium-size jobs. Or you may want to invest about $2000 in a hydraulic snow blade for the front end of your 4WD pickup to plow driveways and parking lots. If the snow comes heavy and fast, you can make big money surprisingly fast.

$ ♿ ■

960 SWAP MEET—FLEA MARKET PROMOTER

Swap meets and flea markets are gatherings of small-time merchants and amateur sellers—and today they are big business! As the organizer you provide a parking lot or other space and begin reaping goodly profits from stall rentals and gate entrance fees. Sellers pay from $4 to $20 for a stall or table from which they can display their wares. Add on food and snack shop sales and you can tally up gross profits of 80 to 85 percent! This new craze can only grow.

$ ♿ ■ ■

961 TAPED WEDDINGS

Many couples treasure a tape recording of their marriage vows for years to come. You can capture the entire wedding and reception on cassette tape and sell copies of it to the couple and their families and guests. Carefully place microphones where the action is—where the marriage vows are spoken, at the head reception table, at the punch bowl, and so on. Capture the serious as well as the lighter moments of the occasion. Watch for notices of marriage licenses in your newspaper for prospective clients. Your best advertising will be when word spreads quickly from one happy customer to the next.

$$ ♿ ▥

962 TAX AXE SERVICE

Selling loopholes is a big money-making business, especially when those loopholes are legal means of avoiding paying excessive taxes. Governments are slow to advise citizens of these legal loopholes, so you can sell this timely information before it is too late for taxpayers, and thereby you can share in the monies saved by your clients. Bone up carefully on the entire tax system so you will have the intricate info readily available for sale without delay. Stress accuracy and observance of legalities for repeat business year after year.

$ ♿ 🔨 ▥▥

963 TEMPORARY-HELP AGENCY

Recruit large numbers of qualified workers who are willing to work part-time. Keep them on standby. An employer contacts you when he or she needs temporary and qualified help right now. It is a question of time. It is cheaper to pay more for a fill-in than to lose production. If the going rate for a given worker is $10 an hour, and a company desperately needs one for a day or a week, it gladly pays much more than $10 an hour. The difference is your temporary-help agency's take. Emphasize top-caliber people, professionalism, and specialization, and all parties will profit well.

$ ♿ 🔨 ▥

964 TOOL AND EQUIPMENT RENTALS

You will cater to contractors, gardeners, do-it-yourself carpenters and masons, and so on. You will be able to capitalize on homeowners who are trying to avoid the high cost of outside labor. Add-ons of chainsaw sales, crane service, and the like are possible. Inventory costs are high, so a silent partner is a possibility to consider.

$$$$$ ▥

965 VIDEOTAPING SERVICE

People are just beginning to realize the astounding possibilities of using videotape for permanent record keeping. You can start up your own very lucrative business easily for under $800. Here are some things you may consider taping for money: weddings, social gatherings, speakers, sporting events, individual efforts, how-to-do-things tapes, legal testimony, wills, sales demonstrations, mechanical operations, assembly techniques, real estate listings, construction projects, selling animals, surgical operations, management "fireside chats," household inventories, art collections, fire scenes, accident footage, and so on. Be totally mobile and on call from your home.

$ ♿ ▞▙

966 WEDDING STORE

Set up as a "one-stop" shopping center for weddings. Offer photography service, consultation service, trousseau and bridal dresses, reception arrangements, showers, mailing of invitations, selection of music, planning the ceremony, arranging for the honeymoon, limousine service, tuxedo, and so on. The average wedding costs $3000 to $6000 and your part could net you an average of $1500! Ring those bells!

$$$$ ▙

967 WINDOW CLEANER

This job is for real. Invest $25 in initial supplies. Use vinegar in your wash water for a nonstreak finish. Have your paper carriers distribute ad circulars to all homes and businesses in your area. Book by phone. Charge about $20 an hour. Keep using circulars to expand. This is a service business nearly everyone can use. You will grow best if you get repeat business from well-satisfied customers.

$ ♿ ◤ ▙

968 WORK SCOUT

In this business, you become a spy or an intelligence operative. You go about your town looking for jobs that need doing—houses that need painting or siding or reroofing, cars that need dents removed and paint touched up, fences that need mending, and so on. Then contact the appropriate businesses specializing in a given type of repair and sell them your list of people needing their type of services. They then have a list of strong prospects they can contact for possible further business.

969 YARD SALE

Many items are just too big and heavy to be handled by secondhand stores or normal yard sales—boats, appliances, wheelbarrows, cement mixers, plumbing fixtures, playground equipment, and so on. You can set up a year-round business in which you specialize in these larger-type items, storing them outdoors under the sky or in open front sheds. Accept the items on consignment so you won't have to invest in anything but a sign and some fencing for security. You will get your income from commissions on each sale. A neat, well-managed business of this type can be very profitable.

970 LASER AND IMPACT PRINTER SERVICE

Wherever you find a computer, you are very likely to find either a laser printer or an impact printer. Millions of impact printers are in operation across North America. Gradually, as prices come down, impact printers are being replaced with laser models, which print much better copy. Most owners of these machines are incapable of fixing them when they malfunction. A nice home business can be set up in which you train yourself to sell and maintain both of these widely used machines. A preventive maintenance program could be included in your services along with sales of toner cartridges and printer papers.

$$ ▞

971 PROPERTY TAX REDUCTION CONSULTANT

Governments at all levels, from the local to the federal, are hard-pressed for revenues to stay afloat. As a result, nearly all taxes everywhere in North America are increasing, many ballistically. These tax grabs are causing many taxpayers to consider tax revolt. If you have the requisite training in the field of property taxes for your locality, you might well consider going into business as an expert who can clearly and legally show clients how to reduce their present property taxes to the minimum. Most taxpayers are unaware of most tax loopholes. You can sell your knowledge of these loopholes to your over-taxed clients. It appears that the market for this valuable service will be bright for years to come.

$ ▞▜

972 PRIVATE POSTAL MAILBOX CENTER

In much of North America it is possible to go into competition with the federal postal service. It is usually less costly to the consumer when public services are privatized. Private contractors have a vested interest in finding unique ways to cut costs without stinting on service. It may be possible where you live to set up your own private postal mailbox center. You will first obtain a block of postal mailboxes from a manufacturer, which you will then install in a building of your choice. You will then rent out these boxes to individuals and businesses for rental fees which are competitive with the public postal service. You can make your service more attractive than the competition by giving special fee reductions, special hours of opening, and other draws.

$$$$$ 🔨 🏭

973 CERTIFIED UTILITY BILL AUDITOR

Most people are on the go these days. They are usually too busy to carefully check their own utility bills for accuracy. This is true of both individuals and businesses. These bills include gas bills, fuel bills, rental bills, phone bills, electricity bills, water bills, cable bills, and others. You can familiarize yourself with the standard billing costs and procedures for all the utilities in your locality. You can then sell this knowledge to clients who are too busy or lack the knowledge to check their own utility bills. You can set up a route of clients whose bills you check each month. You will need a good calculator, a phone, and not much else.

$ ♿ 🔨 🏭

974 FRANCHISING CONSULTANT

Franchises are businesses that have already been more-or-less perfected by someone else. For the right price, you can purchase one all ready to go. There are all kinds of franchises available. Some of them are quite good, while some of them border on being scams. The average person is unable to determine if a given franchise is genuinely a quality business. It takes special expertise to sort them out and to detect weaknesses in franchises that are otherwise reputable and lucrative. If you have a paralegal or legal background and a background in franchising, you may qualify as a franchising consultant. Check your local authorities to see if you qualify for this profitable business.

$$ ♿ 🔨 🏭

975 ENTREPRENEURIAL CONSULTANT

Over one million new businesses will be started this year alone. Most of these new businesspeople will need considerable advice in setting up their new businesses. Many items are available to teach them how. If you have a background as an entrepreneur, you may qualify as a consultant in this rapidly growing field. Extend your expertise by reading everything you can in the field. Consider giving night classes on the subject. You can also sell items, such as this book, that would assist any would-be entrepreneurs.

$

976 SMALL BUSINESS BUSINESS

This business is truly a business business. You will set up to provide any and all the items a small business might conceivably require. This will include business cards, flyers, business forms, business bookkeeping records and journals, rubber stamps, stationery supplies, small business aids such as books, copying services, computer software programs designed for small businesses, and many similar items. You might set up a small printer to print some of the items you'll supply, such as business forms and business cards.

$$$

977 WEEDEATER SERVICE

Weeds will always be with us. They grow nearly everywhere. They can be a nuisance for many homeowners and businesses. They can even pose a real fire hazard in the dry summertime. The easiest way to control them is with a weedeater machine, which can be either electric or gas powered. Use the electric model if noise would be a problem and if electricity is readily available. Most people don't like operating weedeaters because of the noise. Get an industrial grade machine, send out your flyers, and sign up by contract with the exact work required spelled out on the contract.

$

978 POLL-TAKING SERVICE

Polls can be very useful tools. They can indicate what the majority of people think should be done about a given problem, or what their opinions are on a given public issue. You can learn how to take polls so that they cover a good cross-section of the population involved in a particular problem or issue. You can take most polls by phone, and then sell your results to newspapers, to various governing bodies such as city councils, or to groups of concerned citizens. They can be used by the citizenry to fight various governmental bureaucracies that are on the prowl for tax revenue. They can be used to fight oppressive rezoning policies, and so on. A good poll at the right time can be worth a great deal.

$ ♿ ▙▐▌

979 ARBITRATION, MEDIATION, AND NEGOTIATION

Arguments, disagreements, quarrels, bickering, spats, disputes, and verbal wars. These are common in our society today and they seem to be increasing in intensity as the economy worsens. If you have a special talent as a peacemaker and a general background in psychology or an understanding of what makes people tick, and if you have a gift for pouring oil on troubled waters, then perhaps this business is for you. Troubled homes and marriages will be a major opportunity for you, but wherever there is confrontation in society you will find potential clients for your most valuable services.

$ ♿ ▙▐▌

980 MERCHANDISE DEMONSTRATION SERVICE

You have probably seen someone already in this business. Perhaps it was someone giving away free crackers or cheese samples in your local supermarket. He or she was paid for giving away these free samples because they were samples of a new product that was being introduced for the first time. Or it was a product being promoted more aggressively to get the edge over the competition. You can contract to do this same kind of service. Your start-up costs will be very minimal. In most cases you will simply have to dress appropriately for the job. All the materials or supplies you will be demonstrating will be supplied free to you. A real shoestring operation!

$ ♿ ◣ ▙▐▌

981 FORWARDING AGENT

We live in a very mobile society. Many people are constantly on the move, with no fixed address. They have difficulty receiving their mail or receiving freight deliveries required for business operation. As a forwarding agent, you will be hired by these various individuals and businesses to provide a fixed address to which mail and other deliveries will be sent. You will either temporarily store these items securely or forward them to a temporary address for your clients. You can make your service known with flyers and with an entry advertising your business in your local phone book's yellow pages.

$ ▞▌▐

982 HAZARDOUS WASTE DISPOSAL

Industry has produced some sophisticated chemicals and other goods that are a very real threat to human health and life. They may be deadly insecticides, special paints, radioactive products, or waste by-products from some industrial process. There are special procedures that must be followed in the safe transportation, storage, and disposal of these various threatening agents. A thorough knowledge of how to handle these materials is required for this business. You will contract either with industry or government, or both, to properly deal with these goods. Toxic-site cleanup could become a big part of your business.

$$ ◣ ▞▌▐

983 IMMIGRATION CONSULTANT

New immigrants are arriving by the hundreds every day here in North America. Even before arrival, most of them have to deal with immigrant authorities. These exchanges with the authorities can be protracted for many months, in some cases. There is often much confusion in the process. Language difficulties and reels of red tape are common problems. You can educate yourself on how to make the process more hassle free for both parties concerned. With this information, you can start a business as an immigration consultant and act as a go-between.

$ ♿ ◣ ▞▌▐

984 MISSING PERSONS SERVICE

Few things are more frightening to most people than to have a loved one turn up missing. This is particularly true if the loved one is a small child. Most missing persons turn up within a few hours, but this is not always the case. You can build a business around helping clients to find their missing loved ones. You will circulate posters widely, and you will be working with police departments, human resource departments, and similar agencies. You will have to have a telephone which is accessible at all hours of the day. You will employ techniques used by trained detectives. This can be a highly rewarding business in terms of both income and personal satisfaction from helping others.

$ ♿ ◣ ▞▌▐

985 ODOR CONTROL SERVICE

No one likes trying to cope with stubborn, obnoxious odors. These can be caused from cigarette and cigar smoke, spilled liquids, pet urine or worse, vomit, air pollution, fires, grease, exhaust fumes, and the list goes on. You can arm yourself with the know-how of dealing with these odors. You can then advertise your service of controlling or eliminating odor problems. You will be working in homes, in automobiles, in restaurants, in smoke-damaged buildings, and in various other places.

$ ▉▊▐

986 HOMEBOUND RESPONSE

It is difficult to keep tabs on a handicapped or elderly person around the clock, especially if you are holding down a full-time job as well. But there is a way to do it effectively. In fact, you can make a good living keeping track of such people. You must have a computer and a phone. You make contact with the busy people who are responsible for such homebound people. You contract to keep tabs on a given handicapped or elderly person for a certain fee per month. You maintain contact by phone with the person you are looking after, and keep careful records of each call. You may be required to remind the person in your care to take certain medicines on time, or you may check to make sure the person has safely returned after a walk around the block. Each client will require an individualized schedule for these phone checkups.

$$ ♿ ⬧ ▉▊▐

987 LASER PRODUCT CONSULTANT

The invention of the laser is a landmark in civilization. Every day new uses for it are discovered. Lasers are already used in laser copiers, in compact disc machines, in dentistry, in carpentry levels, and in a host of other ways. Few people are trained to maintain and repair this type of equipment. Few people understand how laser equipment can make many jobs easier to perform. You can educate yourself about laser technology and the equipment now available. You can go into business selling, installing, and maintaining this special type of apparatus.

$ ♿ ▉▊▐

988 PROFESSIONAL BILLING SERVICE

Here is a business you can do right from your kitchen table if necessary. Doctors can cut their overhead expenses considerably if they hire someone working at home to process all their medical claims forms. You can learn how to process these forms, and then hire yourself out to perform the required work. If you can work for more than one doctor, you may find yourself working full time, if that is your desire. It is a good business for a single parent who has to keep an eye on younger children still at home. Handicapped people can also do well in this business.

$

989 OPERATING A 900 NUMBER

Numbers of individuals and small companies make their entire living by operating one or more 900 numbers. In this business you will use the phone number to sell information or products to customers who call the number. You will make money off of each call, and the phone company will make money as well. With the right mix of information and products, it is possible to make a handsome living in this business. Contact your local phone company for details.

$$

990 PACKING, UNPACKING, AND SHIPPING SERVICE

Many businesses don't have a proper shipping and receiving department. Private homes aren't much better off. If you understand how to properly pack and ship just about any type of item, this could be a good home business to get into. It doesn't take long to learn the business, and it doesn't take much in the way of start-up costs to get under way. You can do the packing and shipping right in your home. Or you can do it in the back of a mobile van, right in the home of your client. You can also provide unpacking service for those businesses and household movers requiring it.

$

991 SENIOR CARE

There is a large class of seniors who need only minimal care. Most of these people are in reasonable health, but they do need to be watched so that they won't wander off or do something wrong, perhaps because of forgetfulness. Many younger people can't work outside the home because they are tied down watching the seniors individually. It is possible to contract to look after several of these seniors at the same time in your own home during the day. You would be required to look after the individual needs of each senior during this period each day. Usually you could arrange your schedule so that your weekends would be free.

$$

992 WEDDING PLANNING SERVICE

Planning weddings is seldom accomplished with solemnity and style. It is too often a very hectic experience which wearies everyone involved to the bone. The bride is often too exhausted from the ordeal to enjoy her honeymoon. Knowing this, and having an expertise that allows you to take calm control of wedding plans, you can go into business and offer a full service in which you plan weddings for paying clients. You run the command post. You look after any and all details. Your clients just sit back, sigh, relax, and pay your fairly earned bills.

$ ♿ 🎹

993 LOANS CONSULTANT

Many people requiring loans will accept the first loan made available to them. This seems strange because, depending on the size of the loan, big bucks can often be saved by simply shopping around for a loan. If you have a strong background in the loans industry, you can put this valuable knowledge to work for yourself. You can educate yourself about all the possible loan programs available in your locality, as well as any loans which can be accessed over a greater distance. You can then sell your knowledge to prospective loans clients, showing them the very best loan deal available for their particular needs. You will maintain loyalty exclusively to your client in his or her pursuit of the best loan possible.

$ ♿ 🔨 🎹

994 COST CONTROL CONSULTANT

Larger projects, such as building a home or a commercial building, need careful cost control accounting, even while the project is in progress. If you have a background in cost analysis and accounting, and if you have some managerial experience and understand how projects flow together, then you may be qualified to be a consultant in this business. You will probably be able to work right from your own home. The start-up costs are negligible.

$ ♿ 🎹

995 FREIGHT AUDIT

In many businesses, shipping and receiving is taking place at such a hectic rate that auditing the freight billings is overlooked. Mistakes happen at the best of times and with the best of intentions. Where lots of shipping and receiving occurs, the costs caused by mistakes can really add up to sizable sums. If you understand how to audit freight records, you can build a business in which you do the actual auditing. You could contract to do this service with several larger firms in order to keep yourself busy full time.

$

996 PERSONAL MOTIVATION

Procrastination is one form of suicide. Many people waste much if not most of their lives just spinning their wheels and doing nothing. Other people go on lecture circuits, talking to groups of people and simply motivating them to get up and go, and to get things done. These people are motivational experts who know how to overcome procrastination, and they make a good living motivating others to become doers like themselves. You can move into this same kind of business if you are filled with a zest for life and you enjoy encouraging others to move upward and forward.

$ ♿

997 SURFACE RENEWAL

Surfaces under constant wear and tear become degraded. They can use occasional renewal of one form or another. These are the surfaces of items in your home such as doors, cabinets, countertops, appliances, bathtubs, and the like. You can learn how to give a face-lift to these various household items. Then you can run a business in which you go door-to-door selling your money-saving services.

$$

▌▌▌▌▌▌▌TELEPHONE

998 AFTER-HOURS PHONE ORDERS

People are often offended by automatic phone answering services. Most people prefer to deal with a real live human being on the other end of the line. You can open up a personal phone answering service for various businesses, such as department stores, drug stores, and so on, in which you personally take orders for customers after store hours—in the evenings, on Sundays, holidays, and so on. Your number is then listed in the phone book under each business hiring you, with instructions to place after-store hours orders with you. You get paid monthly. A handicapped person could run this business quite successfully.

$ ♿ ▐▜▐▌▐

999 ANSWERING SERVICE (GENERAL)

A handicapped person can be entirely self-supporting by running his or her own telephone answering service. You help out people—such as plumbers, painters, small contractors, small businesspeople, electricians, and so on—who have little or no office staff for answering their own phones. Start about 6:00 A.M. and close down about 6:00 P.M. You can provide alarm clock service as well, as required. Also, you can check in on people by phone, such as special elderly persons. A cheerful, patient and efficient manner will attract a good-paying clientele.

$ ♿ ▐▜▐▌▐

1000 APPOINTMENT SALES BY PHONE

In this business you will sell appointments. Nothing else, just appointments. You first contact firms that employ salespeople. Then you contact the salespeople one-by-one and offer to set up appointments for them by phone. This type of advance screening will be well worth the price per call that they will pay for having you do it. All you will do is to sell the prospective customer on the idea of talking with the salesman, to see if they will be interested enough to give him a bit of their time for an interview. Find out-of-town salesmen also, who are probably looking for someone to set up appointments for them.

$ ♿ ▐▜▐▌▐

1001 BABYSITTER SERVICE

Most parents have had problems finding capable babysitters. You can ease this strain by setting up a business in your locality that provides well-trained babysitters that are bonded! Recruit a number of responsible teens and older people you have personally interviewed. Require them to attend a formal babysitting class in which they master the art and science of babysitting. Bond each graduate and require a health certificate for each one. Advertise your employees as being well-trained and having bonding. You make 20 percent of each transaction. Parents will be happy to pay more than average rates to have the comfort of knowing their children are in the best of care.

$ ♿ ✈ ⛲

1002 BIRD DOG PHONING

Businesses use "bird dogs" to find qualified prospects in the field for salespeople who then follow up the lead to close the deal. It is almost all done by phone. The bird dog may call "cold turkey," which means picking names randomly in the phone book and trying to create interest in a product. Usually the bird dog has a list of names of people to work from, people who have already shown tentative interest. You, the bird dog, set up appointments with prospects for salespeople. You receive commissions on any sales made by the salesperson. Your advantage to the salesperson is in saving him or her from the time-consuming job of making preliminary calls.

$ ♿

1003 BOOSTING SALES BY PHONE

Something for nothing will always bring customers into the store. You use a phone only in this business. You make a contract with, let's say, a dry cleaner manager. You will then methodically phone everyone in the phone book and tell them they can get three garments cleaned and pressed for the price of two. The dry cleaner manager pays you a commission on each sales response. You call one-twelfth of the phone book each month, so you and the dry cleaner can spread out workloads. Next year, you do the same thing, except you change to a different dry cleaner! Work ten different types of businesses simultaneously for really big earnings!

$ ♿ ⛲

1004 CAR SALES BY PHONE

If you have a gift of gab and know the basics of selling, this business may be a natural for you. Contract with your favorite car dealer to sell more cars for him or her by simply using your phone at home. The dealer supplies you with lists of names of people who own cars that are two or more years old. You phone these people at your convenience and in a friendly, tactful manner, sound them out on a new car. You get paid for each phone call plus a healthy commission for each of your contacts resulting in a car sale.

$ ♿ ⚒ 🏙

1005 CATALOG ORDERS

You can get paid well for simply taking catalog orders in your own home. You can contract to work for certain companies who issue catalogs listing hundreds of specialty and novelty products in your area. Simply take catalog orders by phone for these companies in your area and pass the orders onto the companies. These companies then drop-ship their products directly to the customers. You receive commissions on each and every sale you handle. An excellent home business opportunity.

$$ ♿ 🏙

1006 DOCTOR'S PHONE SERVICE

Most doctors are on 24-hour call. Finding them in a hurry can often require a series of harried phone calls. You can set up a central phone answering service, to be used only by doctors, that operates 24 hours a day. Doctors update you constantly of their whereabouts so just one phone call to you will locate a given doctor in a jiffy. Twenty doctors subscribing to your service can give you a fine living and it can even save lives as well as give the doctor's family members more peace and privacy.

$ ♿ 🏙

1007 GOODS PROMOTION BY PHONE

With an interest in good merchandising you can make lucrative headway by using your phone. First you contract with a given business to pay you by the hour to simply call people listed in the phone book and advise them of specials and bargains available at the store you are calling for.

You can do this for any business offering any specials for sale. Contact department stores, furniture stores, appliance stores, and so on. Many will become repeat customers for you. Try to work with the big-ticket items whenever possible. Your client will supply you with all the sales info and details necessary to represent them well.

1008 MARKET SURVEYING BY PHONE

Businesses need feedback from the public so they can better plan for the future. You can open up your own business in which you do nothing but market research. Contract with a firm to collect the information needed. Then call up people on the phone and collect the required information. You then package the information and sell it to the firm you contracted with. Opinions of products, services, TV programs, and so on, will be the type of information you will be collecting. You get paid for each call you make. You will have no selling to do. Most people will willingly answer your questions.

$ ♿ ♮

1009 PHONE FLEA MARKET

Run an ad, "If there is anything under the sun you wish to sell or buy, just call the Phone Flea Market. Phone _____." Example: Client calls you and explains he wants to sell a TV set. You explain that you will list the TV set and you will refer any requests for a TV set to the calling party upon receipt of their fee in the mail. Charge perhaps $1 for items under $30, $2 for items $30 to $100, and $3 for items over $100. No charges to any buyers. Sellers and buyers complete their own deals. You keep two up-to-date accurate filing systems: one for items for sale, and two for items wanted to buy.

1010 TELEPHONE ANSWERING SERVICE

Imagine making a good living just answering the phone for someone who can't do it himself. Today's highly mobile lifestyles coupled with the fast pace of personal and business decision making have made comfortable livings for many who started with just their home phone and then quickly grew until a large switchboard was required. Lucrative add-on services mean even more profits.

$ ♿ ♮

1011 WAKE-UP SERVICE

Telephone wake-up services do nicely. People lose jobs because they don't wake up in time. Valuable appointments can be missed for the same reason. Simply start up with a phone, a reliable clock and an ad in the paper. Have a private phone line, never a party one. With 500 subscribers at $4 a month you will gross $2000! In a smaller city it could be an ideal side business.

$ ♿ ▮▮▮▮

IIIIIIIITRAVEL

1012 BACKPACKING VACATIONS

Many people want to escape from the mundane into something out of the ordinary that offers some exhilaration. They will pay you well to take them on a very rugged and demanding backpacking trip where the soft, plush life is left back in civilization, and where they are pressed to the limits of their endurance and patience. You can lead these vacations and do very well financially. You will need to supply only the basics of tent, food, and so on. The harder the trek, the more your clients will value it, so don't try to pamper them.

$$$

1013 BOAT TOURS

Boating is an enjoyable sport. If you live near a scenic body of water, all you will need to set up a boat tour business is a smaller boat. Perhaps you have access to a city harbor, a lake, river frontage, or a group of islands with wildlife. Whatever it is, most people will welcome leaving their car behind to ship out on a water adventure. You may motor, row, sail, or paddle the boat.

$

1014 CABIN RENTALS

Many people cannot afford motor homes or trailers for vacationing. Yet they can afford to rent small tidy cabins to spend their vacations in, especially if your cabins are surrounded with peace and quiet. You can build small cabins as you can afford to and rent them out to fishers, vacationers, cross-country skiers, and so on. Keep your prices reasonable, and you will enjoy a year-round high occupancy rate with the resulting handsome year-round income.

$$$$$

1015 CAMPGROUND

Camping is a common vacation for many people in North America. From pup tents to elaborate motor homes, millions seek a back-to-nature experience every year. You can turn your rural property into a paying campground business. You will need to provide the basics of access, tables, fire pits, tent sites, toilets, signs, and so on. You may also be able to provide extras such as hiking trails, fishing, berry picking, and so on. Charge the going rates for campgrounds in your area offering similar services.

$$$$

1016 CANOE TRIPS

A canoe trip is one of the most unusual vacations possible in North America. Most people are unfamiliar with how easy and pleasant such a vacation can be. You can start a business in which you organize and guide small canoe parties through beautiful water wilderness areas. Letting them help paddle, make portages, bake bannock, and swap stories around the campfire will build you a repeat clientele for future years. A more inviting business is hard to imagine.

$$

1017 CONVENTION TOURS

Convention tours offer the attendees relief from the drudgery of being lectured to hour after hour. The family members accompanying the conventioneer can also look for a bus tour or a walking tour to help fill their hours of waiting with interesting and entertaining moments. You can run a business organizing and selling these tours for conventions and similar group gatherings. Contact city halls, chambers of commerce, and so on, for dates of these events in your area.

$$

1018 ESCORTED CAMPING TRIPS

Camping trips can be sheer fun! You can make honest money by taking groups of youngsters on such trips. You must like children and be able to take charge of them, and you should know how to live outdoors. Prepare a brochure giving details, dates, and so on. Explain carefully what you will offer. Explain what must be brought and what can not be brought. Provide necessary transportation. Expand by hiring capable young people as leaders and send out many groups at a time. You can easily do very well if you are a good organizer.

$$$$

1019 FARM VACATIONS

City people will often pay small fortunes to be able to spend their vacations as farmers. Set up your farm to accommodate these people so they can live right in the farm house with you, eating your food and observing and taking part in such farm activities as feeding the animals, gathering the eggs, milking, gardening, haying, picking fruit and so on. They help you with any chores, and then you can all go swimming in the pond, horseback riding, berry picking, hiking, or fishing. Give your guests a quiet, relaxed stay away from the noise and confinement of the city, with good food and outdoor life, and they will come back year after year.

$$$ 🏠

1020 FREIGHTER HAND

Work your way around the world as a deckperson or a workaway. A workaway swaps labor for passage and food. Concentrate on foreign vessels. You won't need money or experience or references. Check ship-to-ship talking with captains, or check with the Scandinavian Shipping Office. You will need a passport and a vaccination certificate. Luck, timing, and persistence are assets. Sailors are actually good people to work with. Life at sea is the most relaxing and peaceful life possible. Try it.

$ 🏠

1021 GOLD PROSPECTING TRIP GUIDE

Guide city families on gold prospecting trips back into the beauty of nature. Backpacking your way from gravel bar to gravel bar, your clients can relax with fresh air, clean water, nature lore, and evening campfires. Shaking off stress and getting back to basics pays off, and finding a nugget or two in your goldpan is just a bonus.

$$$ 🏠

1022 HOME TRAVEL AGENCY

Many smaller towns and cities don't have travel agencies. You can easily open such an agency right in your home, and you can conduct nearly the entire business by phone. Become the authorized agent for hotel chains and air, rail, bus and steamship lines. Keep current advertising brochures for prospective travelers. Make total travel arrangements for your customers and charge them absolutely nothing, because the hotels and airlines will be paying you commissions ranging up to 10 percent! This business can thrive even in a smaller town.

$$

1023 INTERVIEW SALES

A cassette tape recorder is all you need for this business. You will make interviews and sell them to companies or organizations. Example: You could interview all the customers coming out of a given supermarket and simply ask them why they shop there, what they like, and what they dislike about the store. Then you sell the tape to the management and they could use it to improve the store.

$

1024 JOBS BY LONG DISTANCE

Many people desire to move to a new region of the country, but because they do not have a new job to move to as well, they hold back. You can operate a mail order service for them in which you simply contract to mail the employment sections of the newspapers in your area to the people located elsewhere. Advertise in national magazines; expect a flood of requests, and a steady income. This business is self-perpetuating because we all know that "the grass is always greener on the other side of the fence"!

$

1025 JOB CREATION

There are thousands of jobs that are never filled simply because people are unaware that they even exist. These jobs exist in every community and they are solutions to real needs. These needs are often never even identified, much less talked about. You can search out these real needs and then create a job for yourself (or whoever) that will fill the needs you have found. This is job creation. First, identify problems. Second, create jobs to solve the problems. You can make a living helping others create their own jobs.

$

1026 JOB FAIR

A job fair is simply a large gathering of employers in separate booths in a large auditorium individually interviewing thousands of job seekers during evening or weekend hours. A convention style of entertainment could be a drawing card. Charge employers about $250 per booth, and job seekers about $5 each for admission. You could provide inexpensive workshops and seminars on being interviewed, good grooming, and the like. This whole affair makes it much easier for job seekers and employers to get things together.

$$ ♿ 🏙

1027 JOBS FOR YOUTH

Young people have great difficulty in finding employment in today's limited job market. You can help yourself by helping them to find jobs. Assemble a list of responsible young people able and willing to do categorized jobs—lawn mowing, yard cleanup, window cleaning, clerking, car washing, and so on. Then run a second ad saying that you will provide teenagers who will perform such services as above. You will need to charge the young people a modest fee for your services, unless you can come up with an alternative method for collecting your fees.

$ ♿ 🏙

1028 LUGGAGE RENTAL SERVICE

Most people do not use their suitcases most of the time. Wise buyers are switching to renting quality luggage for their infrequent travel needs. You can invest in this business and run it from your own home. Simply stock sets of quality matched luggage, advertise your service, and rent the luggage out at reasonable weekly rates. Add on pick-up and delivery if you like. Cultivate travel agents for referral business.

$$$ ♿ 🏙

1029 TRANSLATOR RENTAL AGENCY

A non-English-speaking person or family arrives in your city or town and wants to see your city. Hire out a man or woman who can devote himself or herself to the project in a gracious way. Your hired guides must be able to handle the foreign language as a translator and be able to cheerfully accompany and instruct the lonely traveler or family around your city or area. Tourist centers where there are lots of people with plenty of money will be your best location.

$ ♿ 🏙

1030 TRAVEL AGENCY

Travel around the world FREE with fringe benefits. You will be constantly bombarded with invitations to visit new resorts FREE! Or take cruises FREE! And how could you resist? Go along FREE with tours you have packaged together. Buy "bulk" from airlines and cruise ships, and then resell the space to individuals at a handsome profit! North Americans spent $214 billion last year on travel and your piece of the action could leave you breathless!

$$ ♿ ⛏ 📊

1031 TRAVEL BY TV

The majority of people are becoming weary of the usual TV fare with all the violence, sick comedy and immorality. They long for something worthy of the potential of TV. You would be doing your community and yourself a wonderful favor and service by purchasing a TV channel on which you specialized in showing wholesome travelogues and nature films. You would have a steady clientele that would put the other channels to shame—real shame. You would have no trouble securing sponsoring advertisers. You might even put some of the other channels out of business—which would be splendid!

$$$ ♿ 📊

1032 CRUISE-ONLY TRAVEL AGENCY

There are many different types of travel agencies. But the type of travel agency that yields the best profits is surely a cruise-only agency. These agencies specialize only in selling cruise vacations with various cruise ship companies throughout the world. You sell package cruises that include round-trip airfare. You will usually have most of the vacation already packaged for you, so there is little for you to do except sell the package. As an agent, you can take advantage of cut-rate or even free sample cruises with most cruise ship companies, making it an unusually pleasant business to be in.

 $$ ♿ 📊

▌▌▐▐▐▐TYPING

1033 LEGAL HOME TYPING

If you have had former legal secretarial experience or training, you may be qualified to set up a business in which you type up legal forms for lawyers in your own home! These specialty documents must be typed with great accuracy; many of them are too complicated for the inexperienced. This work can provide a good income for you and can provide lawyers who are just setting up their practices with the help they need.

$ ♿ ▐▀▌▐

1034 SECRETARIAL SERVICE

Contract with salespeople, big corporations, professionals, municipalities, hospitals, and so on, who have enormous transcription and dictation needs on a regular, or on an as-needed, basis. Start small at home with desk, phone, typewriter, and file space. A steady, well-paying job is a high probability. It is possible that you will soon be turning down excessive work.

$ ♿ ▐▀▌▐

1035 STENO SERVICE

Beat the nine-to-five with a typewriter (preferably electric) and a phone and stay at home! Salespeople without secretaries supply you with their business letterhead, and then they call you whenever they get into town and dictate their correspondence to you over the phone. Make three copies of the letter—original mailed to right person, second copy to the salesperson plus your bill to him or her, third copy for your file. Your biggest problem may be to keep your business small enough.

$ ♿ ▐▀▌▐

1036 TYPING INSTRUCTION

At home you can teach others how to type. Many would love to learn typing but have never had the chance. Try to fit your instruction into your client's schedule, perhaps in the evenings. You can offer class instruction to groups or single pupil private instruction. All practice drills are to be done at home on the student's own typewriter and time. With the advent of personal computers, more and more people will need to learn the invaluable skill of typing.

$ ♿ ▐▀▌▐

1037 TYPING SCHOOL PAPERS

With a good electric typewriter (IBM probably has the best) you can make good wages typing papers for students—essays, research papers, postgraduate theses, job résumés, and various other documents that will help students pull in good grades while being on a heavy, rushed schedule. Advertise in student papers and on school bulletin boards. Charge extra for editing services.

$ ♿ ▮▮▮▮

IIIIII||VENDING AND JOBBERS

1038 DUPLICATE KEY STAND
Be a real "key" man. A good location is a must. The percentage of profit is very high, running about 350 percent. Invest a total of about $1000, which will include a key-duplicating machine ($500) and a stock of key blanks. If possible, avoid a fixed overhead by paying rent as a percentage of your take. Don't buy anything until you are sure you have secured a good location.

$$ ♿

1039 FISHING TACKLE VENDING
Many people believe that a fishing pole is a stick with a hook at one end and a fool at the other. There is some truth to this, because fishing equipment commands prices that are normally marked up 100 percent or more. You can get into the market of distributing fishing tackle to retailers and make an excellent income in the process. You must know which products will bring in the fish and thus will sell well. Try to visit marinas and boat ramps and docks and slyly find out from fishermen what lures are working best.

$$$ ♿ ▐▜▐▌

1040 ADVERTISING SPECIALTIES
You have received such things as free ballpoint pens imprinted with the name and address of a business of which you were a customer. Millions of similar items are given away every year—coin holders, key rings, plastic pencil sharpeners, and so on. As a small wholesaler, or jobber, you can buy these advertising items from a manufacturer and sell them to business firms, imprinted with their messages. The manufacturer does the imprinting for you. You just get orders and send them in. You can readily build up a business that can net you $30,000 or more per year.

$$ ♿ ▐▜▐▌

1041 OFFICE SUPPLIES
This business has outstanding potential as a home business. Many office supplies have a hefty markup of 300 percent! You can stock office sup-

plies in your home and undercut all competition because your overhead would be almost nil. Set up a delivery route of smaller offices and business firms, which you can service weekly with a van. You can take orders by phone, thus allowing prompt deliveries. You will have no wages to pay out, no red tape with the government, and none of the usual hassles of running a business. This is an ideal home business.

$$ ♿ 🏭

1042 PACKAGED POPCORN

If local food license regulations allow, you may be able to set up a popcorn factory in your own home. Make several types of popcorn—plain, salted and buttered, caramel corn, and so on. Package same in proper transparent bagging. Offer large- and smaller-size bags. Take samples to merchants. The popcorn should sell itself if you have done your part well. Help merchants set up displays of your products in baskets or bins. You may want to expand by selling to a confectionery wholesaler.

$ ♿ 🪓 🏭

1043 PLASTIC LAMINATING

Individuals and businesses alike have many important documents that need to be preserved. You can purchase a small machine that will encase these valuable documents in laminations or layers of optically clear plastic material. The list of documents is endless—marriage certificates, deeds, menus, social security cards, drivers licenses, car registrations, and so on. You can clear more than $100 a day using this machine door-to-door. The machine uses no heat, chemicals, or even electricity, in its operation. Almost everything you bring in will be clear profit.

$$ ♿ 🏭

1044 POPCORN VENDING

Popcorn has the highest margin of profit of any snack food—with a cost of as little as 8 percent of the retail price. It is easy to start with a good popcorn machine for about $200. A good location will be your main concern. Sales are automatic. Look for heavy foot traffic areas. Be mobile so you can go from event to event. Weekend openings alone should net you from $20,000 on up per year!

1045 PRODUCE VENDOR

If you don't want to be tied to the treadmill, if you would prefer to own a little business that allows you to freely roam around your city or out in the country, in which you can alternate equally between hard work and going fishing, this may be for you. Raise the fruit and veggies if you can, or else buy them from a farmer, and sell them wherever you can. Use organically grown produce whenever possible and advertise as such. Start a door-to-door route and lay back with a paced, predictable income. Offer a list comparing your prices with local supermarket prices.

$$ ♿ ﬔﬕ

1046 RACK MERCHANDISING

Now you can start a real retail chain "store" of your own for about $100! All because even retail merchants like something for nothing—profit without risk or investment! Buy a rack of toys (or stationery, or greeting cards, or panty hose, or whatever) and place your "store" within the bigger retail store. The big store owner gets perhaps 20 percent of your take. (He doesn't know that your profit can be up to 100 percent or more!) Now just collect your share of proceeds and restock the rack. Invest in more racks and expand your chain store!

$$ ♿ ◣ ﬔﬕ

1047 RAWLEIGH, FULLER BRUSH

An ideal way to begin a home business on a shoestring budget is to sell someone else's inventory. You can do this very easily by becoming a dealer for household products with a safe national image such as Fuller Brush or Rawleigh Products. Contact the company of your choice and see how you can set to work for them, and for yourself, almost immediately. Sales experience and ability will be of help. Little else is necessary. Many people do quite well in this type of independent business.

$ ♿ ﬔﬕ

1048 ROSE VENDOR

Make $80,000 a year selling roses? It is a fact! Hire 5 gracious people. Each evening they stop by your house to pick up their night's quota of 200 roses each. Each visits 10 restaurants 5 nights each week. They visit each table where women are seated and ask their escorts if they would like to buy a rose for their lady—for only $1. Each seller sells about 150 roses per week night and about 230 roses each weekend night. You figure it out—if 5 people each sell an average of, say, $950 worth of roses per week, you gross $4750 for the week and you have only worked about two hours! The sellers make $250 each a week and enjoy their work. Everyone gains. Remember this is a cash business!

$$ ♿ ◣ 🏙

1049 SEAFOOD VENDOR
Cutting out the many greedy middle managers between the boat captain who catches the seafood (fish, lobsters, etc.) and the hungry consumer can mean real profits for anyone shrewd enough to seize the chance. Get started for about $800 or less. Operate in rural areas where there will be less red tape. Keep your overhead down by operating out of your truck at roadside. Or fill door-to-door orders arranged earlier by phone.

$ ♿ ◣ 🏙

1050 SHOES
Mason Shoe Sales of Chippewa Falls, Wisconsin has been making top-quality shoes for a good many years. These shoes come in about 400 styles, which are displayed in a 147-page catalog. They have dress and work shoes alike. You can purchase their shoes at decent dealer prices and then resell them in your area for decent profits. The shoes tend to sell themselves because they are made to last year after year. The shoe market is flooded with junk shoes today that wear out in just a few weeks. People are looking for durability at decent prices.

$ ♿ 🏙

1051 SUNGLASSES
This is an easy business to get into with very little cash outlay. A $400 inventory can bring in $125 net profit a day if you work the right locations, such as flea markets, sunbathing beaches, yacht clubs, and the like. Stay mobile—follow big summer events.

$ ♿ 🏙

1052 TOY STUFFED ANIMAL VENDOR
Here is a real easy sleeper! This is a good weekend job that can easily bring in more than your regular job. We have all seen plush toy animals

being sold along the roadside at one time or another. Grossing $40,000 a year is not uncommon, because stuffed toy animals are an impulse item and they obviously sell like hotcakes just about anywhere you could set up.

1053 VENDING MACHINES

Having a string of coin-operated machines is like having coin piggy banks in a great number of places. Start small and expect to grow. Dispense peanuts, candy, capsules, gumballs, wholesome amusements, or whatever is selling. Repair them yourself. The proprietor usually gets 25 percent of profit. Proprietors accept them, as they make money without risk.

1054 WAGON VENDING

Here you own your own wholesale house, and if you are any kind of a salesperson you can start for $300 or so. You will simply buy merchandise from manufacturers and sell it to retail outlets. Small wholesalers are called "jobbers." Some of the biggest wholesalers in North America began as wagon jobbers. You will need business letterheads and goods of your choice. Sell for cash on delivery only. Merchants usually know what will sell, so you rarely have to make sales pitches. The sky's the limit in this business.

1055 PERSONAL CARE VENDING MACHINES

Vending machines sell nearly everything you can imagine. It is now possible to use them to sell personal care items such as deodorant, shampoo, toothpaste, pain reliever, breath freshener, antacid, and a host of other similar products. The items most commonly sold in drug stores can be vended through these machines. Special vending machines designed to accommodate these goods are now available. You can run a home business in which you obtain permission to set up these machines in strategic locations in your area. You will simply resupply them on a regular basis and collect the money.

▌▌▌▌▌║║║WRITING

1056 AD NEWSPAPER COLUMNS

This will be a publishing novelty of sorts for most of your readership. You want to write a newspaper column that will keep bread on your table, so buy the space in the paper yourself. Then sell the column to a different firm each week for writing up their products or services. Give some careful thought and practice to this idea, as it has tremendous possibilities. You may be the next Mark Twain in your area.

$ ♿   ♒♒

1057 BIOGRAPHY WRITING

There are thousands of books waiting to be written. Many of these are the biographies of people who have led unusually interesting lives. Most of these people will enter their graves without having their lives recorded in print, which will be a sad loss to humanity. If you have a knack for writing, you may want to help one or several of these outstanding people record their unique stories. You will need a tape recorder, a typewriter, and a life story worth the special effort it will take. Check elderly residents of nursing homes and similar places for your story. Be prepared to share any monetary proceeds.

$ ♿   ♒♒

1058 BUSINESS RATING GUIDE

Everyone knows the service provided by the magazine *Consumer Reports*. You can publish a book that provides similar info on businesses in your local area and sell it like hotcakes to local subscribers and businesses. In the book, you will provide ratings of local businesses concerning their services, their prices, and their products. These ratings will be the end result of collating info from mass mailings of questionnaires to the consumers. You will hand out roses and brick bats based solely on the opinions of Joe Public.

$$ ♿   ⬉   ♒

1059 CLUB NEWS SERVICE

Social organizations and clubs are held together by good communications. You can make a good living based upon this fact. Contact all the societies, clubs, fraternal groups, and so on, in your area. Offer to write, publish, and circulate a monthly newspaper or bulletin for their group.

Their members report any news and activities to you. You then write up the material in an interesting manner, using your own style. Send copies to each member, charging the organization per copy. You can also reserve space for local advertising, which will add more profits. Work for several clubs each month and expect a good steady income.

$$ [symbols]

1060 COLLECTION LETTER WRITING

You can make a fine living if you have the talent for writing good collection letters. You can sell these letters by contract to small, independent business firms. Your clientele will include electricians, plumbers, servicemen, contractors, small business operators, and the like. These letters will be dealing with very delicate matters, so the ability to be tactful, yet persuasive, is a must. They will require a variety of pressure words to be used with great care—"ask for, insist upon, urge, demand," and so on. You will collect 30 to 50 percent of the money you collect.

$ [symbols]

1061 COMPLAINT SERVICE

Complaints are never pleasant, either in giving them or in receiving them. However, there are many times when complaints are not only justified but called for. Sometimes the most loving thing you can do for a person is to tell him "NO," that you won't tolerate shoddy treatment, or service, or products. Verse yourself on the hundreds of different ways of delivering complaints. Then go into the business of preparing complaints for paying clients and delivering these complaints to the intended receivers.

$ [symbols]

1062 CONDO NEWSLETTER

Buying a condo means beginning a new lifestyle. Condo owners value info that will show them what owning and living in a condo is all about. You can publish a newsletter for your local condo association in which you discuss the following areas: services and supplies at group discount prices, mortgages, when to sell or hold onto a condo, tax changes, financial briefs, redecorating tips, group social events, and so on. You will become the center of condo life in your area. Subscriptions will mount fast.

$$ [symbols]

1063 FREELANCE NEWS REPORTER

This shoestring venture is clean, always interesting, and it will give you prestige wherever you go. Gather news reports, package them, and sell them to radio stations, TV stations, or newspapers on a freelance basis. If you have a "bad" back, this may be for you.

$ ♿ 🎹

1064 GHOST WRITING

Find people who want their special story written and contract to write it for them. It may be a fictional narrative, but it could also be an autobiographical account, even a full autobiography. Record the story in the person's own words, using a tape recorder. Type up several drafts as you proceed, revising as required. Use your skill to maintain momentum in the story by either deleting or spicing up dead spots. Sell the finished manuscript or publish it yourself. Split the proceeds fairly with the storyteller.

$ ♿ 🎹

1065 GUIDEBOOK PUBLISHING

Guidebook publishing is a flexible business that will allow you to live where you want to live and to work flexibly as well. The demand for simple, honest guidebooks is steady, and the supply is surprisingly low. It is a fun challenge. If your local area is worth singing about, then get to know your area intimately, whip out your computer, throw back your head, and sing out with honest gusto! Fill that emptiness!

$$ ♿ 🎹

1066 HAND LETTERING

There is nothing colder than a graduation diploma with your name done in sloppy typing or stark-naked computer printout type. Mechanized documents just won't do for most people. This is where you come in. Hand lettering is easy to learn, it is worth honest money, and it takes us back to a time when folks took pride in appearance. You will need a steady hand, a slight artistic inclination, some good old routine self-discipline, some black India ink, a penholder, and a point (begin with a Speedball C-4). Most people will prefer your fine hand lettering to poorly rendered mechanical substitutes.

$ ♿ 🎹

1067 HANDWRITTEN WORKS

No one likes to receive an impersonal form letter. We accept them as insults to our very existence. Yet in the hurried pace of life they are more and more necessary. You can help solve this problem by contracting to handwrite greeting cards and envelopes, wedding invitations, letters, professional announcements, and political bulk correspondence for clients badly needing to portray a caring, personal image. Good handwriting is a must. A small, continuous ad under "Personal" will keep you more than busy.

$ 🦽 💹

1068 HIKING GUIDEBOOK

Walking is the best all-around exercise possible. More and more people are parking their autos and going hiking. You can explore your own locality and write up descriptions of outstanding possible hikes. You can then publish your collection of possible hikes in one complete volume, calling it a Guidebook to Local Hiking for your area. Provide a variety of hikes—easy ones and harder ones, short ones and longer ones. Try to capture special places of interest for plants and animals, scenery, and so on.

$$ 🦽 💹

1069 HOME HISTORIES

If you like digging into the past, write up histories of houses in your neighborhood and then sell these histories to the people presently living in them. Everyone is curious about how their house came to be and who the former inhabitants were and what they were like. You will have to contact all sorts of people and look through old records to find the needed info. Put the more interesting home biographies together into a book that should sell well to the locals.

$ 🦽 💹

1070 HOUSEHOLD HINTS SERVICE

This can be a wonderful home mail-order business. Collect valuable household hints and sell them. People will respond to your ad, which invites them to become a member of your "household hints club" by paying a specified membership fee. As a member they are entitled to receive 25 (or whatever) helpful and unusual housekeeping suggestions by mail each month. Try to search out potent new suggestions to include in your monthly club bulletins. Use bulk mail to cut down your overhead. Advertise in national women's magazines.

$

1071 INSTANT LANGUAGE BOOKLET

When faced with a language barrier, most people get lost quickly in a standard dual-language dictionary. What is needed is a very simple dictionary that covers quickly and easily only the most needed words and phrases—such as days of the week, numbers, names of rooms, and so on. You can write and publish these basic dictionaries in any language required and sell them at substantial profits over your costs. Be sure to include simple pronunciation guides in each dictionary.

$$

1072 INSTRUCTION MANUAL

This is a publishing business. First run an ad, asking for anyone with anything at all to teach for free or for hire to please forward their teaching subject plus name and address and phone number to you. Then compile the list of instructors and print up a brochure containing the info. Retail the brochure on newsstands and elsewhere. Ask in the booklet to be advised of changes, so you can issue revised editions periodically.

$$

1073 LETTER WRITING SERVICE

The majority of people are able and willing to write their own business and personal letters. However, there are people in every community who need special help in writing these letters from time to time. Perhaps they are too busy, or afraid, or anxious, or incapable because of poor education or foreign language problems. Advertise your services to write these letters and you will likely find yourself quite busy. Work with one client at a time by appointment whenever possible.

$

1074 LITERARY AGENT

Your function is to sell literary material for your clients. You must submit each manuscript that you consider salable to every possible market until a sale has been made. You receive 10 percent of the sales price for your commission. Charge reading fees for the reading of the manuscripts. You must have a good knowledge of the literary marketplace for all types of literary works. Advertise your services. Some agents regularly collect more than $100,000 a year from their "stable" of authors!

$ 🦽 🔨 ▀▜▌

1075 LOGOS

An attractive logo can enhance the image of a business, create an identity for it, and make it memorable and widely known. You can learn logo design in a few short hours and then become a freelance logo designer and consultant. It is not uncommon for a logo to sell for $2000 or more. You will show clients why having a logo is important for effective competition and how to go about utilizing it. Every business is a prospective customer for a new logo. Even well-established logos require updating or replacement from time to time.

$ 🦽 🔨 ▀▜▌

1076 MAGAZINE ARTICLE WRITING

Writing is not one of the easier ways to earn a living. An exception can be writing feature articles for magazines. Study carefully the feature articles in a given magazine and you will discover that there is a pattern to the styles and contents of the articles. You can write articles that fit nicely into this pattern and yet offer some originality of content. These can be sold to that magazine. Once you have sold one article to a magazine, they will usually solicit further manuscripts from you. Once you have broken into the market, you are on your way.

$ 🦽 ▀▜▌

1077 MAIL ADDRESSING

Many businesses send out volume mailings for advertising, billing, and so on. You can contract to do the envelope addressing for them. Advertise: "Envelope Addressing for Volume Mailings. Reasonable Prices. Accurate, Quick Service. Call _____." All the work can be done on your home typewriter. The client will supply needed envelopes. You will charge per address typed. Other typing jobs can easily result from offering this service.

$ 🦽 ▀▜▌

1078 MAILING LISTS COMPOSING

You can, with the use of an inexpensive personal computer, compile and sell up-to-date mailing lists. For example, you can collect the names and addresses of all the firms in North America retailing widgets. Anyone wishing to contact this specific group of widget retailers can purchase the list you have compiled. You can make quite decent wages compiling these lists and selling them by mail direct to individual customers. Or you can market them to mailing list firms who will in turn retail them. This is a superb home business.

$$ 🔥 🏢💼

1079 MANUSCRIPT PREPPING

Many good writers need their rough manuscripts prepared for professional presentation to publishers. Contract out your services to fine-tune the manuscript until it is polished. You may be required to proofread it and make corrections to its grammar, spelling, and punctuation. You may be required to edit it, to criticize it, or to retype it for final copy, ready for submission. It will probably be fair to charge a flat fee per page for specific functions you perform. Advertise in a popular national literary magazine for clients.

$ 🔥 🏢💼

1080 NAME LISTS SALES

Businesses are always on the lookout for prospective customers. You can run a business in which you sell lists of names of strong prospects. Peruse all your local newspapers and compile two main lists: (1) the names and addresses of all newlyweds, and (2) the names and addresses of all new parents. Sell the new lists to your business subscribers each month. Subscribers will be furniture stores, department stores, cleaners, photographers, appliance dealers, and so on. Bill your subscribers monthly based on the number of names you supply each month.

$ 🔥 🏢💼

1081 NEWSLETTER WRITER-PUBLISHER

Compile, write, and publish a newsletter containing two to six typewritten pages of specialized up-to-date info. Example: Publish a food (or whatever) commodity advisory newsletter. Advise on best food buys in a given city. Charge $200 (or whatever) per year. Get 200 subscribers and gross $40,000 a year. Example: Find stores or companies that need a newsletter for public relations purposes and fill their needs. Opportunities abound here. New newsletters pop up every day.

$ 👤 📷

1082 NEWSPAPER COLUMN

The trick in writing newspaper columns is getting your column to "catch on." Your very first column is extremely important—it must grab the reader's attention and hold it from the start. Your column may be in any of your strong areas—philosophical, technical, humorous, domestic, of general or specific interest, sports, or whatever. Prepare a column well in advance so you won't be under the pressures of publishing deadlines. Weekly columns are easier to write than daily columns, which can become stale and monotonous quickly. A good livelihood can be had here.

$ 👤 📷

1083 PARENTS' GUIDE

Parents are faced with constant problems in looking after their children. You can make their job much easier by collecting all of the appropriate information they may need within your local area and then publishing a guide for parents, paid for by advertising from businesses with a vested interest in the information in the guide. You will need oodles of info concerning doctor names, 4H clubs, babysitters, remedial tutors, music teachers, parks available, places of recreation, and so on, in your guide.

$ 👤 📷

1084 PEN PAL MATCHING

People will happily pay you if you can provide them with names and addresses of other people with whom they can strike up correspondence. Your selection and matching of pen pals is based upon common hobbies, inclinations, and so on. People see your ad to join a Pen Pal Club. They pay you a $3 fee and forward info about themselves. You send them three pen pal addresses who share common backgrounds and interests. Pen pals are always interesting and inspirational. You will want to join your own club!

$ 👤 📷

1085 PERSONAL HISTORIES

Many births and birth certificates have never been properly registered. It can be very time consuming and frustrating for people to sort out this problem. You can hire out to search out this type of information through old church and school records, town documents, census records, and so on. It can be an interesting and rewarding side business. You can add the tracing of family trees, coats of arms, and other personal history about the living client or his or her ancestors. Many people will pay well for this service.

$ ♿ ♮♮♮

1086 POETRY

If you have a bent for writing poetry, you should nurture the gift and consider marketing it. Certain magazines solicit original poetry, rhymes, and jingles. Certain greeting card firms advertise for new, original, and humorous ideas for a variety of different greeting cards. You should enclose a self-addressed stamped envelope with each set of material you submit to editors. Equip yourself with a rhyming dictionary, don your thinking cap, and begin to make your talent pay its way.

$ ♿ ♮♮♮

1087 PR BROCHURES

Top-name PR firms command sky-high prices for their promotions. You can undercut their prices drastically and still gain a good profit for yourself. You can arrange the layout and printing of brochures for client businesses, which are in turn given away free to their clients. Example: Publish a colorful, attractive brochure for a bakery, which is given away free to all the patrons of the bakery. The bakery pays for all costs, including a goodly profit for you.

$ ♿ ♮♮♮

1088 RESEARCH SPECIALTY

Many writers, businesspeople, lecturers, tradespeople, professionals, and so on, have problems finding answers to problems because they lack either ability or time to find the answers. You can do the research for these people, find their answers in the local library or wherever, and then collect a fee in exchange for the information. You will need to advertise your services depending on which clients you intend to work for. You will find your services in constant demand, especially if you advertise nationally.

$ ♿ 🍴

1089 RESUME SERVICE

Individuals applying for jobs with larger companies usually need to submit a resume in which they list their general background, education, previous employment, and other qualifications. They may need 100 or more copies of the resume printed. Hire out to help them with typing, editing, writing, grammar, printing, and so on. You will need a typewriter and good writing skills. A larger city will give you full-time work in this business. This is good home side business.

$ ♿ 🍴

1090 RURAL NEWS REPORTER

Big-city newspapers need columns of local interest to attract readers in the smaller villages, suburbs, and round about. You can apply to write a continuing column with a well-written letter and you may land the job. Use the phone to round up most of your local news. You will develop a group of special contacts. With a flair for writing and a nose for news you will do well. Sell your efforts by the word or by the line. The more valid news you can sniff out, the bigger your paycheck will be.

$ ♿ 🍴

1091 SPECIALTY MANUALS

Put your accumulation of expertise and knowledge down on paper. Then publish the info in a brochure, leaving half the spaces available for paid advertising. Circulate the brochure free to all prospective customers of the retailers who paid for the advertising. Example: Write up all your knowledge about new babies and their care. Then get retailers to buy your ad spaces so they can advertise their diapers, baby toiletries, milk, drugs, and so on. Distribute the brochure free to all new parents. Then send monthly bills to the advertisers and collect fees based on the numbers of free books distributed each month.

$ ♿ 🍴

1092 SURVIVAL BOOK

Mt. St. Helens. Chernobyl. The San Andreas fault. These names remind us of disaster. Disasters are unpredictable, and we in North America are not adequately trained and informed by our government officials to cope well with potential disasters. You may have a background in information that shows people how to cope with the real problems that result when disasters strike suddenly. Methodically put all of this info into a book, which should sell well to at least 10 percent of the population who are interested in this.

$ ♿ 🎹👤

1093 TOUR GUIDE

Every community has attractions that outsiders, tourists, and even many locals would like to both see and hear about. You can search out the history of your own area and then get a passenger van or a small school bus. With the information and the transportation, you can then provide a guided tour of your area for interested customers. Your steady narrative as you drive your clients from one place of interest to the next will be the key to your success—make it as informative and entertaining as you can. A good living can be made nearly anywhere in this business.

$ ♿ 🎹👤

1094 WHO'S WHO LOCAL DIRECTORY

Nearly everyone is proud of his or her achievements, no matter how small. Everyone desires an opportunity to be recognized, and seeing his or her own name appear in your local Who's Who guide will make anyone glow inside. Sales often amount to as much as 80 percent of the people listed. Example: 10,000 names, 8,000 sold at $25/copy—$200,000 gross! Collect all your biographies by mail. Print the book and sell it by mail. All you need are enough form letters and a mailing list. Every town/city is a potential fertile market!

$$ ♿ 🎹👤

1095 WRITING SOCIAL LETTERS

Surprisingly, people will actually pay you simply to write them letters once a week (or on a predetermined schedule)! Advertise that you will write friendly letters to anyone anxious to receive them for a subscription fee. You will get responses from elderly people, lonely people, childless couples, divorcees, members of the armed forces, hospitalized patients, and so on, all looking for new interest in life. You can provide them with new interests in your letters. You can introduce new topics or write about topics your clients have introduced.

$ 👤 🏙️

1096 WRITING SPACE FILLERS

Space fillers are brief interesting paragraphs used by editors to fill up space on a page to be printed so it will be balanced in appearance. They enhance the interest of the publication to the reader. They may be quips, recipes, puns, proverbs, unusual facts, questions and answers, medical breakthroughs, household hints, nutritional advice, anecdotes, and so on. Pay for fillers is high compared to other forms of writing. If you are inclined to write for a living, give careful consideration to this possibility. It is well worth investigating further.

$ 👤 🏙️

1097 WRITING SPEECHES

You can be well paid for literally putting your words in other people's mouths! How? By ghost-writing speeches for clients who are unable, because of lack of time or talent, to write their own speeches. Politicians especially, but professionals, businesspeople, and educators will often be happy to hire you to provide them with a speech. Research the required background for the speech and write it along general guidelines laid down by your client. Try to reflect the speaker's character as accurately as possible and you may have a permanent job as his official speechwriter!

$ 👤 🏙️

1098 WRITING STORY PLOTS

Many writers who have exacting literary skills that enable them to write complete stories suitable for publication ironically do not have the ability to conceive good plots for stories. You can sell story plots to these authors if you have a vivid imagination that just pops stories into your mind with little effort. A small ad for your services in a magazine that features the category most suited to your writing is all you will need to find clients who will gladly hire you to help them.

$ 👤

1099 PERSONALIZED BOOKS

Books are special things to most people. But a book that has your very own name in it again and again is a very special thing. And when your very own name is the name of the hero or heroine all the way through the book, then the book simply sells itself. All you have to do is produce the book and hold it out to the eager buyer. The backbone of your business will be a computer that has the text for the book or books already in place. The plot of the book can be your own creation, or you can purchase one on computer software. All you do is type in the purchaser's name and the computer inserts the name in dozens of places throughout the book. Then the book is printed up. For common names, you can have your book or books already printed ahead of marketing time.

$$$ 　

1100 HOME NURSING DIRECTORY

Medical costs have escalated dramatically in recent years. Much nursing that used to be done in hospitals is now being done in homes. This change saves megabucks for the patients. If your locality is a larger center or city, you can collect the names and addresses of all the people in your area who are capable, qualified, and willing to be home nurses. You can then tabulate this information in usable form and print up all the information in a booklet. These booklets can be updated from time to time as needed. They can be sold to individuals looking for home nursing assistance, perhaps by subscription. You may try covering the cost of the booklets by selling display advertising that you print in the booklets.

$$ 　

1101 WRITING BUSINESS PLANS

In order to secure any financing with which to start up a new small business, the entrepreneur must have a well-thought-out business plan drawn up and on paper. All loan officers will ask for it up front. Most people planning to start up a business really don't know how to properly create and print this document. If you have the basics for making up these plans down pat, you could do well for both yourself and prospective businesspeople by setting up a business in which you write up customized business plans for paying clients.

$